# FINDING

Masculinity

## FEMALE TO MALE
## TRANSITION IN ADULTHOOD

### EDITED BY
### ALEXANDER WALKER & EMMETT J. P. LUNDBERG

Foreword by Nick Krieger, author of Nina Here Nor There: My Journey Beyond Gender

MAGNUS BOOKS
An Imprint of Riverdale Ave Books

D1059725

For more information contact:
Riverdale Avenue Books
5676 Riverdale Avenue
Riverdale, NY 10471

www.riverdaleavebooks.com

Design by www.formatting4U.com
Cover by Sheyam Ghieth
Photography by Yana Davis: www.yanadavisphotography.com

Digital ISBN: 9781626011861
Print ISBN: 9781626011878

First Edition May 2015

# TABLE OF CONTENTS

# Foreword
## Nick Krieger

Every so often, I hear the news through the queer grapevine, an acquaintance, or directly from a friend that they or someone we know is transitioning. Whether or not I know the person, I feel a sigh of a relief, the creep of a smile, and a tenderness in my heart. The process of self-discovery and acceptance can take many years, and the willingness to risk all that is known for all that is true can take even longer. The moment a trans person embarks on this journey is, in my opinion, a great celebration.

From my own experience, I know the path for a trans or gender nonconforming person is difficult—family and friends may object, the medical community may put up obstacles, and job and career may be at stake—but the rewards are infinite. Internal ease, physical comfort, and the opportunity to be seen can alter our very constitution, shifting the quality and texture of every moment for the better.

When Alex and Emmett shared with me their idea for an anthology of transition stories, I immediately felt sentimental and nostalgic. The concept thrust me back eight years to my own gender awakening. Back

1

then, I spent many late-night hours clicking around on blogs, watching YouTube videos, and reading piles of gender books stacked by my bedside. Learning about people with various transgender identities opened up a galaxy of possibility for me. I used their language and experiences as a reflection, a disco ball where each mirrored fragment showed me a tiny piece of myself.

I loved reading these stories. They provided me with practical information, empowered me to take action, and invited me into a community. I also hated reading these stories. They triggered self-realizations, presented a daunting future, and caused me to question the validity of any of my gendered experiences that differed from those I read and heard. I slowly discovered that there was no single trans narrative, which was both inspiring and frustrating. The potential to be my own unique self was appealing, but some proof or a test sure would've helped with my certainty.

During my self-inquiry, I struggled to understand why I had not "always known" I was trans, an element that seemed central to the narratives of many. I experienced a girlhood and not a stifled or squashed boyhood. I was equally comfortable as one of the girls and as one of the boys. I have no recollection of believing or wishing that I was a boy. Even now, I do not feel like a man. I do feel embodied, at peace in my skin, and present and available to those around me.

While I often group the emotional, physical, psychological, and social changes associated with a visible shift in my gender under the shorthand of "My Transition," the phrase also implies a linear movement from A to B, or in my case, from female-to-male. This had never been a goal. Instead, I put one foot in front of the other, taking incremental steps, each one independent—choosing the language that suited me, the body that felt comfortable to inhabit, and eventually, the hormones that soothed me. I had no end point in sight, but I had set off a chain reaction whereby each revelation of happiness inspired another step towards happiness. Rather than fight this previously unfathomable level of contentment, I surrendered to its continued unfolding.

Recently, I watched a home video from my first testosterone shot, recorded by an ex-girlfriend who accompanied me to the doctor's office that summer day. When the nurse practitioner hands me the loaded syringe, my chin is quivering. My eyes are steeled. I am intent on my mission. I cock the thing like I'm about to launch a javelin into my thigh. And then I do. As I press the plunger, releasing the hormone into my muscle, I take slow, deep audible breaths. Once I am finished, the nurse practitioner places a Band-Aid over the injection site and exits the room. The second the door clicks shut, I leap off of the table. "I did it! I did it myself!" I cry. My eyes bulge with incredulity. A smile rips across my face. I swivel my hips, shake my butt, and put on a show so unexpected and out of character that I watch the video again and again, just to see my little dance.

The whole clip is less than two minutes. And yet this brief segment captures my entire emotional journey through transition—from abject terror to unfettered joy. At times, the movement was less direct, and the fear and excitement mixed and mingled, seemingly one and the same. For a while, every day was a heart-pumping adventure with some new challenge and some uncertain situation awaiting me.

3

Transition is a long list of firsts. The first time I purchased men's underwear. The first time my friends sang "Happy Birthday, Dear Nick." The first time a lover ran her hands across my flat chest. The first time I showered in the men's locker-room at the gym. The first time I claimed my identity and said, "I am transgender," which also turned out to be the last time I spoke to my dad for several years.

The triumphant moments traded off with awkward moments. Friends tripped over pronouns and tagged me on Facebook in old photos from my Lady Tigers sports teams. A former lover responded to my hello with, "I'm sorry, but do I know you?" On a first date, I walked into the bathroom, bladder bursting, and discovered it only had urinals. The judge at my name-change court hearing asked, "Are you sure it's just Nick? Not Nicholas?"

I understand the urgency felt by many trans folks to get this transition phase over with, for the fuzz of dysphoria to fade and for the reflection in the mirror to match the self-image. For me, I also found it important to recognize, honor, and treasure all the moments, the cringe-worthy and the affirming, during this heightened time of change. I was both participant and witness, a teenager lost in the grand swirl of puberty, and a parent awed by the beauty and vulnerability of a precious child in transformation.

Reading the stories in this book, the rawness of my own personal experience rose to the surface of my memory, this visceral sense of having been there. At the same time, I felt distant from this past, comfortable and firmly rooted in my current body and identity. I no longer read the stories of trans and gender non-

4

conforming folks with trepidation. I read to learn about those with different backgrounds and experiences, to offer a nod and a wink to those with shared histories, and to reignite my connection to community.

As the period of non-stop action, this climactic stretch of "My Transition" recedes, it becomes an increasingly shorter segment on this longer trajectory of my life. Touching back to this time reminds me of all the ways we change, of all the transitions, small and large, that go on within and around us. We transition in our jobs, relationships, living situations, and aging bodies. We transition in our style of dress, eating habits, walking routes, and hobbies. Around us, the seasons come and go, the moon waxes and wanes, the sun rises and sets. We can push and power through the phases we dislike, hoping to arrive at some end point where it will supposedly be easy, or we can lean into the uncertainty and ride these changes as if on an adventure.

Sometimes I wish that everyone received the gift that we trans folks refer to as "My Transition," an opportunity to undergo a change so big it does not need a qualifier. Transition taught me introspection and self-awareness, to honor the truths that live inside of me, and to recognize my fears and still leap. The challenges along the way strengthened my capacity for compassion, and only by experiencing my own suffering could I truly empathize with the suffering of others. Accepting all of my feelings, even and especially the pain, is what let in the blessing of joy. This joy is what I see and look for, what I remember, and what I hope for whenever a trans person shares their story. It is the joy of allowing ourselves to be fully seen. I encourage you to look for this in the following stories and in your own lives.

Nick Krieger
December 2014

# INTRODUCTION

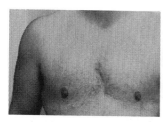

The concept of gender is messy. The majority of global societies have narrowed the definition into two distinct and separate boxes between which there is no space. One is either male or female and is expected to meet the physical, emotional, spiritual, and mental parameters associated with the corresponding box. More socially progressive societies understand that cultural norms surrounding gender are flexible and are often more accepting of those whose body or self-expression defies one or more of the above parameters. Far fewer are the cultures who embrace the understanding of gender as a continuum, or spectrum, rather than the binary that much of the world clings tightly to.

For those of us whose internal self is not aligned with the sex we were assigned at birth, or whose gender does not fit neatly into one of the two boxes, living in a gender-binary based society can be challenging. For many of us, the conflict between how we feel, how we look, and how the rest of the world perceives us starts from the first moments we form conscious memories and thoughts. This is the common tale that is told about people like us; the one that you hear about on morning talk shows and that is often sensationalized in the media. However, for many more of us, the story of how we came to understand this conflict between the outside world, and ourselves, takes years to comprehend and is significantly more complicated.

Finding the path toward feeling more engaged in life often comes with a choice of undergoing some sort of transition from the gender that is associated with one's assigned sex at birth to another state that more closely aligns one's mind with how one is perceived by others in society.

This book was inspired by the stories of those that were assigned female at birth and found transition from our assigned sex to a form of masculinity at later points in adult life; an option that gave us life and livelihood in a way that we hardly dared to hope was possible. When one's mind is more congruent with how one is seen by others, it often creates a sense of self and belonging that was previously diminished, missing or even harmful. We refer to ourselves as transgender, two-spirited, trans, male, queer, gender fluid, genderqueer, ftm, and/or trans-men, among other adjectives.

There is no one "right" way to navigate the process of transition. Some choose to use medical interventions to aid in this process to align our body with our mind. Much of the literature and conversation about female-to-male transition, both from within and from outside our community, focuses on medical transition. Yet, there is often a lack of conversation about how the holistic process of transition, medical and non-medical, impacts less-visible aspects of a person's adult life. The process of exploring one's gender identity and transitioning often has more effect on these less-visible parts of the day-to-day life of a person than their more outward appearance. In many narratives, individuals speak to the physical, and emotional, changes that come with female-to-male medical transition.

As two men of transgender experience, we began to realize that there were many pieces of information lacking in available narratives about how others experience transition in different aspects of their daily life, beyond the most-often discussed medical transition. Through both of our own journeys, we searched for a side of these narratives that were unspoken. How would transitioning to a masculine-identified person affect how we approached the world? How would this process impact our relationships with our friends and significant others? What about our careers and our families?

We were both thankful to have found others within our community to guide us through finding the answers to these questions and provide examples of how one could successfully navigate the many aspects of transition. Still, we felt a strong desire and need to expand the body of literature for individuals both within our community and those seeking to understand and learn about our experiences.

With this mindset, we set out to address six of the areas of life that are often most impacted by transition, aside from the medical process.

First, you will meet the contributors to this anthology through their introductions. Each contributor wrote additional pieces in some of the following categories based on what resonated most with their experience.

## I. Emotional and Spiritual Development

Within this section, contributors share insights and experiences about their spiritual and emotional development during their transition. For some, this involves religion. Others write about their experience in society and how they have aligned themselves emotionally throughout transition.

## II. Family

Who knows us better than our family? Many people of transgender experience have positive, negative or a mix of both experiences with family. Our contributors seek to share these moments of struggle, triumph, and how family relationships have evolved or how they created and developed chosen family to support our development and be a sounding board.

## III. Relationships

Transitioning can be a selfish endeavor. You are growing and changing as a person, as are your perspectives of others and how you relate to them. Through the experiences of people within new, established, and developing romantic relationships, this section explores how couples have grown in their partnerships throughout transition.

## IV. Medical Community

The medical community has grown tremendously to serve transgender needs in many parts of the world, yet we still face difficult decisions about where and how to seek medical treatment, both for transition and for all other types of medical needs. In this section, contributors share their experiences within different systems throughout the world and how to talk to medical professionals, while maintaining dignity and respect for themselves.

## V. Transitioning on The Job

For many of us, the majority of our time is spent working. Many people define themselves within the context of their professional life. In this section, contributors share their personal experiences of transitioning in the workplace. Some of the contributors are out and proud, while others live a life in which identities at work and home are discretely divided.

\*\*\*

As a body of work, we hope that this can serve as insight for individuals who want to engage in learning about how transition from female-to-male affects a person's life. Additionally, we hope that these stories shed light for individuals who have transitioned or are contemplating transition for themselves. We sought a body of diverse men—born and socialized as female, who began their transitions after already establishing individual lives—who are proud to be themselves, and in their own individual ways define being male, men, masculine, queer, trans, two-spirited, transsexual, and however they define themselves along the transmasculine spectrum.

Alexander Walker and Emmett J. P. Lundberg
April 2015

# SECTION I—INTRODUCTIONS

Harvey Katz – Age Thirty-Three,
Athens Boy Choir, Currently Living in Brooklyn, New
York (with roots in Georgia and Miami)

By becoming what, in the end, turned out to be a mostly straight, white man in this world, I've become just about everything else first; a soft butch, a riot grrrl, a dyke, an eternal teenager, a freak, a monster, a faggot, a daughter-gone-missing, and a sister that mysteriously vanished from the retelling of family lore. I have always existed as a whole but my life has been fractured into a schizophrenic retelling. When you're trans, to the people around you there will always be two lives: the one that you live, and the one that you lived.

Unlike most trans narratives I have heard, I couldn't wait for puberty. For most trans masculine people, menstruation is the end of boyhood dreams. Quite literally, it is the period at the end of the sentence. I, on the other hand, couldn't wait to get my first period. I thought that was the only thing standing between me and becoming one of the girls.

I was a late bloomer and was on my way out of the eighth grade before good ol' Aunt Flow made her first trip down south. I had anticipated her visit for years. I would jump the gun, thinking I was getting my first period in class, overtly mouthing "female problems" to my teachers when asking for the bathroom pass. I got a particular thrill doing this during geometry. I had a crush on my teacher and wanted her to know that this boy-girl was soon to be a lady. The only bad side to getting your period, I reckoned, was the supposed connection between having it and having to sit out of gym class.

Last week, for the first time in more than seven years, I had some spotting. It was dark red and foreign. It had been so long since I'd had a period that I'd forgotten that you could bleed without a wound. I'm anxious and dreading going to the gynecologist. My dad's biggest fear all along has been that the testosterone would kill me. God, he's mentioned more than once, doesn't like you to mess with nature.

When I first tried to find a doctor that would help me with my medical transition in Georgia, I discovered that the nature of self-care could get messy as well. It took me a year after getting my approval letter from the psychiatrist to start seeking out medical providers for surgery and hormones. Finding a surgeon was easy. My dad was a wreck. I called him two days before my chest surgery. I hadn't planned on ever telling him. Once, my mom woke up when the anesthesia failed mid-surgery and I feared a similar thing would happen to me, so I called my dad and I believe he cried. He'd forgotten about the letter I had sent him two years prior when I explained I was transgender. I found the letter opened and placed on my childhood desk the next time I visited him. He bought a plane ticket, flew to Georgia the next day and drove me the 90 miles to the strip mall where my doctor rented a surgical suite. He bought frozen peas on the way home. They smelled gross as they melted on my chest.

I hadn't started hormones yet. I didn't know if I ever would, but that feeling didn't last long either.

Testosterone itself is glorious. My appetite for everything grew. I felt feral. I wanted meat and hot sauce. It was like life had an exclamation mark at the end of it. I had spent the last five years looking away from my reflections and now every day I became more inclined to take glimpses of myself in passing.

I'm thirty-three years old now and almost eight years into my medical transition. A few years ago, I was watching *The Biggest Loser* on TV. The massive transition the finalists made awed me. Without a second thought, I turned to my roommate and remarked, "God, I wonder what it would be like to experience such a profound body change." Her silence was audible. No less than fifteen long seconds passed before I remembered, "Oh that's right, I had a sex change." We laughed ourselves off the futon.

I feel like I have completed my transition medically, emotionally and socially. Being a man in this world feels easy and organic for me now. I'm not the antagonist in my own story anymore. I can be kind and good and gentle to myself. I can be naked with myself and feel safe from my own self-destruction. I feel honest and whole. If my life were a movie, I feel like the ending would be boring—and after all that madness, I feel like that's perfect.

## Gabe Pelz – Age Thirty-Two,
## Family Restaurant Cook, South Georgia

When I began my transition, my main concern was, and continues to be, the health and well being of my daughter. Language has been a big part of my transition with her. What does she call me? Does that change? Will this confuse her? These questions have spun around time and time again. But ever since I was a child I knew that inside I felt like a boy. I didn't think I could be a good parent without honoring that feeling inside.

I was born and raised in South Georgia in the early 1980s. I've lived here all of my life and throughout that time, my family and I have been through many challenges. My parents met in Germany when they both were serving in the United States Army. My mother's relationship with her family has been difficult since she announced that she was having a baby and the father was a black man. She is white, and back in the '80s, it wasn't very common to have a biracial child. In fact, southern Georgia was still very segregated. There are certain stereotypes or "right" things to do in the south. Ways that men and women act and what kind of people should be in relationships.

So when she wrote them a letter telling them, they were furious and demanded she get an abortion; she refused. My parents didn't stay together long because of how my dad would have been treated here in the south. I'm sure my mother thought that would be the hardest thing she would face with having me.

Growing up I never felt out of place in my family. I never heard any racist comments until I entered school. In kindergarten, I went to visit my father and missed school for a week. My teachers got word of this and when I returned, several teachers came into my classroom and singled me out, asking about my father's race. One teacher said, "What color is your dad?" Being so young, I didn't understand the big deal and simply said, "He's black." Their reaction was unclear to me, but I knew that they saw this as something wrong. When I got home from school, I told my mom about my day. When I mentioned that the teachers asked me those questions, she was livid. She sat me down and told me if they ever asked me questions like that again to tell them that my dad is "yellow with purple polka dots." The next day she went to handle the situation herself and those teachers never asked me questions like that again. Intrusive questions like these have always been a part of living in the south for me. I don't think I realized it, but in a way, growing up as a minority with a family that wasn't right in society's eyes helped me grow to become a person who can handle a lot. My transition has been difficult, but not impossible. It took me until my late twenties to learn the term transgender.

My first memory of feeling incongruent with the sex I was assigned at birth was in the third grade. I was telling my friend on the playground how I wished I was a boy and hated being a girl. He looked at me and said, "You should get a sex change." Looking back, I was so confused about how in the world he knew what that was. I'd never heard of such a thing. This feeling kept returning like a concentric circle overlapping with normal childhood milestones. The second time I verbalized these feelings was in the fifth grade. I had two best friends. When we played I would always tell them that I was really a boy, but my mom wanted a girl so bad that she made me pretend to be one. Like most kids, my friends didn't know what to do with that information or what it meant so we quickly moved on from the topic.

As I got older, I started to fulfill the desire to display my need to be a boy privately. I would use my allowance money to buy boys' underwear, but hid them so my mom wouldn't find them. Out in public, people in the south always gendered me as male because I kept my hair short. When I opened my mouth, they would correct themselves. This process made me feel sad and disappointed. I wanted to tell them, "No, you were right the first time." I always knew I was a boy, but no one believed me. I spent many times throughout my development wishing and dreaming. There were even times when I was at the mall and I would ask my mother for some change to throw in the fountain. I threw my coin in and said out loud, "I wish I woke up a boy." Slowly I pushed these feelings back and gave up wishing as I entered my teenage years. I didn't have any earthly idea of what could be done.

As I grew out of adolescence, life threw me into a loop—I met someone who I fell in love with. In my twenties, this man made me so happy, but little did I know he had a secret addiction. I was too blind to notice. We later found out I was pregnant, but unfortunately he wasn't able to keep clean and we split up for the well being of my daughter. Rye was born in March 2006. It was the best day of my life. I remember her looking at me with her big eyes and personality. I couldn't have asked for such a gift. I thought I finally had it all, but I still had a secret. Something I had been hiding and pushing away for so long that I almost fell upon it accidentally on the Internet.

One day in late 2010, looking for a stand-to-pee (STP) device for a camping trip, I came across a video of a transman talking about STPs. I watched and instantly knew what was going on with me. I continued watching videos on YouTube about what testosterone does to the body, all the changes that come with it, and how to get it. These videos gave me a sense of hope that my wish in the fountain when I was younger was true; I was a boy. The only issue was I couldn't find a transman on YouTube that had children and many of the guys were younger. That feeling of a lack of visibility among other trans people with children or who weren't in their college years is why I'm so open with my transition. I want to help guys that are in the same shoes I was once in. The information I found was amazing and scared me about my daughter and quality of her life. I began the constant questioning of how I might broach the subject with her. I asked myself so many times: "How will I explain my feelings to her?" She was only four at the time, so I did not want to confuse her. "How will people treat her?" I think this question bothered me the most since I experienced my teachers asking about my dad in school. "Will she hate me?"

It was obvious to me that I had to protect Rye's happiness above all else, so I held back; but I could not stop watching YouTube. Finally in March 2011, I told myself I would go talk to a therapist and just see what they said. Living in the South, it was very hard finding someone who could help me, but I finally did. The sessions were great. We talked about family, my anger issues, and my daughter. The therapist really opened my eyes to see that the world has a variety of people and also genders. All my life, I was taught a person was either male or female. There was no in-between. They told me that transitioning would be hard to do in the south, but not impossible. They also reassured me that my daughter would love me no matter what, and that for me to be the best parent I could be to her, first I needed to be happy. These fears stuck with me, but I knew that if I was going to be a stable parent I needed to be myself authentically. After six months of therapy, I made an appointment with a primary care doctor in Atlanta who I found through other trans guys in the area. But before that, I needed to talk to my parents and daughter about my transition.

In my family, we don't usually talk about personal or tough things unless it's important. So I sat Rye down and told her how mama had always felt like a boy inside, but that my body did not match and I was thinking about changing that soon. I asked how she felt about it and she said, "Okay, so what will I call you?" I told her whatever made her happy. I felt like our conversation went great. For consistency, she continued calling me "mama" for the first two years I medically transitioned.

Next, I had to talk with my mother, and I worried about telling her. I knew she would accept me, but I also knew this would be very hard for her being that I was her first child. We work together, so one day I told her we needed to talk later on. Instantly, she thought the worst and demanded I tell her right then and there. At first it didn't come out right because I was so nervous, and she replied, "I'm going to freaking kill you!" That was definitely not what I was hoping for, so I sat her down to explain my feelings. She instantly went back to when we were at the fountain in the mall. She understood right away. Then she asked about my daughter. I told her that I had already discussed it with Rye and that we would work through things as they came up, but that she understood. After that we watched talk shows, YouTube videos and read books about being transgender. Now she refers to me as Gabe, her son.

Before I started testosterone, I wanted to get my family together to tell them. In my head, I thought that since we are all close, it would be okay and that they would love me no matter what. Unfortunately, that was not the case.

It all happened quicker than I expected so I didn't have the chance before beginning my medical transition. When I went to Atlanta for my appointment, I began testosterone the next day. My cousin knew my about my transgender identity. My cousin told my family before I had a chance to, so a war broke out. I begged for them to listen to me, to let me explain, but to them I had committed the ultimate sin. Half of my family are hardcore Christian, and the other half rarely attends church. It got so heated that the Bible was thrown around a lot, which was scary. A gay family member told me to wait for them to cool down and suggested I give it a few months. After a while, I called my aunt who I had always been close with. I was about three months on testosterone. She had no clue who I was on the phone. "Who is this?" she asked. She began to cry when I told her and said I was never going to be a man; I would always be a freak. She refused to accept me, told me she'd never call me her nephew, and hung up the phone. This broke my heart into pieces. I spent so many nights crying myself to sleep thinking about how I lost my family. I wondered, was all of this really worth it? Now we speak maybe twice a year.

I had experienced so much loss from my family I began to worry about work, but knew that I needed to be up front and honest about transitioning. I'm a cook at a local family restaurant. We all work very close together. This tight-knit setting can be both a blessing and a curse. My work has no protection for me as an employee. When I came out, my initial experience was okay, but has become increasingly volatile over the last four years. I'm constantly being called by my old name in addition to an onslaught of LGBTQ bashing. I sometimes wonder how much more I can handle. I have to keep my job, though, because as with anything else, my daughter comes first. She keeps me going and pushes me to work through the challenging times.

When I think about it, it's funny how my daughter has changed over time throughout my transition. At two years on testosterone, we were in

Wal-Mart when the cashier said, "Here you go, sir"; my daughter turned and said, "Actually it's ma'am." The cashier was just as embarrassed as I was, and she apologized. I wanted out of there as fast as I could. That night at dinner I told her we should come up with a word to call me that only she and I knew the meaning of. This excited her since it would be a secret between us. I felt that neither one of us was comfortable with me being "Dad" just yet. After so many silly names we decided on MOPS. That day forward it has been MOPS. My transition is about me, but it is also about being a strong and good parent for my child. Transitioning has helped me become a better version of myself for Rye.

## Jack Elliott – Age Forty-One, Writer/Producer/Project Manager, Brooklyn, New York

My account, as I recollect, began with a dollhouse. It was just one of many unwanted little-girl gifts. Evidence left over from the pile of Christmases that had gone terribly wrong for me. It was too big to stuff under the bed or in the back of the closet like the dolls and pink things that came before it. It stood in the middle of the room taunting me with its feminine mystique. It took up real estate in my bedroom, and in my mind. It was a classic Victorian, tall and green with black shutters. I held the Oriental rugs in the palm of my hand. I stuck both my feet in the first floor pushing my way past the staircase. Toes pressed up against the wainscoting. The structure could not house my size. I pushed, and shoved in anyway. And so my life began, cramming into something pretty. Shoving, contorting myself into what looked fantastic, but felt like shit. Elbows poked through tiny windows, legs that wanted nothing more than to stretch, instead they were held knees to chin.

The beginning of me took place in Brooklyn, New York in the early seventies. Graffiti-filled subway cars squirmed through the underbelly and I was on them. Paper-bag covered bottles rolled back and forth beneath my feet at each stop. My only job was to lift my feet slightly so as to not get in the way of motion. The smell of pizza hung outside our fourth-floor window, trapped inside a cloud of sewer steam. The stucco walls in our apartment guarded like barbed-wire fences. Sharp and unforgiving, it was the twenty-four hour watchman who assured there would be no roughhousing indoors. Buses hissed to their stops, and horns tried to out-honk each other. Kids rounded bases made of fire hydrants and lawn chairs. Voices rose up, crashed hard on the pavement and shattered. The days were big, loud, and left a layer of proof on your skin that they existed.

I know we didn't have a lot of money, but I never remember wanting for anything. If there was struggle, we were kept separate from it. My memories are soft, dimly lit, and torn around the edges. For the most part, those were not happy times, but I have washed them over with better lighting, and turned the volume down to an acceptable pitch.

I could sense the times that were happening around me even if I was too small to comprehend them. The adult 1970's things were sequined, shiny, and thumped to the bass. Blouses flowed, jewelry glistened, and everything was brown and deep gold. All of our parents commuted to the city. I watched the army of secretaries and mid-level management march to and from the subway. Some had ambition, and some would have never equated such a thing with a steady paycheck.

Both my parents worked full-time so my dad's father watched us every day after school; I have very simple memories of him. They appear in my mind like an old-timey telegram: Picked me up from school - (STOP)- Went for ice cream cone at Carvel -(STOP)- Went to his local bar so he could get a drink (or several) -(STOP)- We threw a Nerf football at his newspaper while he read -(STOP)- Parents came home -(STOP).

While I was busy attending to the business of being a kid, my body had already begun to betray me. Clothes wore me. Dresses felt like costumes. Mary Janes held my feet captive like prisoners. My Catholic-school uniform restricted normal movement—I wanted to tear the threads piece-by-piece and watch plaid turn into nothing.

Things began to be expected of me, to act in a way that felt strange and uncomfortable. My six-year—old mind had no language for this. These feelings were giant, free-floating objects with no particular place to go. I just batted them around in the air like a balloon that is not supposed to touch the ground. Girls to the left, boys to the right; it was clear to me that under no circumstances was I allowed to go to the right. A world forever separated in two directions, and I was a girl. What did this mean for me? The unspeakable. Of course it was, I was six. Everything that represented my six-year—old life was based on gender. Life was categorized by a certain set of color codes and norms. I was to be friends with the little girls and prepare for my future in the way of plastic babies and ovens. How did they get it wrong? I was screaming so loudly even though my mouth was shut.

I didn't realize it at the time, but my response to all of it was to create a second self, a subterranean part of me that was locked away and fed scraps. I tried to tend to his needs at first. I played in the dirt, chose trucks over dolls, and ran shirtless. I insisted on dirty sneakers, and worked hard on the healing and re-healing of the scrapes on my knees. I rejected frilly things, and chose rough over soft. I knew it made me different. I had the sense that people were actively allowing me to act that way, as if there was something wrong with it. At that point, I had confidence, and it made me feel powerful.

Instead of merging these two selves, I decided to just play the part on the outside that was dutifully assigned to me. I was uncomfortable with the in between; the girl who looked and acted like a boy. It left me exposed and vulnerable, this secret boy self. It felt dirty and shameful. So I got myself a multicolored order form for those cookies, and joined the girl scouts like everyone else.

We were: Mom, Dad, and my brother who was four and a half years my senior. On special occasions our family of four ate dinner on a foldout table in front of the television. Our chairs dug into the deep carpet leaving temporary marks. There were sounds of silverware and serving spoons hitting plates, chewing, and swallowing but little else. I didn't know it yet, but our family was disappearing into the sounds of *Love Boat*, and *Fantasy Island*. I don't remember any big fights, and there were no epic family tragedies playing out in our apartment. Life seemed manageable, and small enough to contain in a fourth-floor walk up.

I felt very separate from my family. I don't know whether this was of my own design. There was a system of operations that was developing. Everyone began training for his or her position. My father began his emotional disappearing act, and my mother soon followed. I've only come to realize now that they were in their twenties at the time. Oh, the gravity of fucking kids playing house.

My brother and I were close during those years. We invented a game called "Joe and John." Two regular guys doing odd jobs and getting into shenanigans just like regular ol' guys do. We didn't pretend to be super heroes or have any interest in saving the world. On any given day Joe and John were electricians called to a house to fix an electrical problem. We kept our fantasies at bay in a very manageable blue collar way. I, of course, had to be the one who stuck the fork into the socket to check things out. Or I'd have to be taken to the fake hospital to remove my cast made from an entire roll of masking tape. But why did brother John see me as Joe, and no one else did? It wasn't a conscious decision we made that I was never to be a Jane.

As the '70s were coming to an end, our family moved to a tiny town in Orange County, New York. My parents' marriage began to deteriorate and my father spent his time back in Brooklyn most nights. One of my mother's goals for moving to the suburbs was to save us from being stoop kids. She feared the kids with dirty jeans and hair; the unsupervised kids with foul mouths had too much time on their hands. In reality, asshole kids have nothing to do with geography. But soon, woods replaced pavement-covered playgrounds. Porches became a part of the house instead of a place to meet and hang out. Our new house was on the middle of a hill, not the kind that builds with anticipation but a teasing incline that gave way to the sight of our house without warning. This is when things really started to unravel.

In December of 1980 my parents were finally

getting a divorce and my mother needed respite. We went to the farm where we spent every summer with my grandparents. That December on the farm there were private adult conversations, but I could not understand the words so they just became rhythms. It was the melodic sound of the end. Fried chicken, mashed potatoes and apple pie were our guests at the feast celebrating the end of our family.

After dinner I moved myself outside to the snow. I began to see myself as unrecognizable in this landscape, as I was in my own body. I remember staring at my legs for hours. The silence was so loud it broke something loose, and it traveled through every part of me. I was so tiny and not yet a complete person. These thoughts of losing my family, confusion about my gender, they were so much bigger than me. But it was there in that snow bank that I was forced to grow big enough around all of it. It was then that I decided to acknowledge my secret boy self. I spoke the words out loud and I would do everything in my power to hide and protect them.

I realized my body was different and separate from me. I had no idea that nature was being kind to my eight-year old body, because in a few years the straight lines turned into curves, what was flat became round, and the hard turned into soft. Eventually my hormones took their rightful ownership of me.

But he was on the inside, and I was forced to carry him around underneath an uncomfortable girl suit.

The work that needed to be done in keeping this boy inside of me was a secret project with no adult supervision. There was no architectural plan or directions on how to not be a girl without anyone noticing. From what I could tell this was a deep-cover solitary mission. How could I construct a person within a person? How to exist only in my mind with skateboards, BMX bikes, and monsters while living dolls, dresses, and fairies? I thought this as my little-girl arms dangled Barbie in hand from underneath a sundress. Each self had its own experience, and the boy one would have to be filed away for use later in life. I learned to have some level of joy even if it had its physical limitations. I could not take my shirt off and run through the streets. My body did not move or behave the way I wanted it to—or more specifically how I was told it should. But in my mind I could run free, and so I did just that. It's only now I realize that in reality I was standing still. I couldn't have known it then, but I'd end up spending most of my life that way.

Being a teenager was one big toothy grin of a blur like something out of a John Hughes movie. It was the '80s, I was popular, did okay in school, excelled both at sports and at being normal. Everything looks normal clothed in a smart V-neck sweater and a turtleneck. Any and all feelings that I had suspected to be true about myself began to be shooed away like a newspaper at a bad dog. I thought, "What would life mean if I truly admitted to myself that I was born in the wrong body?" As I feared I would be exposed, the notion became absurd to me, almost fantastical. So the charade continued.

My twenties became about coming out the first time. The liberation of saying I was gay with confidence even though something about it never felt quite right. It was one step closer; the once unspeakable had a voice even if it really wasn't speaking truth.

Most transmen I know had to go through the

33

experience of being a gay woman before transitioning; an obvious choice. It was a tight-knit community but it ended up feeling isolating and confusing. How could it be that I didn't belong in the midst of a community that itself didn't belong? My options were dwindling.

My early thirties became about career and direction in so much as that meant a further distraction of inner self. My angry-boy self that had certainly not matured at the same rate as my other self was getting restless. At the age of thirty-four, life finally came around, gently tapped me on the shoulder and told me there was such a thing. An option.

The funny thing is, as soon as the knowledge came to me that I could in fact transition there wasn't an existential crisis or long drawn-out deliberation asking myself if I could do this. Regardless of the unknown both physically and mentally, the decision was immediate, and it was absolute.

Even though transitioning has felt like being thrown out of a helicopter in the middle of the jungle, armed only with good intentions, a dull knife and the will to survive, I wouldn't change a thing. It has made me strong, introspective, thoughtful, emotional, empathetic, curious, forgiving, motivated, confident and resolute.

What shaped my experience was the fact that I grew up thinking transitioning wasn't a possibility; what's worse, there wasn't even a choice. The trans narrative is part of a larger cultural conversation now. Transitioning is now politicized and editorialized but ultimately the process is still about people and their stories, secret selves, discovery, strength and unimaginable courage to live the lives we were meant to live.

### Mitch Kellaway – Age Twenty-Five, Assistant Editor – Transgress Press, Boston, Massachusetts

My mind has returned often to the pivotal moment I first read the word *transgender*—what my queer friends jokingly refer to as my "root." I wonder what impelled me to neatly fold trans into a prepackaged visual, instead of allowing it to undo messily and rebuild my core self image. I came upon it in the school library one day when, acting as the proper Gay/Straight Alliance leader I prided myself on being; I decided to research an upcoming bulletin-board display. I thought I was learning about it because I found the thought of gender transition intriguing, and it was my duty, as a club chair, to be well informed.

Back then—and I'm not sure it's so popular now—gender nonconformity was presented as a "Transgender Umbrella." The image was simple, eye catching, and what's more, I could decorate it with rainbows and make a cute exhibit. I did just that and for the whole semester it remained standing. It successfully captured the attention of a certain receptive, though limited, student body: me. My eye was snagged every time I passed.

My relatively early self-awareness of my own transness was made possible by trans activists before me; their work allowed me to grow up in a world where some cultural concept of "transgender" has always existed. Whether or not I always knew what it was—and I didn't fully until I reached age seventeen and was poised to leap over the adolescent cliff into young adulthood—it was nonetheless lying in wait for my discovery.

With each year that passes, I become more aware of how privileged I was to respectfully learn in a public school what being transgender meant. In many ways, my experience was exceptional. I attended an institution with one of the United States' first Gay/Straight Alliances. Our colorful group of teens, fluctuating between five and twenty attendees each week, was afforded enough space, acknowledgement, and faculty support as any other club. We even got to start planning a mural for the wall outside our advisor's classroom (and took equal advantage of the opportunity to abandon such a large project). Teachers encouraged us to engage in lively events outside of school where we proudly carried a rainbow flag emblazoned with our high school's name.

Even to this day, I can count on seeing younger students march by carrying that same banner each year as I stand on the sidewalk observing the annual Pride parade. Despite how my appearance has changed over the years, I'm still spotted by my former faculty advisor who waves me closer for a hug. The beard lining my jaw, my surgically flattened chest, and the baritone I now use to cheer can't keep my mentor from recognizing me. A couple of years ago, he even pulled me into the crowd to march alongside for the last few blocks, back among my Gay/Straight Alliance again; beside me marched another teacher, newly out as a transgender woman. My school couldn't have been more supportive.

Yet, I'm not sure I could have ever come out as transgender back when I was a teenager. This had as much to do with the timing of my self discovery—the last semester of high school, just as I was making the enormous life change of graduating and approaching college—as it did with how very out I already was. For my last two years of school, I was very public about being a gay woman. My visibility was an intentional political statement: it's okay to love the same gender. Being a part of that cause was a vital part of my evolving sense of what I had to offer the world as an emerging adult.

Being gay was how I came to know myself as an activist and—though, again, I didn't have the exact word then—a feminist. When I first fell in love with a female classmate, I logically assumed I was a lesbian. Each day I sat next to her in math class, my pounding heart and sweaty palms seemed to confirm it. I was raised, as most young people are, to believe that possessing certain body parts (breasts, ovaries, etc.) and being socialized into femininity meant that I was naturally and permanently female. I'm grateful that I was in an environment where everyone was taught that being a woman-loving woman was perfectly acceptable, and that I had the time to figure out if that was truly who I am. It wasn't, in the end—but I can't regret it.

Experiencing same-sex attraction caused me to think critically about my sexuality; that first act of gender transgression opened up my mind to what a social fiction gender norms are. I was so convinced of it that—following a queer poet's last-minute cancellation on our annual Transgender, Bisexual, Gay, and Lesbian Awareness Day (ToBeGLAD)—I announced I was gay to a group of fifty classmates. The school newspaper followed up the next month by publishing an interview with me. A year later, I staged a well-attended protest of the Westboro Baptist Church after they threatened to picket outside our school's production of *The Laramie Project*. I could not have been a bigger poster child for adolescent homosexuality if I tried.

I had every reason to be pleased and proud of myself, and I was. It made me so deeply happy to be an out gay activist that I resisted the internal whispers telling me this self-exploration wasn't complete. I first heard that voice when I came across transgender activist/writer Leslie Feinberg's *Transgender Warriors* listed in my school's library catalogue, as I was gathering materials for my Trans Umbrella display. My curiosity piqued, I went to the history section, only to find the book was checked out. Mentioning this discovery casually to my GSA advisor the next day, I noticed a flash of anxiety in his eyes.

"That's odd that it's out," he said uneasily. He explained how he'd helped to make sure funds were allotted for gay and transgender-focused books for our library—an anomaly among high school collections, even now. It struck me as odd that he was so worried about someone actually using the book he'd helped buy, but I was quick enough to read the subtext: he thought someone had destroyed it. He wanted that transgender book to be there for the future, but was worried that it wouldn't survive current social attitudes to trans folks.

Now I needed to know what precious words were in that book. I asked the librarian—herself a lesbian, and a great ally to a queer bookworm like me—to let me know when the book resurfaced. It wasn't long before she informed me that someone had borrowed Transgender Warriors for a research project on Joan of Arc, a historical gender rebel. Soon enough I held it, clean and undefiled: an oversized neon-green volume, its author's masculine face a shadow staring intensely from the cover. Reading about gender outlaws throughout history, I felt electrified. I felt mirrored. Something primordial stirred within me.

It took me another year to recognize that this unshakeable feeling was more than the joy of learning something new: I was a transgender man. I tested the theory, as I'd been dutifully taught in grade school, by mentally producing hypotheses of my future self. Somehow, I just couldn't imagine living the rest of my life as a woman, even as I lamented the thought of losing my dear-held lesbian identity. But if living out loud throughout adolescence had taught me anything, it was that I had to be real with myself. I quietly announced my plan to transition—though I set it far off in the future, erroneously believing I shouldn't transition socially before I could afford hormone therapy and surgery—to a few friends on AOL Instant Messenger. It wasn't the large audience I was used to, but it was enough. Every little step I took towards my transition— actually, more like years of stagnation, then one huge leap—was enough until, one day, seven years later, I looked in the mirror and saw the man I always suspected I'd grow up to be.

## Rae Larson – Age Twenty-Three, Secretary for Metro Trans Umbrella Group, St. Louis, Missouri

My whole life feels like a contradiction. I'm an old soul in a twenty-two-year-old vessel. I'm a heavy left-wing liberal with devout Christian beliefs. I don't believe in war or funding militant behavior but I am an Airman serving actively in the Air Force. I want to make my father proud more than anything, but everything about my life is displeasing in his eyes. I am a boy in a female's body. Twenty-four months ago, if you told me I would conquer the truths I've since faced, I would have questioned your sanity. There is nothing scarier than being honest with yourself. My personal development in all aspects of my life has shaken my foundation, challenged my thinking and evolved my true happiness—and let me tell you, for a kid brought up in a strict, military, Christian home, selflessly aiming to please, that was not easy to overcome.

I think the most relevant place to start is back in January 2010—the time I left home for basic training. Military training is like all new things in life— impossibly challenging at first and all you want to do is go back to "how it was," but you get used to it as you go along. Shortly after training I received my orders to Scott Air Force Base in Middle-of-Nowhere, Illinois. For my first year and half at Scott, I had but two friends; one of them happened to be a drag king. She took me to my very first drag show and I immediately fell in love. It took me about a half a second to know I wanted to perform, three weeks to muster up the courage to sign up and two months to wait for my first show. My friend told me, "Doing drag is going to teach you so much about yourself...much more than you realize." At the time I didn't think much of the words; now I think about them almost every day.

I was twenty when I met Sean, a queer trans kid well known for his drag presence in the Saint Louis LGBT community. I had heard a lot about him prior to talking with him and I'd seen him perform on a few occasions. I knew he identified as male even though he wasn't assigned that way at birth, but I didn't know much more than that, and quite frankly, I didn't care. We performed in a few drag shows together before finally exchanging numbers. He said he wanted to have coffee sometime, and since he was such a huge local celebrity, I was honored.

When we met for coffee I wasn't really sure what to expect. We sat down and had a few minutes of small talk before the conversation took a sharp turn toward intense. He started telling me about his life, his story, but mostly his trans identity and what that meant. He said he was a boy with a vagina that he loved, who did drag as a boy and embraced his feminine side. He said he didn't always feel that he was a boy and that it didn't matter—trans is all-inclusive and can be defined differently for everyone. I had no idea why he was telling me any of this. All I could think was, "Wow, that's awesome, dude. Good for you!" I mean, what else was I supposed to say? What was he expecting?

After that initial meeting, he was constantly checking in on me, asking me how I was feeling, if I had done any research on my own, if I wanted to talk more. He asked me if he could use male pronouns with me because it just felt more natural—I didn't really care so I let him. I remember feeling annoyed by him and that was what drove me to actually do research on my own. I figured maybe if I watched a couple of YouTube videos, he'd get off my back about it. One of the first videos I watched—*How I Knew I Was Trans*—made something inside me stir. A lot of trans individuals talk about their "moment," the time when it hit them so hard they couldn't deny it, the time their entire lives flashed before their eyes and they saw everything so clearly. The YouTuber was describing his story but at the same time he wasn't…he was describing my story. I began to sob—I was terrified, liberated, electrified and dejected all in one instant. I could see every single moment of my entire life all connected to one underlying issue that was pressing at my heart from my very first memories—I was a boy. I had always been and had always known.

When I first came to terms with my transgender identity the only thought that rattled me more than uprooting my entire life was knowing how displeased my father would be. Because of this fear I sought therapy. The first therapy session I went to was a travesty. The appointment was in a military hospital; the hallways filled with clean, pressed uniforms and hard faces. I was already nervous enough to talk about my gender for the first time with a complete stranger, but the fact that I felt like I was at war made it worse. I guess, in a way, I was at war; I was about to "out" myself to someone who may have been obligated to turn me in to my commander—being transgender is considered a mental illness in the military and is grounds for medical discharge. I sat awkwardly erect in a cold, dark, unfriendly room, unnervingly concentrated on the thought of the worst-case scenario. The therapist walked in, shook my hand like it was made of glass, and said, "What can I help you through today?" Though I felt our initial greeting was very off-putting, I spilled my guts to her. I didn't cry but I made myself incredibly vulnerable, hoping she could help me.

About thirty-five minutes later, when I stopped talking, she sat in silence for a very long moment. She looked me deep in the eyes, let out a little breath, and squinted her face so much it seemed like maybe she thought the more creases in her forehead, the more likely she'd know what to say. She opened and closed her mouth a couple times before slowly forcing out: "How long...have you known you like women?" Mind you, the only thing I had mentioned about sexuality was that I came out as a lesbian to my dad when I was fifteen. I was completely shocked and I don't know why...I should have known better. I responded with, "I'm sorry?" "Well, you know...it's hard these days... to be... a lesbian," she said. I only went to the mental health clinic on base because I knew I couldn't use my health insurance to cover my therapy sessions without getting approval through the military doctor. I also knew that most transgender individuals in the military are too scared to talk to mental health workers for fear of losing their jobs. I left that initial therapy session feeling defeated.

I had to seek help from somewhere else. Sean suggested I talk to his therapist—which is what I ended up doing. I started seeing my current therapist in May of 2012. During the initial visit, I was asked to elaborate on my goals and what I wanted to accomplish through therapy. Other than starting my medical transition and maintaining my emotional health, the reason I wanted to go to therapy was because I needed to figure out how to come out to my family—specifically my dad. I knew I wanted to start hormones close to my birthday, so that gave me about six months to prepare to come out.

My current therapist has been a godsend. I've learned so much by focusing on just one aspect of myself with intense scrutiny. I think that's the thing most people will never have in life—a deep understanding of "self" and what it means to be completely honest and vulnerable with yourself. Therapy helped me obtain a mental state where I was prepared to let my family go.

My parents' faith was just starting to blossom when I was born and they tried very hard to raise me the way they imagined God wanted me to be raised. I will never, ever question the notion that my parents did their very best, because I truly believe it. But to say I've never held resentment in my heart toward them would be a bold-faced lie.

45

My earliest memories are of trying to convey my gender "confusion" (to me, the world was confused) to my parents. I fought them to no avail with the clothes I wore, the toys I played with, the friends I had, the activities I participated in and the way I expressed myself. I really did not understand why everyone seemed to fight me on my gender. I knew I was a boy, so why didn't everyone else? The day I figured out what society was fussing about is still so clear in my memory. My dad and I were playing "tickle monster" and he was chasing me around the house. One of the closets in the room we were goofing around in had a cupboard above it that was just large enough for me to fit in. My dad grabbed me and put me in the cupboard while I laughed and laughed. There was a book sitting in there with me, and out of curiosity I picked it up. It was a cartoon book that displayed the anatomy of men and women. My parents were probably going to use it to help explain the body and sex to me and my siblings. The page I opened to had a female body on one side and a male body on the other. It was then that I realized the part I was missing and I was completely devastated.

From ages four to ten I would pray every single night that I would "wake up as a boy." My mom kept my favorite Barney towel on the towel rack facing the toilet. I would lock myself in the bathroom and stare at it. I spent a good 20 to 30 minutes a day looking deep into Barney's eyes and pleading with him to use his magic to "make me a boy."

When I entered middle school I learned that 11:11 is a lucky time of day. I set my watch alarm for 11:11; when it would go off, I would wish that tomorrow, I'd wake up and be a boy and that everyone would be okay with it.

I came out as a lesbian at fifteen. I had myself fooled that it wasn't that I wanted to be a boy; it was just that I wanted to like girls. Coming out as a lesbian was completely life altering. My first girlfriend and I dated for a year before I realized how much I had always liked women—my first baby sitter, my kindergarten teacher, all of my best friends. I'd just thought I really, really admired them. Being a part of the LGBT community was so liberating. Feeling like I "fit in" somewhere and knowing that others felt the things that I had felt was incredible. But something was still off. Why was it that in a group of women, even lesbians, I still felt like the "odd man out"?

My dad and I argued over my lesbian identity for seven years. My dad is a very black-and-white kind of guy. I held onto my Christian identity while still holding onto my lesbian identity and he could not fathom that, so in my mind, coming out as transgender to him would be devastating to our relationship. His initial reaction was much worse than I could have ever imagined. He said some incredibly hurtful and ignorant things and I was sure that his love for me would end there…but fortunately it didn't.

It took him about two weeks to come around. He wrote me an email saying that though he didn't support it, he thought he could understand where I was coming from and he could respect me for it. He has completely stopped arguing with me—we have never once debated my identity since that day. And though he still gets my preferred name and pronouns wrong more times than he gets them right, he is trying. My little sister said that, in a heated argument, he admitted that I was his favorite child. He must respect me a whole lot for never backing down from what I felt was true, even when he came at me, guns blazing.

Just like with my dad, my relationship with the rest of my immediate family has only strengthened by leaps and bounds. Some took longer to come around but they are all trying to be as supportive as possible and our bonds only feel stronger as the days go by. It hasn't been sprinkles and cupcakes the whole time, but each time they get my name right it tastes sweeter and sweeter.

Initially I believed in God because my parents told me to, but as I grew older I undeniably experienced the presence of a higher power not of this world. I used this faith to crush the hopes and dreams of everyone I could—because after feeling these unexplainable things, I looked to self-righteous people to tell me what to do with my faith. I was taught to place judgment, deny love, and bash those who didn't believe what I did. When I came to terms with my queer identity at fifteen, things really had to change for me. How could I be an extreme Christian and an extreme homosexual at the same time? Thus began the evolution of my faith.

I believe that faith is different for everyone; I have experienced things that not everyone has or will experience. I only know what is true for me, and those principles will not ring true for everyone. I have also learned that I can't stand most "Christians" and I relate a lot better to my atheist friends (even more contradictions). Upright morals, acceptance and unconditional love are not taught in church today—or at least not in the hundreds of churches I've attended in my life. Churches hide behind their Bibles, picking and choosing what to harp on and what to ignore. These are not things I can relate to. Everyone has certain things in their life they feel strongly about and I would never try to tell someone they are wrong in those feelings. Believing in God and having faith is right for me.

A lot of people are curious about being trans in the military. Because of this, I get frequent messages from people who want to join the military but identify as trans. To me, that is equivalent to a scenario in which I had cancer and people were coming to me saying they were curious about having cancer and how would I suggest they go about picking it up as well? Being trans in the military means having to live a secret life that could end your career and also ruin your future career opportunities. If you try to start medically transitioning on your own dollar—which is how most in the military do it—you are essentially destroying government property. The military owns its people—we are property, not employees. We have no life outside of what the government says is okay. Seeking medical attention that the government is not moderating is considered mutiny and is grounds for dishonorable discharge. Try to get a job at McDonald's after a dishonorable discharge, and then let me know how unemployment is treating you. I should tell you that there are some trans individuals who are in the military and whose leadership is completely fine with them identifying however they want. The problem is that in the military you are likely to be moved every two to four years, at least. On top of that, leadership is being cycled in and out, as are the people you work with. All it takes is one person to speak out and you are done. It's an incredibly huge risk to be out as trans in the military.

There comes a point in everyone's life where you can't hide anymore. After another incident in which the government reminded me that they owned me, I decided I couldn't put my life on hold any longer. I sought medical transition out of my own pocket to include therapy, blood work, physicals and hormones. I did not tell anyone I was working with and have only had a few people asking questions and a couple of close calls. More times than not, people see what they want to see. If you go over to a stranger's house and they keep calling their cat a dog, you're probably going to go along with it.

Being closeted is one thing, but fear of losing my job over being true to myself is a whole new ball game. I have no desire to be secretive about my life. I have learned where my true liberation lies and I am forced to pretend that doesn't exist for more than forty hours a week. I feel so helpless and caged in. Every time I use the women's restroom at work, every time I hear "ma'am," every time I put on my "women's uniform," I am conflicted, angry, and ashamed. I have to submit to the will of those who believe my happiness is a mental disorder. I am fighting for the freedom of others, a freedom I myself am not allowed to enjoy. I feel as though I am a child at Disney World for the first time but I'm locked in a glass box in the middle of the park.

Without the trans community here in Saint Louis, I would be an incredibly unhappy female—lost and confused by the fact that nothing felt "worth it." I could very well be dead.

Though it is great that it exists at all, the trans community is still somewhat disorganized in the metro area. I wanted to help others grow as I had, so, along with some close trans-identified friends, I decided to start a non-profit group to promote education, visibility and a sense of community for trans individuals.

Through my work with the Metro Trans Umbrella Group, I have connected and networked beyond my wildest dreams. I have never felt so supported in my entire life, and I know that I will only build a stronger support system as my work continues.

I am constantly and rapidly evolving. Every day I feel farther and farther from the weak, confused, closed-off person I was before. I have meaning and purpose now, and that's what most people would call "living." When I first started coming to terms with my trans identity, I become completely preoccupied by a need to know myself. Allowing myself to be consumed by this drive for liberation, I have experienced so many personal revelations that have set me free.

I am passionate about making a difference in whatever way I possibly can. I am taking steps towards strengthening my faith. I am pushing myself to exercise and eat better. I am diligently building my relationships with family and friends. I'm striving to be a better version of myself. It's so easy to feel excited about living when your life feels like your own. After you've been trying for so long to make a square peg fit into a round hole, it's utter liberation.

I can't really identify with the person I was two years ago, but in essence, I have always been who I am now.

## Will Krisanda, Age Thirty-One, Freelance Writer/Billing Specialist, Scranton, Pennslyvania

The swishing sound of leather against nylon rope immediately followed dinner time on Wagon Road. It felt natural each time I picked up the basketball and tossed it into the net from the imaginary free throw line in our driveway. I could dribble between my legs at a young age and thought someday I would play basketball like Michael Jordan.

Being a twelve-year-old girl, standing 5'2" and being twenty pounds overweight made it impossible to dunk from any line on the court, but it didn't stop me from wondering what it felt like to fly through the air and hear that swish up close.

Pimple-faced boys watched me play in gym class and shouted in their cracked voices, "You play like a boy!" I continued playing, dribbling near them with my head facing downward, wishing they would leave me alone and quietly say under my breath as I passed them, "I feel like a boy, so why wouldn't I play like one, dummies?"

A few years later one of the girls in my grade caught on. In freshman typing class, I sat next to

Angela Kane. She wore turtlenecks every day, even in the summer. She had thick brown hair, so thick it made her head look freakishly large. Her skin was pale, she had a small, stubby nose and always sat with perfect posture. While waiting for the teacher to come back, I slouched in my seat, with one arm stretched out over the empty seat next to me, one leg propped up with my foot resting on the other leg's thigh.

Angela glared at me. Her gaze started at my face and followed the length of my arm and down toward my feet.

"You know what?" Angela said while studying me closely.

I looked over at her and shrugged.

"You would make a better boy," she said with a know-it-all attitude.

Before I could contemplate what she said, I let out a nervous laugh and the teacher came in, asked us to sit up straight in our chairs and place our hands on the home keys.

She was right.

When I hit puberty things got very confusing.

"Mom, I got my period *again*," I said the second day of having it.

"Meg, you'll be getting it for a few days each month for a long time," she said reassuringly.

I said okay and with my basketball in hand, went back to practicing my lay-up. I didn't understand what was happening to my body and I didn't care to know any more about it.

Sometimes I thought my parents were keeping a secret from me, a secret too controversial for someone my age to understand. I thought they had my penis surgically removed when I was a baby because they already had two boys. In the shower, I would search for the scar, looking to find any evidence to help me understand.

Scars would come later.

"I just thought you'd be gay. You enjoyed playing with the boys the most. That's when you were happiest so I thought you'd be a lesbian, but this? This I didn't suspect," said my mom.

She was half right. I came out as a lesbian when I was seventeen. It made the most sense at the time. I was attracted to women and the word transgender didn't exist in my world yet. I dated a few women for the next several years and confused everyone, including myself, when I fell in love with a boy sometime in between it all. But something still didn't feel exactly the way it should. Something was missing.

I first heard people transitioned their sex when I discovered the movie *Boys Don't Cry*. I made whoever I was dating at the time, as well as my mom and all my friends, watch and re-watch it with me. This isn't a movie that should be re-watched, it is a tough movie to sit through, given the tragic story of Brandon's transition but something inside my stomach stirred quietly, moving its way up to my throat whenever I watched it. I bought the Brandon Teena documentary and a book about another man who had transitioned that I later saw on the daytime talk show *The View*. Again, my stomach was in knots.

Finally, it took reading an article to push me to make active steps toward transitioning. At age twenty-six, I read an op-ed article about Thomas Beatie, the transman who got pregnant, in my colleges newspaper.

The author of the article condemned him for his decision to become pregnant. The author was very adamant that Mr. Beatie would never truly be a man no matter how many hormones or surgeries he would undergo. Along with my knotted stomach, my body was filled with heated rage. I re-read the article a dozen times, underlining sentences, making notes in the margins, circling words.

I decided to write a letter to the editor. I felt the author of the piece was not educated enough on trans issues and he said some really offensive things. I included some books and names of websites about transgender information in my response, expressed my feelings about the piece and I signed it with my birth name and "as someone in the trans community."

Shortly after, I made the leap and decided tell my family, friends and co-workers that I planned to begin hormone therapy. I wrote a letter to everyone explaining my intentions because writing has always been the best way to explain this journey. I visited Philadelphia for their annual Trans Health Conference to gain as much information as possible. Everything started to happen so quickly.

My aunt Nini was the first person of my extended family to call and wish me luck. I stood in my bedroom, looking out the window and cried as she said, "We love you no matter what."

My mom cried every night for the first few months. Initially, she was shocked and concerned for my safety. She didn't know what the response would be from others and feared for my well being. She also blamed herself for not being prepared for it. She wanted a daughter and was afraid of losing the relationship we've shared for the past twenty-six years. But nothing has really changed other than now she compliments how much hair is growing on my legs or my face.

Once the hormone therapy began, I expected the changes to happen quickly and when they didn't, I became increasingly impatient, which led to an overwhelming feeling of frustration and depression. I wanted to be seen as a man the day I told everyone. I wanted to erase the past and start over.

The positive side of the impatience was how it made me realize this was a process. It forced me to try and focus on the present moment even though I fought it as much as I could. I wanted my life to be in the next chapter, but I hadn't finished the first page yet.

My first day of work as Will, I was welcomed by the owner of the company at the door. She led me through each department introducing me as Will. My name had been changed on my badge and my e-mail. I had learned later that she spoke with all the supervisors informing them of my change and instituted a "zero tolerance" policy regarding discrimination toward me.

A few older women I work with hugged me and one of them came up to me, with her glasses hanging low on her nose, her white puffy hair, perfectly ironed beige cardigan sweater. She came up close to me, stopped and said in the sweetest voice and genuine tone,

"Sometimes even God makes mistakes, Will. I wish you the best."

And she hugged me.

I am one of the luckier ones that hasn't been thrown out of their house, fired, broken up with, or denied healthcare because of my transition. Family and friend support is the biggest factor in a safe and smooth transition and without it I imagine I would be in a very different place.

After four years of hormones, a name change, a double mastectomy and a legal sex change, I am just starting to live the way I've envisioned in my head all these years. Growing up and imagining myself as a boy was an exhilarating experience. I spent hours in the bathroom wearing my brother's clothes and covering the mirrors so my reflection wasn't visible. I was playing out what was going on in my head, practicing. It was my secret. It was something I treasured and never intended on sharing it until it became something that was much bigger than me.

Living out something you've spent countless hours daydreaming about and wondering about is an experience that isn't easily put into words.

For me, transitioning my sex is always a work in progress, especially now as I continue to discover how I fit into this new body and self-image in a world which saw me as something completely different than what I felt inside.

I still can't and never will dunk from any line on the court and I'm okay with that.

## Emmett J. P. Lundberg, Age Thirty,
### Writer/Director/Filmmaker, Brooklyn, New York

This is the second version of my story. The first one wasn't very authentic. Not that I didn't tell the truth, but rather, that I put on a façade. Part of being transgender involves trying to be something you don't feel completely congruent with. So many years are spent in an act of survival, of putting on airs just to get through the day that I think sometimes it's almost second nature to show people what they expect to see.

If you ask me who I am, I could be any number of things at any given moment. At the core, I am energy. I believe that everything in this world is made up of the same stuff, so I am no different than you, nor am I different than the trees, or the air, or the cars on the street. I am a philosopher at heart, if that wasn't obvious. I am a time traveler, but don't ask me about that because I'd have to kill you. I am an X-Phile; no explanation needed because my fellow Philes will know what I mean. I am a lover; of people, of things, of ideas, of Cats. I am a writer, an artist of the written word, learning to adapt to different platforms. And I am a trans man. I am all of these things and none of them at once. I am more than just a label, an identity, or a name. I am, in this very moment, the sum of every other moment in my life.

Let me give you my story in quantities; I'm thirty years old, I've been on testosterone for sixteen months and I had top surgery a mere seven months ago. This still doesn't tell you the truth about when my transition began. Even I don't know the absolute truth to that. When I was young I liked being set apart from the other girls. I took pride in my abnormally large feet and husky voice. I liked being compared to the boys. I wanted to be seen in that way, even if I had no idea what it meant. In fact, I think I continued to brag about my shoe size right up until I started my transition. My mom told me recently about a time we went shoe shopping when I was in elementary school. The sales clerk commented on the enormity of my feet. My mom was offended. I was thrilled. But I never had that moment as a child where I "knew" I was a different gender than I was told. It wasn't something I could have told you when I was five years old. To me, it feels more like an evolution into who I am today.

I've been extremely lucky, not only in my transition, but throughout my life. I was born into an exceptionally artistic family and have always been supported in my pursuits. My parents have never been anything but encouraging and supportive in every possible way. When I was old enough to talk, my mom took me clothes shopping. We wandered through the little girls department and I turned to her with a puzzled look on my face. "Why does everything have flowers on it?" I asked. From that moment forward she allowed me to choose my own outfits. Suffice it to say, there were no more flowers from that point on.

Each of my family members boasts at least one artistic ability. While my younger years were spent on the suburban blocks of a town of no more than 50,000 people, I spread my wings for high school, auditioning for, and being accepted into, Milwaukee's High School of the Arts. Still living in the suburbs, I caught the "little" bus at 4:30 a.m. to travel into the city and spend several hours a day devoted to my chosen major, theatre production. While our academic record wasn't necessarily stellar, I don't think enough can be said for giving students the chance to be creative for a large part of their day. Though at times I feel that my school smarts could have been better developed, my emotional, spiritual and creative IQs are all off the charts.

It was during my time at MHSA that I became conscious of the attraction I had to women. Not knowing that I could be anything other than the gender I was born into, I deduced that I must be a lesbian and came out as such. I certainly wasn't the only queer-identified person at the school, which made it an iota easier. The other schools in our district, and even some of our own student body, jokingly referred to us as MHS-Gay. While my time in the lesbian community was not in any way devastating, I still had the pang of something not quite being right.

A common theme among LGBT youth is depression, and I certainly was no exception. Before I had much of my own identity figured out, I was despondent. Not everyone will understand, but, even before you have the vocabulary, sometimes you just know that you don't feel right. On top of that, being someone who is perceived as female bodied, as a

61

teenager in this world, is far from easy. I struggled with female friendships, particularly in middle school, when I was accused of being a lesbian after expressing my deep (friendly, as far as I knew) love for a classmate. This set off a string of events that ended with the loss of more than one friend. For the first time in my life, I entertained thoughts of suicide. To clarify: I make a distinction between the act of thinking about suicide and the drive to want to go through with it. I don't think I ever got to that point, even at my worst, when I thought life would not continue after my heart was broken.

When it came time to apply to college, I was hell bent on New York. There was literally no other option for me. The only place I applied was to NYU, early decision. Thank God I was accepted, despite my less-than-dynamic SAT scores. I majored in Film and Television Production and minored in Philosophy [insert completely unemployable joke here]. Since graduating in 2006, I have been pretty steadily employed in the industry, as I work toward doing exactly what I want to be doing. I am thankful for that. It has allowed me to remain here. I don't think the beginning of my medical transition would have been quite so smooth had I been somewhere outside of the city.

It was in my early twenties that I first heard and digested the word *transgender*. Once it was in me, I couldn't get it out. I was obsessed. I searched the Internet, read all the books I could get my hands on, anything I could do to learn more about this fascinating topic. I found out later that this is not uncommon among trans folks, but it would still take me another six or seven years to actually accept that this was the identity that best fit me.

I hesitate to base the history of discovering or validating my trans identity on those I have been with but how can we know ourselves without seeing the reflection of who we are in the eyes of those around us? It was towards the end of my five-and-a-half-year relationship with a woman I grew up with that I realized I truly needed medical transition for my own well-being. While she was not always supportive of this because of her own fears and insecurities, she had to admit that even when we first met I had expressed feelings to her about not identifying with what it meant to be female. Knowing in the depths of my being, a place a friend of mine calls "The Gut," that this next part of my life did not and could not include her was one of hardest decisions I have ever had to make. I'd like to be able to say that now, more than two and a half years after our separation, we are friendly as can be, but that would be a lie. That is the one part of the process that I may never come to terms with. It's one thing to lose a lover; it's another to lose a best friend.

After that, I dated a woman who intellectually understood my desire to transition and who was completely supportive, but who I felt never saw me as the guy I could see inside myself. I'm sure it was merely internal, since our time together was nothing but good, but that was not enough. I learned from, and am thankful for, that experience. I gained the clarity I needed to move forward in my journey.

Then, in the late summer months of 2012, you know, that time when New York is so hot the sidewalks are radiating, I met a woman who would be integral to the courage I needed to take the next step. She was the first person to truly see me as male, before I had taken any medical steps—before I even had a chance to come out to her, as I was not out on the job at the time. With her support, I began telling more people in my work environment. She used a shortened version of my name in the office, as it was more comfortable for me than my full female name, and eschewed pronouns entirely to both eliminate female pronouns and not out me with male pronouns. Outside of the office and when she'd introduce me to her friends she used male pronouns, and it was exciting and liberating. She knew that I still had a few months until my planned T-date, but she encouraged me to reconsider delaying. I used the job as an excuse to mask my fear, but she urged me to face it. With her support I had my first T shot on October 12, 2012. For those additional three months, I am forever in her debt.

I never imagined being on this side of things. I was always on the outside looking in. And now, here I am, someone that those early in their own transitions can look to. The first year on T goes by fast and the second seems to go even faster. It just becomes part of life and you start to forget that you have to give yourself an injection every week to continue living what feels so undeniably true. Every day I feel more comfortable than I did before. My mind has cleared space for creative projects and things that are really important in life. And now, I have these grand moments, usually as I'm listening to music and traveling through the city, when I feel full of everything that is good in the universe and that anything is possible. I can't wait to see what my life, this life brings.

## Dylan Farnsworth – Age Twenty-Eight, Research Biologist, Washington State

I don't know at what age we begin to form our identities, but I think that at some point in our development we all must face the discrepancy between the vision we have of ourselves, and what the world sees. Looking back I can see in sharp and poignant relief the moment in which I was faced with this realization. I was in kindergarten or first grade, happily playing toy monster trucks with some of my male classmates. From atop a small playground platform above me came a mocking inquiry from three older girls as to why I was playing trucks with boys. The implication of course being that I was a girl, and shouldn't be acting like a boy. In response to their teasing I gripped my monster truck in hand and defiantly thrust it skyward retorting: 'Would a girl have this!?' There was a pause, followed by laughter: 'You think you're a boy??'' My response to their jeer seemed perfectly rational to me at the time. I recall believing that I could truly convince them I was a boy because I was in possession of a boy's toy, playing with other boys. That somehow, by sheer force of will, I could make them see me so. It didn't work. Whatever it was that marked me out as a girl was apparent and visible to the world, but I could not see it. I don't know how soon after that the innocent beliefs I held about myself were consumed by self-awareness, but I cherish that memory—for in that moment I stood as a child and told the world who I wanted to be, and I, for one, believed it.

My best friend Sally, who lived next door to me for our first fifteen years of life, was my constant companion. When we played Barbies I was Ken. When we played Legos I was the male Lego character. Some years later, with the acquisition of a VHS video recorder (I know, I just dated myself), the imaginary games of our childhood became the recorded skits of our youth. These *Saturday Night Live*-style recorded skits were known by both families for their silliness, extravagance, and humor. No effort was spared on hair, make-up, or costume. Though it should be noted that silliness was the goal, and so our makeup was by no means skillfully applied, nor were our costumes ever intentionally well implemented; the more ridiculous the better. Beyond the fun we had I think we were both drawn to the idea of stepping outside of our own lives and experiencing things we otherwise could not have. I don't know which roles Sally found to be the most authenticating and validating, but mine are certainly no secret. Throughout the years our roles varied widely, but I always leapt at the opportunity to play a male part. The goofiness of applying absurd makeup barely concealed my exhilaration at being permitted to draw facial hair on my chin. These were moments of joy in my young life—these were moments when society gave its permission for me to explore my gender in a safe and unconfined space.

Would that all children experienced such freedom in their lives, and that it could have been incorporated more into my own.

My confused childhood evolved into a tormented adolescence. I knew that my attraction to girls was in conflict with the teachings of the Mormon faith in which I'd been raised. I came out as a lesbian to my friends at age thirteen and then to my family at age fifteen. This put a great deal of strain on my relationship with my family, and as time went by I retreated further and further from them. I experienced a great deal of self-loathing and shame during these years and began to exhibit serious mental health issues. I stopped sleeping regularly and my inner turmoil expressed itself as an erratic mix of mania and depression. This resulted in my being absent from school more often than not. My defense against these overwhelming emotions was to become apathetic and disconnected from the world around me. When I was sixteen I left my home, church, and culture, determined to make it on my own. I knew without a doubt that my family loved me, but you can love someone and hurt them at the same time. I felt crushed by the weight of their judgment. Telling someone that you 'Love the sinner but hate the sin' is commensurate with punching someone in the gut very politely. I needed to break free and live my life without the guilt and shame that had confined me for so long. Upon leaving the church I had a final interview with my bishop. When I told him that I didn't think that being gay was a sin he looked at me with incredulity. I truly don't think he knew how to counsel me to repentance when I rejected the initial premise of his position.

I joined the military at age seventeen and excelled. It was the first time I'd been in the position to compete and be challenged in a masculine setting, and I thrived in that environment. Despite being the youngest person in my platoon during basic combat training, and female as well, I was selected for the leadership position. The apathy I'd felt for so long was shattered as I discovered just how much I was capable of. My newfound purpose was not long lived. After a year of dealing with the realities of the Don't Ask, Don't Tell (DADT) policy, I could stomach it no longer. I had left my home and church because of the discrimination I faced there and replaced it with an institution that was just as judgmental. They weren't supposed to seek out gay soldiers, but they did. I was discharged under DADT and received a general discharge with Honor. I still feel a deep sense of loss at losing the right to call myself a soldier.

After receiving my discharge I worked some and then enrolled in college. I became a more active member of the gay community, which helped a little with my feelings of isolation. But I still felt a deep uneasiness within myself, a sadness that was palpable, but that I could not explain. However, following my first year something incredible happened—my girlfriend at the time introduced me to a man who had been born female-bodied, and suddenly the puzzle that had been my life came together perfectly. I was not gay at all; I too had been born in the wrong gender. The awkwardness I had felt since childhood vanished and a penetrating sense of calm and certainty came over me. I knew immediately what had been wrong my entire life. After I found out that transitioning was possible it was less than a month before I began my medical transition.

That first trans encounter and the month that followed were hectic. Once I realized the potential of what I could be, I didn't want to wait any more to begin my transition. I was told that you needed to see a therapist for several months before a doctor could prescribe hormone therapy. As is no doubt evident by now, patience and acquiescing to restrictions that I find burdensome and unnecessary are not my strong suits. At this time the resources that now exist in abundance online were not available to me, and I had no idea how to begin the process of going from where I was to where I wanted to be. I was told that I could order testosterone online from Europe while I went through the process of getting therapist approval, and so I did, not realizing until much later the incredible lack of prudence that I exhibited in making this decision. There was no way for me to know whether the company I was ordering from was legitimate or if the product was safe, and in the end I only ever received two out of the three vials I ordered. In no uncertain terms let me say that I do not endorse taking this route, especially now that there is so much information about how to do things correctly and safely.

I began my medical transition before I told anyone in my family, because I knew they would object. I was right, and after telling them they applied a tremendous amount of pressure for me to stop. Eventually I decided that I had to get away from it all, so I went on a road trip by myself. I resolved that on this road trip I had to face my anxiety over using nonsingle person men's rooms. This was a scary thing for me to do, since I still looked very androgynous. Scary too because they were trucker stops. I knew that if I could face that fear and conquer it alone then I could do everything else necessary alone, and I didn't need the support of my family. I drove from Washington to Arizona where I visited my dear friend Becca, who was one of the first people to truly treat me as a man. She helped me a great deal to find the strength and courage to return home and face down the criticisms that awaited me. Upon returning home I continued my transition and never looked back again. Josh Groban's song "Let Me Fall "became my theme song, and in many ways still is.

There was a very significant person in my life during this time, her name was Kathryn and she is now my wife. We met at the BBQ of a mutual friend and got along very well. Over the course of the next nine months our friendship grew ever stronger. She was unaware of the depth of my feelings for her during this time; she was alluring and beautiful and intelligent, and I could not escape the gravity of her. In April of 2007 Kathryn deployed to Iraq, a deployment that would last fifteen months. I went to see her off before she left and was tormented by my inability to hold her in my arms and say the goodbye that I so desperately desired. Throughout her deployment we texted, called, wrote letters, and Skyped. We shared everything with one another, forming a deeper and more honest connection than we'd ever experienced before. Ten months into her deployment Kathryn got two weeks of leave and we went to Kaua'i together. It was then that we both became certain that something profound had changed. Our love, born of friendship and forged through the separation of war, could not be held back. I proposed during a camping trip the summer after she returned and we were married that fall. Even now I am in awe of her capacity to love. Even though the majority of my physical changes occurred while she was gone, that didn't make a difference to her. At some point I wrote this to her: "You met me at a very strange time in my life. The changing of a season, the breaking of a cocoon encasing an imperfect life. You witnessed my change, my metamorphosis. You watched me evolve and allowed your love to evolve with me." We all change throughout our lives, and we all must allow our love to evolve with those we cherish.

I will not pretend that everything was resolved when I began my transition. I was excited and determined and happy to be making progress, but I was also disheartened that my journey would fall short of the destination I hoped to reach. The limitations of current medical technology made me feel as though I'd been sentenced to a life as half a man. I felt consumed by a darkness, overwhelmed with despair. I could not get over the idea that no matter how hard I worked, no matter what I did, there was nothing that I could do to make things completely right.

It was then that I decided to go back to school to study biology, in the hope that someday I would be able to make a positive difference for transgender patients in the field of regenerative medicine. The hope that this research could actually result in tangible therapies in my lifetime was akin to falling off of a cliff and grabbing onto a tuft of grass. I didn't truly believe it, but I needed to do something. I have been studying biology for the past several years and I'm happy to say that my tuft of grass has become a reliable lifeline. Due to the tragedy of war the Department of Defense is funding a great deal of research in regenerative medicine.. Included in this research is the goal of regenerating urogenital structures, and they've already made progress. Nobody would fund this kind of research for the transgender community, but that doesn't matter; we will benefit from it someday.

As I progressed in my studies and with each transitional milestone the darkness inside of me retreated somewhat. I could feel the body that I loathed being stripped away and was seeing myself emerge from within it, and as I emerged, peace of mind and confidence that had always been absent grew within me. I cannot overstate how significantly my surgeries have changed my life. Even having a hysterectomy, which had absolutely no impact on my external body, surprised me by how big a difference it made in my mind. I also learned that being angry, however justified, doesn't produce any useful outcome. That doesn't mean I'm not angry sometimes, it doesn't mean it's not okay to feel angry—it just means that you have to give your anger its own space, and separate it from the rest of your life. Otherwise it taints all the other things around you and puts a barrier between you and your ability to find peace. I set aside time where I allow myself to feel those things, and sequester it from the rest of my life.

Alongside the physical transition, all sorts of behavioral and social cues had to be relearned, everything from posture to bathroom etiquette. At the outset, in my determination to be perceived as male, I overcompensated. I pretended to like all things male just to fit in and prove myself. Over time I've realized that one need not incorporate all things masculine in order to be fully male. You must find your own balance and be true to your own character instead of striving for some cultural expectation of what being male is supposed to look like. The entire point of this is to be authentic, not to trade one socially confining stereotype for another.

For complicated legal reasons involving the military and the Defense of Marriage Act (DOMA) I was completely stealth for the first five years of my marriage to Kathryn. I was okay with this for the most part because I didn't really identify as trans; I identified as male. I have been confronted by the notion that living 'stealth' is a negative thing, like hiding and being ashamed. For a long time I could not comprehend the opposite viewpoint, why would you be proud of being born incorrectly? It took me many years to fully understand what transgender pride is: it isn't about being proud of being born incorrectly, it's about being proud that you stood up to the world and defied them all, you found your truth and had the courage to live an authentic life. And that is something to be proud of indeed.

Since the Supreme Court ruled that DOMA was unconstitutional we have been less concerned that the military will bother us about our marriage. After all I was legally male when we got married, and the federal government recognizes it, so we probably didn't have anything to worry about in the first place - but we weren't sure. Shortly after that ruling, after knowing Kathryn's family for seven years, I came out to them. We haven't spoken of it in the year since then, and I know that some of their religious beliefs are no doubt in conflict with this situation, but to their credit they have shown me no difference in their interactions with me. I'm also happy to report that the relationships with my own family members which were so strained during earlier years have not only been mended but have grown very dear to me. I would like to think that they see how happy and stable I am now compared to the troubled volatility of my youth, and realize that this is a far better life for me. I must say that the support that was most unexpected came from my old fashioned, religious, conservative grandparents. The first time they saw me after I began transitioning my grandfather looked me up and down and said "Well hey there, son." He smiled, we hugged, and that was that. From then on I was his grandson.

I do not think that we ever stop evolving as individuals throughout our lives, so it's somewhat arbitrary to decide when my transition was complete, or if it ever will be. What I do know is that I now feel more at peace with myself than I ever have before. I do still have moments were I become disheartened that I will never be completely what I want to be. For example, my wife and I are planning to have a child, but fathering a child in a conventional sense is impossible for me. I have to remind myself that biology is not what makes a father—that comes through love, dedication, and selflessness. One of the most important lessons that I have learned throughout this entire process is this: Just because you can't be everything you want to be does not mean you can't be more than you are right now. Apathy saps possibility from your life, and desperation kills the soul.

One social shift that has been challenging for me to come to terms with is the fact that I have inherited the male legacy. There are definitely both benefits and drawbacks to transitioning into a male social role. The inequality in our society means that I, as a trans man, often have an easier time than do trans women. While the transgender community experiences the highest rates of discrimination and violence in the LGBT community, trans women, especially trans women of color, bear the brunt of that negativity. I do not apologize for the privilege that I have inherited, for casting blame and shame is no way to effectively pursue a solution. This is a status quo that needs to be challenged from both sides, and I am an active promoter of gender equality wherever I can be. The only way to combat this legacy is for men of honor to stand up to their peers and tell them that the degradation of others, even as a joke, is unacceptable. I have great hope for the future, when there is so much social pressure against the misogynist attitude that those who exhibit such feelings are cast out in shame.

Looking back at my transition I must say that it has been an incredible aggregation of loneliness, solidarity, despair, hope, darkness, and joy. During those years, with the ever-present support of my wife, I forged myself into a person that I can love and respect. In the end it is the journey that make us who we are, more so than the destination. Now I am ready to face the next chapters of my life, supporting and advocating for other members of the transgender community, educating as many people as I can about transgender issues, making a meaningful contribution to the field of biology, continuing to cultivate a happy and meaningful relationship with my wife, and someday becoming a father.

Eli Bradford – Age Forty-One,
Full Time Working Dad Of Two Boston
Massachusetts

I was doomed before birth.

I grew up in a town just northwest of Boston in 1973. This was a place that was not ready for diversity. Our community was surrounded with homophobic, transphobic, and racist folks including ... my very own family.

My mother wanted a girl, and only a girl. So much so that she refused to put a blue johnnie on in the hospital when I was being delivered because she didn't want to jinx the stars. Sometimes I think she actually wanted a doll. She had my first and middle name picked out by the time she was sixteen, and gave birth to me when she was twenty-four. Despite my temper tantrums, she insisted on dressing me like Shirley Temple, with fluffy lace-like dresses and big-ass curls; it was seriously torture. On the good ship lollipop, I was not. Even at such a young age, I was humiliated. The pictures that were captured of me during this time show mostly tears because I was not allowed to be myself.

From the youngest age I can remember, I thought

of myself as a boy. The harsh reality of it crushed me each and every time someone called me a pretty little girl. In grade school I always played with the boys. I was fortunate enough to be naturally athletic so they wanted me on their teams. Along with this came fist fighting, which I never loved, but did not shy away from when confronted. I didn't always win, but that was okay because it was a way of proving myself as one of the "real boys," and I could hold my own.

Even though my male peers on the playground accepted me, home was a different story. Struggle was a constant. I wanted to play hockey; my mom signed me up for figure skating. I wanted to join karate; my mom signed me up for dancing. She was always battling the boy inside me. This was difficult for me because I was not dainty or graceful, nor did I want to be. This affected my self-esteem, and to this day I wonder if it's contributed to the panic attacks I've suffered since the age of six.

I thought I had made a breakthrough when my mom finally allowed me cut my hair short; years after telling me that I would look fat if I cut my hair—mind you, I've always been the skinniest kid in the class! The only catch was that it had to be a bowl cut like the figure skater Dorothy Hamill. My mom also made sure she was in control of purchasing all of my clothing. Needless to say, I was only allowed to shop in the girls' department and pick out things with bright colors; Rainbow Bright it was. There were times that I left the house in one outfit and arrived at school in another because I was embarrassed by what my mother thought was appropriate. Her desire to push stereotypical female traits and behaviors on me was alarming.

By the time puberty hit, I no longer fit in with the boys. My body betrayed me, and I could no longer conceal it enough for my male peers to know I wasn't one of them. At this point, I also did not fit in with the girls. In middle I became a loner and held onto a lot of anger. I had made a couple of friends but they weren't real friendships. I tried to pull off the "girl thing" as much as I could tolerate, which meant growing my hair out and wearing eyeliner. I got myself a boyfriend, which didn't go so well. We broke up every other month until we graduated high school when the relationship finally came to a true end. Although I loved him for those six years, I didn't know how to explain that I would never have sex with him. It was better to go our separate ways, so we did.

I started at a local community college after high school, but had a great deal of depression that hindered my focus on academia. Instead of flunking my first semester, a couple of my professors gave me incompletes so that my GPA wouldn't be affected. During this same time, my mother discovered that I was dating a woman and kicked me out of the house. I literally had nowhere to go so I camped out in my car at the local supermarket parking lot. New England winters were no fun, especially when you lived in a car. I had no choice but to drop out of school. I never realized how difficult it would be to find a bathroom, or a place to shower, and as a result, I lost my part-time job as well. My mom finally asked me to come home a month or so later, but the damage was already done.

No longer comfortable in my own body, I contemplated suicide, but feared my attempt would not be successful and I would suffer even more as a consequence. I came to the conclusion that I must be gay, so I turned to the GLBT community and found an extreme amount of acceptance and support. For the first time, I felt that it was safe for me to be me. I cut off all of my hair and bought the clothes I really wanted from the boys' department. At nineteen, I finally felt a sense of true identity and happiness.

My wife and I fell in love in 2004 and married in 2012. She gave birth to our two little boys, who are now two and five. I never imagined that I would be so blessed as to have my own family. Experiencing a real sense of belonging and unconditional love was all I ever wanted, but I was still struggling with not feeling like I fit in.

I decided to examine this further. Other than the lifelong issues with my physical body, I remember thinking when my partner at the time first got pregnant, "What would I be called?" Mommy? Mama? Mom? I did want any of those; I wanted to be the dad. Family members from both sides told me, "You can't be a dad. You're a woman." Ouch! I deferred to Mama because my wife wanted to be called Mommy.

When we were planning our wedding, being in a same-sex relationship, our wedding planner assumed we would both be brides. Excuse me, do I look like a bride to you?! I don't think so! I will be the groom at my wedding—end of story. When I told my mom the news, she was so distraught that I thought she wouldn't attend the ceremony. She reiterated, "Only men can be grooms, and you are not a man." Here we go again—forty years later, my mother is still trying to tell me I'm female!

This is when my dysphoria became overwhelming. It constantly ate away at me. I can't tell you how many times I've asked God, "Why?" Why couldn't I have been born a "real boy?" I resorted to telling myself each and every day; "I'm just going to be a boy in my next life." The funny thing is, this self-talk worked for almost forty years! Forget the fact that I won't be aware of my next life, but worse, what if there is no next life? I no longer want to promise myself something that I won't recall, or that might never be. I'm worth more than that, and I deserve more than that. I came to the conclusion that life is too short to just daydream it away.

I'm not entirely sure what changed in me allowing for this decision today because up until last year, I was living in complete fear. The thought of transitioning was the furthest thing from my mind, but never entirely absent. I thought the only way I could possibly transition would be to live on the moon. My fear was literally beyond comprehension; fear of losing my family, my children, my friends, my job, my community, myself, all in order to live my life as my true self. I had to be okay with losing all of these things and knowing it was very possible that I could end up on the streets, homeless and desperate. Fortunately, in my case, this is not what happened, but I had to be emotionally prepared for a complete loss. In most cases, the fear in our minds is always worse than what actually is. I know that I cannot control how others will react, and I'm finally at a place where I am okay with that.

Rediscovering myself and admitting my truth to those I loved most was incredibly scary. Unable to conceal myself for one minute longer, I told my wife.

This was not easy for her to hear, though I think a part of her has known all along. After the initial shock, she embraced me with acceptance and love. We decided to tell our families before our children. My mother and sister have taken the news the hardest since they've known me the longest. I'm hopeful that once they see that I am still the same person, but happier, they'll come around. I will do my best to approach them and each situation after that with love and understanding knowing that this will take time for people to fully absorb. Our children are still adjusting from Mama to *Aba* (father in Hebrew), but it's happening. We have to remind ourselves that change doesn't happen overnight. We take the bumps in stride, giggling each time we stumble on a wrong name or pronoun.

I may have been doomed before birth, but I'm making the most of it today. My decision to medically transition has given me new life. I started my first shot of testosterone in February and have scheduled top surgery for this May (2014). Soon, I will be living my life full-time as a trans guy—no longer ashamed of living as someone I am not. I'm excited for the physical changes and for what the future holds. I am also excited to see our community and society evolve. The world has much diversity to offer, and my hope is that society will eventually be as excited as I am to embrace these differences.

Ian H. Carter – Age Thirty-Four,
Marriage and Family Therapist, Personal Services
Coordinator, Oakland, California

I am not known for being able to easily define,
categorize, or label. I have spent most of my life
feeling like an outsider, trying to find exactly where I
fit in, only to find that the answer is "nowhere." I
cannot define who I am, and frankly I'm tired of
trying.

The facts: I was born Kirsten Hunt Smith at 12:00
p.m. on December 18, 1979 at Methodist Hospital in
Indianapolis, Indiana; a place not widely known for its
acceptance of that which does not fit neatly into [a
box], or in my case, gender. I was born seemingly
"normal"; all of my body parts were anatomically
correct and in the right places. In my parents' eyes, I
was their beautiful little baby... girl, which meant I had
a uterus, a vagina, a cervix, ovaries, and an estrogen
level that later on in life would help me to grow two
small sacks of fat on my chest. The joy. But there was
one thing "wrong" with me. I was born with an
inguinal hernia in my lower abdomen. A hernia that I
found is most common in males, ironically enough.
Was that hernia an indicator of the heavy burden I was

already carrying inside my mother's womb? A predictive metaphor for the feeling I would have while growing up, constantly wanting to rip through and jump out of my skin? Or maybe it was just a hernia.

More facts: I was an unexpected pregnancy, and the third child born to Janet and Mark Smith, but, I was not "unwanted" as my mom has reassured me in recent years. I have an older brother and sister, nine and five years apart from me, respectively. As a child, they would both torture me incessantly, forcing me to do things like lay down on the floor inside the sleeper sofa, and then closing me up inside of it. They would proceed to watch a movie and "forget" I was there despite my high-pitched screaming and crying—as if being trapped inside a foreign body wasn't enough to make me feel like I was constantly suffocating. I was the youngest, so of course it was their duty to make my life difficult and absolutely terrifying. My mom would tell me, "These are things that older brothers and sisters have to do to the youngest sibling. It's in their contract." I didn't buy it, but that was my family, and we weren't really that dysfunctional, yet. Leave it to me, the baby, to shake things up.

By the time I came along, my mom and dad were both working full-time jobs; my father was in health insurance and my mother a German teacher. Their free time was often consumed by driving my sister and brother to and from dance and gymnastics—my family seemed to eat, breathe, sleep, and even shit dance and gymnastics. My mom and dad were a little "too busy" for me the first few years of my life, so I often stayed with my grandparents. They were the ones that truly raised me. I was over there so much that I accidentally started calling my grandma "Mom." She was the one who helped me build a capacity for unconditional love, compassion, respect and understanding for everyone. She showed me what it meant to share your heart and soul with another human being. She shared her soul with me and poured out her love to me in such a way, in such a consistent way, that to this day my heart still overflows, with every cell, every atom of my being. I wished it were enough to kill the pain I carried inside of me every day, but it wasn't.

Eventually, I would feel the pain so strongly that I would find myself literally dying for help—more on that later.

Pay close attention here; this is very important information for anyone who wants to peek inside my heart, mind and soul to try to figure out who I am. I was born and raised in a middle-class Lutheran family. I had to go to church every Sunday with my dad—my mom pretty much never went when I was a child. I hated going to church; it was boring, and even at a young age, the idea of church seemed so nonsensical to me. This does not mean, however, that I did not have a relationship with God; that would be furthest from the truth. Ever since I can remember, I've had a connection to a higher being; something bigger than myself, bigger than this universe, that connects all space and time together and causes everyone's path to intertwine in such a way that destiny is created and each person's fate is eventually met. This is my belief system. I am not religious by any means, but God has always and will always be the biggest influence on the decisions I make. God's unwavering presence in my life has guided me through so many times of struggle, so many moments of pain, both emotional and physical. Pain that I never thought I would survive. But here I am.

I was four years old when I felt the first real ping of internal pain. This is when I realized I wasn't quite like the other girls, or boys. I didn't have a definition for it, or know if it was right or wrong. I didn't know "what God thought about it," or whether God thought about it at all. What I did know was that I liked girls; I was attracted to them. I knew I felt weird inside my own body, as if something was really, really off. Whatever was going on with me, it was a painful experience because I couldn't simply get a new body, and I couldn't feel okay in the one I was currently occupying either. As the days went by, I found myself wishing more and more that I was a boy and wondering why I didn't have the same "parts" that other boys had. When anyone would ask me what I wanted to be when I grew up, I'd say without any hesitation, "a boy." They would laugh and say, "Oh, she's so cute." I thought, "Cute? I'm not trying to be cute. I'm trapped inside this body, and I need help! But you are not listening!" I prayed to God every night that I would wake up as a boy. When I awoke to find no change, I would be overwhelmed with disappointment. At seven, the pain became so much that I decided that if I couldn't be a boy then I would just be gay; a girl who likes other girls. It wasn't exactly what I wanted, but I told myself that I would get used to it and eventually I'd be okay. Unfortunately, this optimism didn't last long.

I remember the first suicide attempt the clearest. I grabbed a large butcher knife from the kitchen and went back to my room. My Bible was on the floor opened to Leviticus 20:13, which states, "If a man also lie with mankind, as he lieth with a woman, both of them have committed an abomination: they shall surely be put to death; their blood shall be upon them." I read that verse over and over again after learning about it while watching one of those evangelical shows on TV. I always enjoyed the way they preached and wanted to be just like them when I spoke to a crowd—passionate and moving. I was completely devastated. "God? God would hate me? The God that loves me so much...the One I tell all of my secrets to...the One I spend so much time with? God would disown me? Send me to hell?" I was such a shy, introverted child; God was all I had besides my grandmother. I grabbed that knife with the intention of stabbing myself. I ran the blade across my stomach trying to work up the nerve to end my life just as my sister happened to pass by my doorway. She ran into my room, hands flailing over my body, screaming, "DON'T YOU EVEN THINK ABOUT IT!" Somehow, that was enough. With shame and embarrassment, I walked back to the kitchen and put the knife away. We have never discussed it since.

From then on, I tried to live a "normal," heterosexual female childhood. I had a lot of boyfriends and boy crushes by the time I was sixteen years old. I look back and wonder, 'How the hell did I have so many boyfriends when I was nine or ten years old??' I would've done anything to feel normal; to feel like the other girls. I would've made out with any boy who I thought might be able to take the pain away. Secretly, though, I crushed hard on girls. I wrote poems and stories about us falling in love, but I would lock them away in my filing cabinet. In all of my fantasies with these girls, I was always the boy. As I got older, I kept pushing these thoughts and feelings away, and began to convince myself that I was just a lesbian. I was able to deal better with the idea of me being a lesbian as I learned to develop my own relationship with God, which did not include religion, the Bible or church. At sixteen years old, I found myself in my first lesbian relationship. There was drama. Lots and lots of drama and pain, and even death threats made by her parents. By mid-senior year I was feeling incredibly depressed, and began experiencing intense panic attacks that would cause me to black out and forget where I was for minutes at a time. Again, I found myself contemplating suicide as I continued to feel like I was, at any second, going to rip through my skin and tear off this body. It wasn't that I wanted to die, I just didn't know how else to stop the pain, and refused to admit I was trapped inside the wrong body.

I dove deeper into my depression. I lost twelve pounds in two weeks, bringing my body weight down to a shocking eighty-eight pounds. I was once one of the top swimmers in my state but could barely finish races any more because I was literally too weak to push myself up over the ledge and out of the water. At eighteen, I made my second suicide attempt, trying to suffocate myself in the middle of the night. I just wanted it all to go away. Thankfully, it didn't work, due to divine intervention—or maybe I just didn't have it in me to finish the job. I woke up the next morning and with tears in my eyes confessed my intentions to my mom. This was what brought me to the world of psychotherapy and psychiatric medications. Despite the ups and downs of my experiences with the mental health system, the help I received was enough to get me through the rest of my senior year alive.

After high school, I left Indiana to attend college at Northern Arizona University in Flagstaff, Arizona. The first two years I spent mostly alone. The last two years I was in a relationship with a woman. Despite being in a relationship, I knew I would never feel completely satisfied because something was missing in all my relationships: me. After I graduated from NAU with a B.S. degree in Electronic Media and Psychology, my relationship ended and I moved down to Phoenix to start my life as a young adult.

I enjoyed living in Phoenix, however my career sucked, because I graduated right after September 11, 2001. There were no jobs in my field for someone who only held a Bachelor's degree, so I settled for a retail supervisor position for the next nine years. During my time in Phoenix I started to grow into the more masculine version of my lesbian self, which brought its own trials; getting kicked out of restrooms and not being served at restaurants for looking too "butch." On the positive side of this "new" me, I experienced more relationships with women, mostly straight, feminine women. These relationships led me to the realization that straight women were attracted to me, to the more masculine version of myself. Awesome.

This was where I would meet the woman to whom I was engaged for four years. Due to circumstances in her life, we moved to California, where she was originally from. This fulfilled my dream of making it to the west coast. I'm going to fast-forward through this relationship, though; by simply stating it was intense, wrong and absolute hell in every way imaginable. The one good thing I got out of it was the motivation to go back to school in 2007 for my Master's degree in Psychology, with an emphasis on Marriage and Family Therapy. That relationship ended in 2009 and I haven't been in a real relationship since then, but don't pity me! This has been a great period for me because I continued on toward my postgraduate degree and I have used these past four years very wisely.

Over the course of graduate school and while becoming adapted to the single life, I spent a lot of time with myself. I learned to open myself up to more possibilities. I learned more about culture and diversity in regards to gender and sexuality. I learned how to use discernment when it came to others' beliefs and opinions about these concepts (especially in relation to God). Most importantly I learned how to think for myself and to speak up, and I was able to come to terms with who I was as a person, someone who did not fit the gender binary. By the time I graduated, I had done so much research on gender and sexuality that I was blown away by how "normal" I just might be in relation to the lifelong struggles I've had with my body! It still took me a couple more years to make the leap to the other side, however—the much more male side that is.

Over the next two years of my life, I began my first job as a mental health professional. I was finally making a decent living financially and feeling more confident about myself in relation to my career, though I continued to procrastinate about coming out as transgender. This led to another yearlong battle with severe depression, and downing anti-depressants and anti-anxiety pills as I continued to fight my inner war. I finally realized I had nothing to lose. Okay, I had a LOT to lose, but sometimes the pain gets to a point where it just doesn't matter anymore. I was at a crossroads. These were my choices; to take a risk so that I could continue to live, and, possibly after all the challenges and scary shit that comes with transitioning, be happy, or...I could die. I had learned enough about depression and suicide by this point that I knew I would be successful if I chose to take my own life.

In November 2012, I chose to live. I was done with misery. I began to plan my transition and to reveal the truth about who I was to my closest friends and family. For everyone else in my life, I decided to do it up big. On January 1, 2013, I posted a video on YouTube and Facebook, where I came out as a transgender person and introduced the world to the real me: Mr. Ian Carter. No more anger, no more fear, no more pain, no more trying to rip through my body like an inguinal hernia. I stitched myself up and placed myself into my rightful position... as a human being.

After I posted that video, I sat there, took a deep breath through my tears, smiled and laughed quietly to myself as all the messages from friends and family came pouring in. It was at that moment that I realized: regardless of the challenges, the fears, the twists and turns of this journey that now lay before me, this is where my life gets good.

Alexander Walker – Age Twenty-Seven,
Special Educator, K -12 Education, Writer/Editor,
Boston, Massachusetts

In the summer of 2007, I walked out the door of my cabin at the summer camp where I worked and took a deep, contemplative breath. The night before, a new friend had asked what seemed, to her, like a respectful question: "What pronouns do you prefer?" In the moment, I was completely bewildered and asked, "What do you mean?" She apologized and explained. Even though at the age of twenty I had never heard the term 'transgender,' this question, and the subsequent conversation, made something deep inside me click. Finally, there seemed to be a potential word for the dissonance I felt inside, which only became stronger as the summer went on; this terrified me to no end.

Today, I'm a twenty-seven-year-old transman who is a dog lover, husband, musician, elementary school special educator, writer, and an introvert. I live with my wife, Eleanor, who, as luck would have it, is the friend who asked the above question that summer at camp, and with our two dogs.

Let's back up, though. I was born in the mid-1980s to a Midwestern family with myriad diverse circumstances and dynamics. I don't remember much from my childhood. I know that I moved more than ten times before the age of eighteen. I was always a good kid who tried to do the right thing. I had a lot of responsibility from a young age in the form of caring for my sisters, due in part to my mother's undiagnosed mental illness. We lived in a double standard kind of situation. Most of my childhood was spent living in poverty, but when I visited my father's family, we had privilege. When visiting my father's parents I had a home that met all human needs and was filled with comfort. I thrived on my visits with them. They gave me the opportunity to attend camps and play the trumpet. I got to see my dad less often. He lived and worked in a different state. As a child I knew he loved me, but we didn't really get to know one another until I was an adult. This side of my family constantly worried about my life living with my mother, but in the '80s and '90s custody aired on the side with the mother. With that privilege, often came societal standards of "fitting in" with my other female assigned at birth counter parts. With three sisters, all whom possess a sense of fierce femininity, I stuck out like a sore thumb. When living my daily life with my mom, there was little parental supervision. I had free reign to wear whatever I wanted to and do whatever I felt like. This freedom gave me the ability to dress in boy clothes and run around with my shirt off during the summer. My mother had very few expectations about what my future held, or my identity, mostly due to the fact that she was present in some ways and not in others. This freedom was as much of a blessing as it was a curse as I entered my teenage years.

I spent my middle and high school years battling severe social anxiety and depression. Doctors told my family, without my knowledge, that my depression and anxiety was due to my sexual orientation. No one questioned the doctors' assumptions. My family told me that they loved me for who I was and rarely mentioned it again. We have a habit of developing patterns in my family; we don't talk about things.

During that time, I was also put on an anti-anxiety drug that did not help much and slowed down my emotional development. I spent several years feeling simply disassociated from life. At the age of seventeen, I quit the medication cold turkey and finally felt alive again.

Soon after my anxiety diagnosis, I began playing the trumpet. I had found little relief in caring for others or expressing myself throughout childhood. I needed an outlet, something that I was proud of and could be my own. Beginning in 6th grade, I attended an arts middle school. At this school, I found my niche. Sitting behind a trumpet, I began to feel something that would last forever. I went on to attend an arts high school and continued playing my trumpet and other music. Eventually, I had to leave due to circumstances of home instability, and attended two more high schools before graduating. Still, I continued to play trumpet.

Trumpet became a means of expression. It wasn't about how high, fast, or exact I could play. I didn't possess the macho attitude of many of the male counterparts in the brass section. For me, it was sharing emotion and evoking something from within me. I'm a sensitive, gentle soul. Still though, as I sat in the back of a band or orchestra, I felt like one of the guys. Music also gave me the opportunity to leave my family and start my own life. Academics weren't my thing for most of high school, although that has changed, as I became more authentically myself. Trumpet gave me a shot at college, which eventually led me to education school and now advanced degrees in education.

During my high school years, I started to realize that I was attracted to women. I was unaware of the "diagnosis" I had previously received but that my family apparently knew about. The people around me assumed that I was part of the lesbian community. I went with it; feeling like having a label would be better than feeling like an alien in the world of social dynamics. In some ways, I fit in with the lesbian community, but in others I felt strangely different from all of my other lesbian-identified peers. Eventually, I began to realize that all of my lesbian friends enjoyed the fact that they were women and embraced their femininity in some way. I did not feel the same way about my gender at all.

To hide this femininity and cope with other challenges in life, I spent much of my high school and early adult years self-soothing with over eating. This caused me to be extremely overweight. There were many reasons for my unhealthy diet—lack of nutritional understanding, the inability to access nutritious food, and inability to stop myself. Eating helped me push down my anxieties and depression. By the age of sixteen, I was 275 pounds. My five foot six inch stature held it well, but I had a wake up call. I felt bad about myself. I had no pride. With weight, I felt like I could just meld in and not be questioned about who I was. I often passed as male in public, but was ridiculed for being fat. Between the ages of sixteen and twenty, I changed my life in terms of my weight. But instead of becoming healthy, I became addicted to a male physique. I ran harder, faster, and more often with little nutrition. I went from 275 pounds to 137 pounds. I couldn't find the balance. Eventually, I wised up, but struggled again gaining too much weight.

At that time, I didn't realize I was searching for inner peace. I had no name or understanding of the possibility of being able to transition to male. Until my viewpoint and understanding of possibilities was opened in 2007 by that one question, I held on to the little identity I had. After 2007, as my identity of being transgender evolved, my weight and health improved. I realized that I had been distorting my self-image to see more of what I heard and felt inside. I had to learn how to build my body to fit my vision. Weight and food, along with anxiety and social interactions, will always be challenges in my journey. It ebbs and flows with what I'm currently going through, but I can be a part of life now. I am my own person and as I walk through the streets I feel comfortable in my own skin. To create this change, I had to identify what I was actually fighting against. I like to think about it as unpacking my two-ton backpack.

That two-ton backpack got heavier after leaving my first college where I had pursued a music degree, but left after two years with most of my course work completed. Instead, I wanted to pursue elementary education. Upon starting this new degree, I began to struggle in a way that I hadn't in music school. School was never an easy thing for me; I have several learning disabilities. I am a person who happens to have dyslexia, a form of dyscalculia, and ADHD. I learned this at the age of twenty-one. I like learning now, but without the knowledge of how I learned or accommodations I needed, learning became a battle in college. Understanding contextual meaning, numbers, and piecing through content is challenging for me. Like any other big thing in life, this could feel like a burden or you can use it to empower you. In the beginning, I broke down, felt defeated. I was ready to quit. Then I had someone walk into my life that helped me harness it. A math professor extended her hand wanted to help me find a way to harness my learning to work for me and utilize my strengths to make learning accessible.

You may be wondering, how does a learning disability effect being transgender? Well, as I questioned my identity and began to develop one for the first time, I had to research and put what being transgender meant in context for me. That was not an easy task. I learn in non-traditional ways. I have to experience things first hand, watch, listen, and then revisit them several times over and over to really internally grasp and understand something. Had I not tackled my learning disabilities and found success strategies in college, I don't know that I would have had the ability to do the research I need to do to reach out to the right professionals, especially those that had experience with working with people with learning disabilities, when I was ready to explore my gender identity. I harness my learning style as part of my identity and it drives me when I work with students in special education, but also educate others on finding their path in life whatever that may be.

Back to 2007, when my future wife, Eleanor, confronted me with, "What pronouns do you prefer," it finally occurred to me that I had never identified as a girl, or as a boy for that matter. That question stuck with me, and, over time, forced me to realize that I was living in a state of feeling that was incongruent with the sex determined for me at birth. But emotionally, I wasn't at all ready to take any steps. I needed time to really figure out what this meant.

I felt that I occupied some unknown space in the middle; there were some parts of me that most of society would identify as female and some that many would identify as male. It was as if I was sitting on the fifty-yard line of the gender football field. Though I did not have the words to express it at the time, I wondered what it felt like to live with a gender identify that fit into one end zone or the other. Did I want to live my life with a gender identity that was not one of the two acceptable choices in our society? Did I want to pick an end zone? What would that mean for me and for my life? I lived with this wonder and constant internal dissonance through my early twenties.

Throughout the five years that I spent considering the above, I was overwhelmed by fear of the "what ifs?" What if I was never respected in the field of education? What if my family rejected me? Would Eleanor still love me as I changed? Would I still have friends? What kind of parent would I be?

For a long time, I let these questions swirl in my

mind but avoided actually dealing with them. That was until I walked into my first teaching job—a class of first graders. They knew to call me "Ms." but would sometimes accidentally refer to me as "Mr." Some children even went as far as to ask, "Are you a boy or a girl?" This caused something deep down inside of me to burn. I often felt completely disconnected from the world, as if I was going through a set of motions, rather than engaging with life.

After four years of pushing through this intense burning, Eleanor and I decided to move out of the Midwest in pursuit of better career opportunities. I felt that this was my moment to "try on" what I already knew to be true. In the summer of 2011, I began living full time as a male. I became "Mr." at my new school and asked my friends to use male pronouns. There were many trying moments during those first few months, as people did not know exactly how to interpret me. However, I finally felt like I was developing an outer persona that aligned with the way I perceived myself internally. I started to consider medically transitioning.

During this time, my family was unaware of my identity. I wasn't ready to risk losing my connection with them, especially my father's family when we'd only just begun to get to know each other. Two weeks prior to my top surgery in 2012, I told my father, my sisters, my father's family, as well as Eleanor's family. They had questions, but took it in stride, and made it clear that they loved and supported me no matter what. They have continued this support throughout my transition. Subsequently, I have arrived at a new, deeper level of relationship with them. I often wondered if this would have happened if I had not taken the leap to finally live authentically.

As I sit here today, I realize that none my of "what if" fears ever came to fruition. I am gainfully employed as a teacher and love my job. I have a loving and supportive wife, who was the first person to really see me. I have a great community of friends, some of whom know my story and some of whom do not. But even more importantly, I am continuing to evolve.

This book is important to me because along my journey of self exploration, I found I wanted to hear more about other transgender people's relationships, emotional transitions, and a variety of stories that weren't accessible at the time. I hope that this book can be explored within the transgender community, in classrooms, and by others wanting to better understand a different kind of self-exploration.

## Leng Montgomery – Age Thirty,
## Trans Advocate/Blogger, London, England

The decision to transition was something that took me a while to come to. In some ways I feel that I transitioned as part of a fundamental series of changes that were put into motion following a break-up. There was something about my old life that I needed to step away from. The summer of 2009 was the catalyst of all this.

Since I was young I have always felt male; I was a little boy for a number of years. That identity lived inside my head however, as on the other side of the mirror, I was a girl. It was confusing to be born in a gender that wasn't my own. My mind and interests were never female. I grew up surrounded by strong women and adored being in the company of them, but at the same time it was impossible to feel as if I was the same; something wasn't right.

At school, the first thing I got in trouble for was "pretending" to be a boy by my refusal to wear a female bathing suit to the swimming pool. Having to wear a swimsuit that wasn't like the boys' distressed me greatly. Any overtly feminine clothing felt oppressive and abusive to me. It was not what I was supposed to be wearing. Fortunately, my mother never forced me to wear dresses or skirts. She began buying gender-neutral and boys' clothing for me, as she knew there was little point in making me wear clothes I wouldn't. She didn't like to see me get so distressed either.

I remember people often saying that I was a girl who wanted to be a boy. From what I overheard, I was always confused about why this wasn't an option, or why there was anything wrong with that. I wanted to be a guy, to have a wife, to be someone's boyfriend, and eventually, husband.

Puberty was a cruel reminder that my desire to be who I felt I was would not come to be. It was like my worst nightmares were all coming true. My body started feminizing more, painful periods started, I put on weight that gave me curves, and my breasts started developing. I didn't just grow breasts though: I seemed to grow watermelons. I ended up with a chest size of 38DD, which made me feel miserable, emotionally and physically. Naturally, a large chest drew attention to me that I didn't want. Both girls and boys would comment, while sometimes trying to grab me. I hated it.

When I was fifteen I came out of "the closet." I thought I must be gay and in many ways I definitely felt comfortable being a lesbian. I liked gay women, I liked gay culture, queer spaces and being around people who weren't straight. I would talk to people online, using my pocket money to buy credits at the local internet café. Sometimes I would meet people but I never told them my age, nor would I see them again if we'd had any type of encounter.

This was a very dark time for me—I felt suicidal

and miserable. I felt ugly all the time and experienced complete unease in my own body.

By the time I was eighteen I had my first relationship, in which I was expected to be as feminine as possible. That definitely did not come naturally to me. The relationship ended, and by the time I was twenty I started to cultivate a more masculine look; the first step was having short hair. This was something that made me feel happier and I was pleased that it made me a more identifiable lesbian, which at the time gave me some form of identity I could feel connected to. I immersed myself in the lesbian scene, going out regularly, feeling popular, and drinking a lot. Most of my life centered on drinking and trying to fit in.

Being in mostly female spaces made me feel like I was out of place, while simultaneously feeling that they were one of the few places I was meant to fit in. It was during this time that I started doing photography and would photograph in bars and clubs. My work started to be featured in magazines for venues in London. The camera provided me with a legitimate reason to be somewhere, and also acted as a barrier between the people I interacted with and myself. I had a reason to go over to someone and say, "Hi," without fear of rejection.

I had a couple of relationships over the next few years that were mostly filled with one-night stands. Overall, I found that connecting with people was hard, but when I experienced love, it was enriching and very powerful. That was not enough though, as I often felt that there was something missing, and that ache just got worse and worse over time. I realized I needed to be alone for a while.

I didn't know what it was exactly, but the dysmorphic feelings in my body and mind were becoming more intense by the day; I would cover mirrors in my house because I couldn't stand to see my reflection. I felt trapped in my own body. I was overweight. I started to exercise, which seemed to help, and I lost a lot of weight because of a painful break up. Even in my new, slimmer body I didn't feel comfortable; there was still something missing.

September 18, 2009 was the day that changed everything. A friend I was staying with in Berkeley gave me my very first binder and as soon as I put it on, I felt like a new person. I could stand up straight and proud; I felt more handsome. This was the body shape I'd always craved. The missing parts of me felt more connected and from that day forward I was never without the binder. I knew then that I wanted to be addressed in a male way. I felt reborn. It was an almost spiritual experience; something changed in me forever and some of the pain and torment that had engulfed my heart and mind started to clear.

When I returned to London all of my friends commented on how great I looked and how content I seemed. I definitely was, but I also knew that if I was going to change my gender, I would have to have no doubt in my mind that this was what I wanted to do. Instead of worrying about what others would think, I started to focus more on what I wanted. I took control of my own life and gave myself the power to do what I needed.

Surgery was something I knew I would want, but it was a question of when because I was in no rush. I knew the social side of transition would be the hardest so I elected to concentrate on that first.

It was almost a year and a half before I changed my name legally. After I did that, I saw a private doctor to discuss what options were available to me in terms of starting hormones and what I needed to do to get a passport with my new gender marker in it. Once I did those things, I entered the NHS gender system. The wait times to see doctors were incredibly long, and the system itself was complicated, but I made my way in.

The only thing holding me back was surgery. My case was not handled correctly and there were many complications because of it. Administrative errors lead to my being called 'Miss Leng Leng' for over six months. My application for chest surgery on the NHS was first rejected and then later accepted, though I couldn't use the surgeon I wanted.

If it had not been for me keeping a blog along with a random act of kindness, I would not have had my long-awaited chest surgery, which finally happened on December 5, 2012. This was another awakening moment. I felt physically complete following the surgery. I finally felt like I stopped transitioning and started living as the person I am now.

Piece by piece a symbiotic relationship started to emerge between my mind, body and soul. I can swim in public places without worrying that I need to hide somewhere or feel like a fraud. It's so comforting and reassuring to have a smooth chest and to not feel imprisoned by a large pair of breasts. Having pectorals and facial hair is what feels right to me.

Finally, I can be someone's boyfriend, and maybe someday I will be a husband, but regardless of those things, being a man and someone's man really makes me happy. It satisfies my soul. Even if things are hard, I know that going through the process of transition has defined me. It's enabled me to love myself, which has consequently affected how I relate to others. I'm able to feel love, which was something I had struggled with immensely.

## Kai Scott – Age Thirty-Four,
## Social Scientist and Engagement Specialist With
## Dialetic Services, Inc.,
## Vancouver, British Columbia

My name is Kai Emery Scott. I am a transgender male. After I was born in Seattle, Washington, I moved around almost every year of my life, to places that included Canada, the United States, Germany and the United Kingdom. I grew up with my parents and younger sister. I currently work as a consultant to the Canadian mining industry on social, cultural and economic issues. I lead an active and engaged life that includes running, hiking, backpacking, traveling, going to concerts, plays, movies, volunteering, and attending functions with my family and network of friends.

My preparedness for transition occurred well before I was ready to admit to myself—and to others—that I was transgender. In December 2010, I began a three-year process of healing from past trauma and pain, as well as seeking professional, spiritual and peer support. It was through this iterative process that I began to have an ever-increasing clarity and understanding of myself. It took significant work and time to achieve the serenity and inner strength to take an honest look at my gender, which had been safely tucked away for decades. When the issues of gender came to the surface, I had the tools to move through the range of emotions that came up when I delved into the heart of it. I was ready and I did not resist.

A key part of my gender journey was prayer and meditation. While I felt guided and led to take this course, I did not want to influence the outcome with preconceived ideas and notions of what it should look like or how it should go. I wanted to be free of any assumptions and expectations. This ensured the least amount of frustration and disappointment, as well as the most authentic process and evolution. After many decades of pretending, blending in, and being a chameleon, I wanted my gender journey to be nothing like my previous approach.

Going through medical transition has strengthened and deepened my spirituality. I am full of gratitude for my Higher Power for showing me the way and giving me the strength and courage to do it. This has translated into a spirit of giving and service. My happiness has increased and the energy that used to be tied up in dysphoria has been freed up. My way of giving thanks is to give back by helping someone who is struggling, volunteering for several causes, and being more present in the lives of my family and friends. I also trust my Higher Power much more and am more willing to give the contents of my life over to the greater flow and design. I recognize that I am a small but important part of the universal plan and I seek daily guidance for how I may align my actions, thoughts, and words to it. I practice minimizing my resistance, fear and denial of what I am intended to do or to be.

I first started to have a clue that I was transgender when I was growing up. Before hitting puberty, I cut my hair short and wore boys' clothes. I mostly played with boys. I felt like a part of my group of guy friends. I was frequently mistaken for a boy and did not correct people, but I knew that something was not adding up. My mom and I often had disagreements about clothing. She suggested dresses and I wanted baggy clothes like my friends. I loved sports and excelled at running, feeling most at home in competition with others guys.

Things got bad during puberty. I started developing in ways that definitely did not compute and I was distraught. I dreamt of becoming a guy like the life-size poster of Michael Jordan I had in my bedroom. I was even sadder when my guy friends noticed the changes, labeled me as a girl and started treating me differently. I felt completely left behind and embarrassed. I got teased a lot. I figured I could not do much about these feelings and stuffed them deep down. I thought I had to accept the cards I had been dealt, so I started to try and play the part. I did that for a long time and I was able to distract myself from the underlying anxiety and discomfort with my body. For many years, I was completely disassociated from my body. This allowed me to do things like wear dresses and act in a particular way that does not resonate internally. I abused alcohol to deal with my pain and confusion. I lost myself in relationships.

Things started to shift when I saw my life spinning out of control from alcohol abuse. I stopped drinking with the help of a 12-step peer support group and I started to work closely with a therapist. She helped me heal many deep wounds from my past. I have now been sober for nearly four years. I started to run again and lost a lot of weight. This gave me a more boyish figure and I began to recognize myself.

Then, I met my transgender friend. Last year, I helped him undergo his surgeries and watched him transition from female-to-male. He shared a lot of his story with me and much of what he said resonated deeply. That scared me. After his top surgery, I was hit the hardest with the realization that this was what I had wanted so badly since puberty. I could not ignore it anymore, so I started to explore and implement non-permanent changes to see how it felt. My inner circle of friends called me Scott (my last name) and used male pronouns. I cut my hair. I bought a binder. Everything I implemented felt like home. I cried a lot with relief that I had found and reconnected with what I felt in earlier years but never had the strength or language to fulfill. I have been on this course of gradual transition since November 2012.

I implemented all the possible non-permanent changes, wrote about how I felt and recorded videos of my reactions. I wanted to be really solid in these changes before going on to semi- and fully-permanent changes. At the end of the day, before starting testosterone, I could not say with 100% certainty that it was going to work or be right for me. It's like Attention Deficit Disorder (ADD) in the sense that you cannot actually diagnose it; the only way you know you have it is when you start treatment and it works. I felt comfortable starting because the changes are so gradual and subtle at first, and I could safely stop at any time if I did not feel the changes matched my internal sensibility. My first shot of testosterone was a surreal experience. I felt so calm inside for the first time. It felt right. Since then, I have been so excited by all my physical changes that I've known that this was the way to go for me.

Surgery was a bit trickier. I knew I liked the look of my flat chest in a binder under my clothes. It felt like coming home and I got lots of psychological relief from wearing it. But as much as it helped me, it also hindered and frustrated me. I could not run as fast; I was gasping for air, trailing behind my running buddies. It hurt and rubbed my skin raw. I felt trapped in search of a solution. Even though I never "hated" the lumps on my chest, I was getting more and more agitated by having them there, and that scared me. I had ignored them for so long to cope with my dysphoria that when I finally examined them for the first time, I started to feel a sense of urgency about getting rid of them. I could handle the discomfort and stress, but I knew I would be miserable in the long run if I did not do something. That's when I knew in my heart that surgery was the next step. I started to do a lot of research about surgeons and different results and procedures. I got more and more comfortable with imagining the scars and excited about the new nipple placement and pecs! I played around in Photoshop, taking pictures of my chest and "removing" the breasts. Anything to help prepare my mind for the change I wanted and needed so badly. It was still the scariest decision I ever made because of the risks and uncertainty. I truly did not know 100% if this was right for me; I had an idea it might be a good solution, but I just did not know for sure.

My parents and sister are still in the process of coming to terms with my transgender identity. I told my sister as soon as possible, but she had a lot invested in my gender being a particular way. She has understandable ideals about the closeness and intimacy between sisters and she worried about the erasure of past experience growing up. What did it all mean? Why so suddenly and unexpectedly? Would she still recognize me in a male form? How would things be different if we had grown up as brother and sister? I completely understood and held space for her anger, disbelief and sadness. I continued to show up with an open heart and mind, and a willingness to listen and explain in more depth. Her love for me shone through when I went to Florida for my top surgery. She did not understand or agree with what I was doing, but she was willing to accompany and help me with post-surgical care. To me, that is the epitome of love and I am eternally grateful to her for doing so. I think that whole process helped us grow closer. It helped her to understand what top surgery meant to me, and I, as the older sibling, needed her help and support. We were both outside of our comfort zone.

I told my parents one month before top surgery. I appreciated the fact that they did not have a lot of time to digest a large dose of reality. They went through waves of disbelief, strong resistance, redirection and pleading. I had the capacity to hold space for them in their confusion and frustration. Their initial response was to say that what I was really looking for was God and they sent me a series of Jesus-converting texts. In the past this would have made me upset and irate, but I had no time or desire to fight. I saw that they truly loved me, and the only way they knew how to express that is from their belief system. They were offering me their best (i.e., their God), because they wanted the best for me. My mom had the hardest time, or at least she was the best at expressing it. I wonder if the parent whose gender the child is departing from has a more challenging task of trying to understand, because they are (most likely) completely at ease and comfortable with their gender and may not see how someone would want to modify their body (e.g., mutilate their breasts.). My mom called me frequently before the surgery, crying and begging me not to proceed. It was hard for me to hear her hurting based on the actions I was undertaking. I wanted to help her, but I had to save myself. I explained to her that I did not want to hurt anyone and that I had a strong sense that "I was a bother," which prevented me from getting the help I needed in the past. It took everything in me to override my natural tendency to accommodate other people's needs before my own. The night before my surgery, she called one last time to dissuade me. I listened for a bit and then had to calmly and compassionately tell her that I could no longer talk as I had enough anxiety about the impending surgical procedure and needed to conserve my energy to get to the operating table. It was hard to tell her that, but I trusted that she had the resources and support to get the help she needed.

Since surgery, my relationship with my parents continues to evolve and improve. I think they recognize that they know very little about me and that they can either continue to miss out on my evolution or become more active participants in my life; both of them email and text me more regularly now. We have enjoyable family gatherings. They ask more detailed questions about my life, including my love life, which used to be a taboo topic. They still call me by my birth name and use female pronouns but I figure it will sort itself out eventually, especially when I have a deeper voice and they call me a female name in public. It will look odd, and the discomfort may promote change more naturally than by me demanding it.

I am not currently in a romantic relationship. I think this has been key to my smooth transition. If I had a partner, I may have delayed, accelerated and/or modified my transition based on their reaction and feelings. I recognize my past habits and tendencies and know that I would have been challenged to be completely authentic. I have been able to explore, implement and try everything I needed to without worrying about another person's feelings and needs. This has been freeing and exciting.

Several things have changed in terms of a sense of community. I have developed connections with the trans communities in Vancouver, Seattle, and Portland. I have met many amazing trans individuals and benefited from sharing my story, as well as hearing their stories. I am a member of the Trans and Gender Variant Working Group, which is part of the Vancouver Parks Board that works to increase trans inclusivity in recreational facilities and programming. Developing recommendations for the Parks Board is rewarding and interesting work. I participated in my first Trans Pride Parade, which had an impressive 300 participants this year. I have added many trans individuals to my friendship circle. My sense of community has also expanded to virtual relationships through posting videos on YouTube and interactive comments. I have met several of these trans guys and their loved ones in person, which has been fun, interesting and delightful.

I have also solidified and clarified my membership in queer male spaces. I am part of a running club made up of mainly gay men. For several years, I was the only consistent female-appearing person in the club. I had a hard time explaining to myself, and to others, why I felt a part of this group. Now I am able to understand that I saw myself as an effeminate man, while they had seen me as a feminine lesbian. It wasn't until I undertook my transition that my running buddies understood and saw me the way I felt. They are also supportive and respectful. I feel even more rooted in this club now that my outsides match my insides and others see it too.

My medical transition has been relatively quick and easy compared to the standard public health care route in British Columbia, which can be quite circuitous and drawn out. Even in a country that pays for gender-confirming surgeries, I found the healthcare system to be convoluted, unclear and constantly changing. The two-year waiting list for top surgery scared me. Answers were hard to come by. I think I recognized this pretty quickly and knew that I had to take matters into my own hands. Thankfully, I had the financial resources to skip the run around. I knew my mental and physical health depended on it. I worked with a gender specialist in Vancouver who did a psychological assessment and wrote me the necessary paperwork to start testosterone and to have top surgery in Florida in May 2013. Additionally, I am grateful for the doctors specializing in transgender health at Three Bridge Community Clinic. I did not need to convince or train them that I was transgender. They are knowledgeable and passionate about trans-specific issues. It has been easy to have matter-of-fact conversations with them about transition-related matters. And they were genuinely happy for me when I came in with a lower voice and sprouting more hair.

Jaguar – Age Thirty-Six,
Graphic Designer, Los Angeles, California

As I write this it has been five years, six months and eighteen days since I began my medical transition. I was thirty at the time; I'm thirty-six now. At this time, I identify as a gay man. However, my journey didn't start within any of these contexts. It was a winding road of exploration with no real end in sight.

First though, let me start by introducing myself. My name is Jaguar, Jag for short. As a transman, it's sort of ironic that my name was from a lesbian Holocaust love story, "Aimee and Jaguar." It was one of my favorite movies and I had used the name before I even medically transitioned. I am a graphic designer by day and a Netflix addict by night. As a local Angeleno, it's not uncommon to see a melting pot of ethnic backgrounds. I am a mix of Filipino, Spanish, Chinese, and Hawaiian, although culturally, I am Filipino. My parents were transplants from the Philippines.

My journey of exploration began in 1999. I was in my second year at a local community college. It was the beginning of spring semester and we were introducing ourselves to one another in art class. A

119

baby-faced, boyish-looking "girl" introduced himself to me. This is when I met Alex. I was drawn to become friends with him. There was something I needed to learn. Although at that time, I couldn't put a phrase, name, or finger on it; he opened Pandora's box in to a world I had no context. Over time, he told me he was transgender although I didn't quite know what that meant at the time; this term stuck with me and I began to gain a context of something I felt inside but had no term for describing.

During my adult life, I identified as a lesbian and was very comfortable identifying as female. I was so proud of being a woman that I actually didn't like being mistaken for a boy. Perhaps this was also rooted in being a young feminist lesbian at the time. However, I cannot escape being mistaken for a boy— because of my petite stature, and my buzzed hair I resembled a little boy upon quick passing. It offended me when my straight guy friends would rough house with me and jokingly say: "C'mon you're one of the guys anyway"—assuming that because I dressed "boyishly" that I identified with them. My daily attire consisted of a pair of jeans, tennis shoes or boots, a T-shirt/ button down shirt. It wasn't because I wanted to be a boy or present as one, it was because this attire was what I felt comfortable wearing. At work however, given that I worked in a conservative office environment at the time, I could sometimes be found in a skirt and blouse; at times, even in high heels. I was very content in my own skin. I was 100% *womyn*, or so I thought. I felt happy and content with where I was.

I think my upbringing gives a lot of insight as to

how I blinded myself from these feelings of incongruence with my identity. My parents are conservative Catholic Filipinos. They used God to condemn my feelings about my gender and sexuality. As someone who is God fearing, I took their word for it. I set aside these feelings. Tucked them away under the rug and never looked to question it.

Growing up as Filipino here in America means there were a lot of cultural differences to deal with. My parents are old-fashioned Filipino with a strong Catholic upbringing. The father is the head of the household. There is a hierarchy within siblings. Meaning as the youngest, I have little or no say in the family. My eldest brother was the voice of reason. However, my other older brother and I have less input (or at least we did when we were growing up). This is slowly changing, as we are now adults, but not entirely. There is still a certain level of "respect your elders" in our culture. Even if the older brother is wrong, he is still right and we are not allowed to contest.

As a Filipino-American, I view life much more liberally than my parents and am a bit more open minded than my brothers. Perhaps, as a transgender person, I've had to be a little more open minded. My eldest brother doesn't respect my transition and still calls me his sister, even after five years on testosterone. My other older brother (the middle child) does refer to me as "Uncle Jag" and uses male pronouns when he talks about me to his son, my nephew.

Fast forward to when I was twenty-one and I learned that one could transition from female-to-male.

All those nightly prayers of begging and pleading to God during my adolescent years to make me wake up as a boy came rushing back. How can I deny myself the ability to be the old man I've always seen myself becoming? There was a light at the end of the tunnel. I thought to myself, I have a chance.

Alex, and I became friends as the semester continued; he was a guide informing me in his process of transitioning from female-to-male. Interacting with him caused my mind to generate a bazillion questions. I'm surprised he continued to talk with me!

During the course of our friendship, I was able to see him morph from female-to-male. In some ways, it was challenging to watch someone change and begin to grieve something that was missing inside. I wasn't ready though, to take any steps. With this friendship in 1999 began the following nine years of gender bending and exploring to figure out my identity.

As my friend's transitioning stories were shared, they sounded so familiar. Alex in particular shared how he always felt like a boy. I would look back at my childhood and though, as an adult I was comfortable to say I was female, I did have those feelings when I was little kid. I began to wonder: was I just brainwashed to accept my female gender, although there were clear signs of me protesting my gender as early as five years old? When I was a kid, my parents had caught me multiple times peeing standing up, or refusing to wear dresses. Time and again, I was yelled at and shamed for doing "boy" things. My parents would ask me, "Are you a boy or a girl?" Of course, in my head I wanted to say "boy" but I knew I would get in trouble, perhaps even be punished. So I said "girl." This fight went on and even caused a lot of resentment towards my parents. It wasn't until I was nineteen that I moved out and wrote a letter to my mom saying that I was a lesbian. After that, I think they understood the dresses would have no room in my closet. But even during this time, my mom would still ask me, "Why can't you be the 'girl' in a relationship?"

Why it took me nine years to finally medically transition was something more personal. During these years, I found how very valuable it was that I felt secure in my identity and in loving my body before I could finally transition medically. Throughout this time, I began to hate my body. I began to dislike myself for being born a girl. Dysphoria crept into my life and affected my relationships. Sex was no longer enjoyable and I wasn't comfortable being seen naked. I felt miserable about myself. "Is this part of the process?" I asked Alex. I was told that it was.

At least I had a network of support, three transitioning transmen: Alex, Albert and James. All were changing into the men they are meant to be and I felt torn by this continuous question. Do I medically transition? But I refused to for a long time. I couldn't become a happy person by simply injecting a drug, so I refused to start injecting testosterone. I knew there was something deeper.

I feel that I have transitioned twice. The first time was learning to love my body and be comfortable for with what I had. This transition was almost aided in the fact that transitioning wasn't a viable choice due to the high costs of medical care and treatment options. Hormones needed to be purchased, and in the early 2000s, doctors didn't prescribe them easily. Chest surgery was expensive; where was I going to get the money to get that done? So I knew if I was going to transition, I needed to love myself with what I had, and, if ever I could transition, then it would be a bonus. So that's what I did. Throughout this time, I was determined to save up so that I could have that option if I wanted. I also knew I needed to prepare my body mentally and physically. I stopped smoking. I drank moderately. I also enjoyed gender bending.

I began to closely observe models of transgender people, including the three transmen I was around and the ones I followed on LiveJournal. Almost everyone was clearly masculine. I wasn't. I still remember the horrifying day when I went to visit James and Alex was there. Alex and another guy were "playing"—they were punching each other on the face to see which one will call the first quits. There was blood. Alex explained to me that testosterone made him aggressive and that he just wanted to punch things. This actually set me back. I thought to myself: if this is the result of testosterone, then I don't want it.

I've always been the kind of guy who wasn't into sports. I only played basketball for fun with my brothers and guy friends but I wasn't competitive. I gravitate towards the arts much more. When I witnessed my friends' aggression, it exhibited a very ugly picture of what I could become. I didn't want to take testosterone and become abusive. These made my fears grow inside. I spent many nights, battling back and forth, wondering how could I feel incongruent, but not know what would happen or how I would feel with testosterone in my body.

What led me to finally go on testosterone was

turning thirty. I wasn't getting any younger and when I closed my eyes and envisioned myself aging I saw a man, not a woman. I began to feel that I was at peace with myself as I was. I felt like I had accepted me as a person of transgender experience. I knew that I could begin my medical transition. Although, even with all of my preparations, I still struggled with testosterone and the adjustment of how society would perceive me as a person.

Testosterone was a mixed bag of good, difficult, and everything in between for me. The most difficult were the changes I went through psychologically. Even though I prepared myself for many years it was an all-encompassing experience. When one's life truly is being turned upside down, you have to find a space of meditation and start to process everything that is happening. I was gender bending for many years, living 50% male, and 50% female, depending on my mood. To have the courage to live completely male 100% of the time was a challenge.

The first year of my transition was the toughest for me, tougher than the time when I was feeling dysphoric about my body. That only lasted a very short time and I was able to accept myself easily. When I was being read 90-100% male, it was a struggle for me. Perhaps the most difficult was being read male, even amongst lesbians. In passing, pre-transition, when I crossed paths with another lesbian, there was a simple camaraderie of smiles that we would exchange. Sort of saying: "Hi, I see you, and you're not alone." After few months on hormones these interactions changed. I was invisible in their eyes. Perhaps because I identified as a lesbian for such a long portion of my adult life, it was difficult to swallow that I was just 'another guy' to my "sisters".

The small things I could get away with as a girl, I couldn't do as a male. I had to learn how to navigate the world as a thirty-year-old male and put aside everything that I'd learned when I lived as a woman. I even remember breaking down alone in my room almost at my one-year mark and deciding to "detransition." On New Years of 2010, instead of stopping, I went ahead and continued my shot anyway. From then on, I knew this would be a lifelong decision.

The trouble was, perhaps I contributed to the internal struggle in my first year by gauging my manhood by comparing myself to others. I needed to get back to my center and process who I was, not who other people were or what they thought of me. I know now that men come in all different shapes and sizes.

Five years later, sometimes even I forget I was born female. I feel this is how I've always looked, this is how I've always sounded, this is how I've always been: the man I have become. I'm still not into sports. I didn't experience any type of aggression, or any of those transitional myths. I learned through this process that I cannot compare my journey to others. It is solely my own. The only thing I can do is become a better man than I was yesterday. The journey never stops with taking hormone shots, after chest surgery, after passing 100%. It continues today is a new day.

## Nathan Ezekiel – Age Thirty-Six, Neuroscientist, Cambridge Massachusetts

At age thirty-four, the realization that I am male, and that I would transition medically and socially, felt like it came out of nowhere: an unwelcome and overwhelming realization dropped suddenly into a life that I had thought was working just fine. My wife, Angela, and I had been together for over ten years and married for seven. We enjoyed parenting our two children together, then ages five and two. We had a close network of supportive friends and were both doing work we enjoyed, she as a math professor and me in research neuroscience. On a whim, I had recently joined a brass band, picking up the trumpet that I had played seriously through my early 20s, but had set down in adulthood when time got scarce. Life was good.

Looking back, my realization was not sudden. At times in my past, in childhood and young adulthood, the knowledge had been crisp, in the foreground of my awareness. In middle school, when I won a big event at our neighborhood track club summer meet, a coach joked "Well, if you keep beating the boys at everything none of them will marry you!" As an adult,

I can see how problematic this comment was, but at the time, I was ecstatic. I understood that if I beat the boys, I was more like one of them—so much so that I wouldn't have to marry one. While I can't credit that comment as the sole source, throughout much of my schooling and work life, I've sought to excel at things I saw mostly boys or men doing. As a child I was a faster runner. As a teenager I was a better trumpet player. In college I was better at math. If I couldn't be a guy, I would do what they do and I would try to do it better.

I was raised in a deeply Christian middle-class family. In many ways, my family was functional and loving. My parents taught my two sisters and me to work hard and live ethical lives. They provided for our material needs without overindulgence. No matter what they were doing, they always tried their best, and they expected the same of us. But in other important ways, my family was a poor fit for a young queer kid, especially one as introspective and intense as I was. By the time I truly understood that I was queer, in my late teens, I had lived through years of dinnertime discussions and sermons that made it clear rejection was inevitable. I had internalized an understanding of myself as a sinner, someone who was fundamentally and irreversibly flawed. I knew my desires fell well outside of what was permissible and that to come out would fundamentally change my relationship with my family. I would have to be ready to go it alone.

At the time, I understood myself as a lesbian, both because I was attracted to women and because that identity gave me space for a more masculine presentation. When I came out to my parents during my first year of college, at age eighteen, the rejection was sharp and swift. My parents were devastated. I was bitter and angry. They were reluctant to help pay for my schooling and I was reluctant to take their support when their rejection was so clear. I dropped out of the Baltimore music conservatory I'd been attending and moved back to Denver, where I had grown up. I found work doing handwork in a textile repair shop and lived on my own. I was determined to make it without them, on my own terms. For two years we barely spoke.

Shortly after I came out as a lesbian, I met a young man at a party. I mistook him for a dyke. He corrected me, saying "Well, actually, I'm a guy. I'm trans." I had a sinking feeling. I had never met someone like this before. I felt like I'd been punched in the gut and didn't speak to him for the rest of the night. Later, to my roommate, I said, "I met a trans guy at that party. I think I might be like that." I thought about it for weeks. Wondering. But I chose to set this glimmer of understanding to the side, unable to see how I could resolve this new possibility with a body and a life that seemed unchangeable. Sometimes I wonder what might have happened if I had talked to this young man, asked about what he meant, about how what he said could be true, about what he was going to do. Other than this brief encounter, I had never heard of any other trans men. I didn't understand what was possible.

After I came out to my parents, even as I pulled away from them, and they pushed, I craved their love and connection. The solid base they had provided was simply gone. I had underestimated how disorienting that would be, even though I knew I needed to pull away in order to survive.

After two years on my own, I was struggling enough to seek help at the counseling center at the commuter college where I had returned to school on a music scholarship while still supporting myself on part time work. They referred me to my HMO mental-health clinic, that it took me two hours to reach by bus. I've gone over my medical records from that time, and none of my care providers seem to have considered the depth of rejection I'd experienced from my family, and how that might have affected me, though they did take care to note my masculine presentation. They offered me psychiatric medications and not much more. After a few sessions I was diagnosed with bipolar disorder, a diagnosis that was becoming more common and was beginning to be applied to a much broader class of struggles than it had historically.

Though I was initially reluctant, this moment, the one where I said, "Yes, I agree, I'm sick, I need to take medications" was a crucial turning point. I didn't see any other path forward. My emotions felt so unmanageable and intense. I hoped desperately that the medications and framework of understanding that a diagnosis offered would help.

With that decision, something amazing happened. I got my parents back. Once I was their sick kid, they knew what to do. They needed to take care of me. I knew what to do, too—I needed to accept their care and be a good patient, following instructions and taking my medications. I saw them more. We talked more. They were concerned about me and that concern felt like the love I was missing. I think my diagnosis may have also let my parents explain away my queerness as part of a sickness, just another part of what was wrong with me, and maybe what had always been wrong with me.

Throughout college and into graduate school, I was on a rotating array of antidepressants, anti-anxiety agents, anticonvulsants, and ultimately antipsychotics, up to four at a time. Never once during this time was I hospitalized for psychiatric symptoms, nor did I ever display classic behavioral signs of mania like overspending or risky behavior. I earned excellent grades and performed well at work. While I didn't display signs of profound mental illness, I did struggle, in particular with longstanding anxiety that seemed to persist no matter how many medications I tried.

After about five years of an ever-increasing medication load, when I was twenty-five, I made the decision to attempt to stop taking one of my four medications. After some research, I had decided that one in particular might not be worth the risks and side effects, including constant fatigue and profound weight gain.

At the time, this seemed like a straightforward choice, but weaning off of that medication turned out to be the most physically and mentally challenging task I had yet attempted in my life. The effects of discontinuation, including panic attacks, profound sleep disturbances and tremors that made writing and even eating difficult, symptoms that I had not had prior to taking this medication, lasted for about six months. As I gradually readjusted, these symptoms slowly faded and I felt my body and mind emerge. My range of emotions expanded. I experienced deeper joy and stronger connections to my friends and family. Angela and I had been together for about two and a half years by this time, and until it was gone, neither she nor I had realized how much had been lost to this pharmacological dulling of my emotions and senses.

Over the next three and a half years I gradually reduced my remaining three medications with medical supervision. I was completely off of all medications by the age of twenty-nine, when our oldest child was about five months old. The process was physically grueling. Each different medication withdrawal introduced a new slate of discontinuation symptoms to manage— including persistent headaches and sleep problems that could last for months after even small reductions in dose. But I went gradually, working my way bit-by-bit off of everything. I had not started out this process intending to live completely free of medications. I had assumed that what I had been told when I was first diagnosed was true, that I would need them forever. But over time, as I felt the new texture of my life emerge, as I felt greater happiness and love, and learned skills to manage painful emotions in new ways, I realized that I was stronger and more resilient without psychiatric medication. Indeed, it seemed the medication may have been causing more emotional problems than they solved. Eventually, it became clear, and my doctor agreed, that I had likely never been bipolar in the first place. Aspects of my life had been very hard, even traumatic. I had certainly been struggling, due to both my own internal identity and emotional life, and external factors, but the answer was not medications.

I've thought back over this time a great deal, and I don't have all the answers for why I was so complicit in treatment that did not help me, and even hurt me. I think part of why I took so many medications for so long, and part of why my life felt so unmanageable in the first place, was that I am trans. The journals I kept at the time I was diagnosed describe conflict and struggle with my body. I spoke vividly of an ongoing and unstoppable fight between my body and my mind. I couldn't keep fighting. I was so tired and I was all alone. Some people drink. Some people turn to illegal drugs. As a white, educated young person with access to medical care, I had psychiatrists ready and willing to provide other ways for me to give up.

So much has happened in my life since I first reduced my medication. I reconciled with my parents, who now warmly embrace and support our family, and are wonderful doting grandparents. Angela and I built our own family and found our footing as parents. I developed strong relationships with both of our kids, taking great joy in seeing them grow and understand themselves and their world. I found deep wells of resilience I had not known I possessed. I have sought what is true, what brings me closer to the people I love, and to a life that I can live fully. It surprised me at the time, but it is actually no surprise that the truth I had been fighting to suppress eventually pushed to the surface unbidden.

Though I was not always visible, I am a man. In looking back, I count my first step of transition, not as the day I first heard my name or that first shot of hormones, but as the first day I took a smaller pill. I had no idea where that action would ultimately take me, but that day marks the first step on a path to live as my whole self.

On hearing my story, it is tempting to try to reassure ourselves that what happened to me in the psychiatric system was an exception, or perhaps ultimately not that big of a deal. We might reassure ourselves that mental health care providers know better now, or that ultimately no real harm came to me since I was able to come off medications and am doing well now. Some might even argue medication may have helped me in a time of distress, even if I didn't end up needing it forever.

But as a whole, mental health providers don't know better now. If anything, we are medicating people, and in particular Trans and LGBQ youth, at far higher rates than we were in 1998 when I was diagnosed. My doctors were not worse than other doctors. My therapists were not more clueless. They were trying to help me with the limited tools that they had, tools that truly do help some people. What was unique about my situation was not that I was misdiagnosed and overmedicated, but rather that I got out.

Even though I was able to successfully come off medications and recover, real harm was done. The eight years I spent medicated left a permanent mark on my physical and mental health. During discontinuation I suffered both physical and emotional pain that was far worse that the original distress the medications had been prescribed to alleviate. If I had been less stubborn, had understood less of the science, had a spouse who was less supportive, or hadn't had the education and background that allowed my later doctors to more easily agree to my attempts at medication reduction, I might not have made it. I likely would have assumed that my severe discontinuation symptoms were a sign that I actually needed those medications, instead of holding on and waiting to see how I fared over the long-term.

Like so many people of trans experience, I grew up in a world that did not reflect who I was back to me. As I have navigated transition, I have experienced what it is to have a cohesive self, a connection between who I feel myself to be, my experience of my physical body, and how I am perceived by those around me. I can now look back and know that for so much of my life, I desperately needed to be seen. Living as a fractured self made everything so much harder and my life so much harder to understand, not just for myself, but also for my parents, and later, my doctors. We tried so many ways to put me together, and my life bears the marks of those missteps, but I made it. I am here and I am whole.

# SECTION II—EMOTIONAL & SPIRITUAL TRANSITION

What happens to our souls when we align the external with the internal?

Emotional development is an ongoing process, and particularly prevalent during transition. For some, it comes with developing a spiritual practice that helps them attain community and sense of self.

It is also a time of deep reflection to unlock something individuals may have repressed or ignored for many years. For many of our contributors, it was a combination of the two.

Within this section, these individuals discuss the varying emotions that came along with the whole experience of transition; prior to, during and after. Anxiety, substance abuse, panic, peacefulness, development, and strength are some themes found in the following pages.

The resounding message is that most people are in a better place now than they were before. By becoming an authentic version of themselves they were able to find a sense of inner peace that allowed them to and develop a happier sense of self.

## Will Krisanda

I began to breathe easier as the ace bandage loosened around my chest while the layers peeled off, one by one. My doctor sat on a stool in front of me and I towered over her, standing with my arms stretched out to each side. My eyes forward, looking at the door, I continued to breathe in and out. My heart was beating faster as I felt the bandages unravel. My doctor's gloved hands did some sort of sign language around my body, opening up the treasure chest behind the bandages and gauze pads.

"Almost there. Only a few final layers to go," Dr. M. said.

My mother and girlfriend stood to the side with wide eyes. It was like Christmas morning and the last gift was ready to be opened. They waited patiently.

The final layer was pulled off my sweaty, hunched body. After seven days of binding with tubes coming out of my chest, and no showers, I was sore and dirty.

"Oh my God, Will. It looks great!" my mom said in a cheerful tone.

My girlfriend wiped tears off her cheeks and echoed my mom's compliments.

I smiled. I felt so relieved and ready to start my life without needing extra layers or a binder.

In my peripheral vision, I could see the landscape of my new chest, but nervousness and a slight feeling of nausea kept me from looking down. I wanted to wait until the drains were pulled out and the small gauze pads were taken off my nipples. Dr. M. talked me through the next step where she'd remove the tubes that were collecting the fluid from my chest over the past seven days.

She asked me to take several deep breaths as she gently removed the plastic tubes from my chest. I didn't feel a thing other than a slight tickle. Too much for my mother to stomach, she left the room until the tubes were completely out.

"All right, just for the gauze around your nipples, and we're ready for the mirror," Dr. M. said.

My knees felt weak and I'm sure I was pale, but I finally looked downward and saw flatness along with markings from where she drew lines with marker where the incisions would be. It was flat!

Dr. M. motioned me toward the mirror and I walked over gingerly. My body was not used to the freedom yet. The last few seconds before I saw my reflection were bittersweet. From that point on I no longer needed a binder, but I worried the results wouldn't match my expectations and I would be disappointed.

At my most vulnerable, I looked at my body in the mirror's reflection, staring at the black marker lines at the edges of the thick red scars where tiny black stitches peaked out of and much smaller black nipples placed above the two scars like the finishing touch to dotting an "I."

I was to treat my nipples like they were two eggs lying on my chest. Not to break them or else revisions would be needed.

"These grafts must take, so please be very careful with what comes in contact with your chest. No pets jumping up on you, no children jumping on you, no lifting your arms over your head. Button-down shirts for the next few weeks and no lifting anything over five pounds for at least four-to-six weeks."

I can do all that, doc. That was the easy stuff.

The truth was I was a little disappointed. Although my reflection showed something I'd been waiting for, it strangely reminded me that I wasn't quite there yet. My breasts were gone but my hips now looked even bigger. Should I get liposuction next? Should I get a tattoo across my chest to cover the scars? Are my nipples supposed to be there? Is that one kind of off? There was no end to this.

About a year before my surgery, a few months on testosterone, I was sitting in my car on a summer night where I found enough motivation to drive to the gym but I couldn't get out of the car. I was crying uncontrollably.

"I have no idea why I'm feeling like this. I can't go in there. I can't," I said to my girlfriend over the telephone.

"Will, honey, calm down. It's going to be okay. It's probably your hormones. They're all over the place. Just breathe," my girlfriend tried to reassure me that what I was feeling was normal and it would pass.

But I didn't budge. Streams of tears fell onto my lap. The inside of my car never heard such screams. I stayed in the car, looking at the numbers on the clock turn, minute after minute passing and I wasn't feeling any better.

I felt I couldn't wait any longer for my transition to be over with. I needed to feel better and I needed my surgery, name change, sex change to happen right then, at that very moment.

*NOW! I am almost twenty-seven years old and I can't wait any longer. I can't be seen as female anymore. Not even one more day. What the fuck is wrong with me? What kind of man I am? Who is going to love me?*

My thoughts raced.

I didn't make it into the gym that night. I drove home with a stomach full of confusion and anxiety. My face was red and my eyes were swollen until the next morning.

Arriving back home to my parents' house, I went upstairs and stayed in my room the rest of the night. Isolation was always, and still sometimes is, my reaction to complete, utter vulnerability and fear. If I just lock myself in my room, I am safe from everything and everyone. That night I wrote, "I want to die right now" in my journal.

As the months passed and my emotions began to settle, I noticed my voice dropped, the shape of my face changed and I grew hair all over. All of these changes were helping my mood become more stable but my ego began to inflate again. My number one goal was to pass all the time and when I didn't, I turned inward, locking myself away in my room, in my car, in any place that kept me from dealing with it the possibility of being seen as anything but a man.

"Ma'am, your car will be ready in two hours,"

said the mechanic after I dropped my car off to get inspected.

*WHAT THE FUCK!? Ma'am?! I'm wearing a baseball hat, jeans, a binder, and an oversized hoodie. How do I look like a ma'am to you!?*

My high cheekbones. That's what did it I thought. I began walking with my head facing downward.

Bathrooms were a challenge too. I opted out of hanging out with my friends if I knew we would be going to a place that didn't have a trans-friendly bathroom, which was unfortunately more often than not.

There will always be those moments where I am re-learning something I thought I had figured out in terms of how to navigate this transition and all of the emotions that encompass it. As the years go by, I'm still figuring it all out.

My nipples didn't crack like an egg, they grafted to my newly formed chest, turned from black to pink, and are nickel-sized. My hips got smaller without liposuction and my chest remains tattoo-free.

The hardest part now is maintaining a mindset of acceptance of my body in its new form and avoiding isolation and comparison. It would be so much easier if I were born with the gender that my brain was configured with from the beginning, but I would have missed out on a perspective that has helped shape who I am today. I will always be happier that my story is a little different than the majority of folks.

Eventually all the anxiety and worry passed when I stopped trying so hard at defining myself and abide by gender roles.

I sometimes relate my transition to flying geese.

When I look up at a pack of geese flying in the sky, I notice how they start off somewhat scattered throughout the sky, a few of them might be aligned with each other but there's always a couple that take a little bit longer to join the rest of the group in the V formation. Every spring, I hear them coming back and look up at them with this feeling of wonderment and excitement. I never really understood why I liked looking at them so much but now I think it gives me a sense of peace. It's never going to start off perfectly, there's always going to be those times where I have to catch up to the others and figure out exactly where I fit into the line of things, but I'm still there, flying through it and hoping I'm not alone.

Harvey Katz

Distance makes the heart grow fonder. The further I get from the beginning of my transition the more it seems as if I'm telling somebody else's story. It's like watching your favorite childhood sitcom star go through puberty during the fourth season. You feel emotionally invested in the person and root for their success, feeling the highest level of empathy for them when their voice cracks during the Christmas concert solo or when their mom catches them washing their sheets again. The humor part of the transition process only comes later when you're recalling yourself being mortified, this time with the benefit of nostalgia.

Transition is a tricky term because it implies you are becoming someone else. One of the hardest parts of the transition process is convincing people that you aren't actually changing at all; that you are just trying to become the truest, most authentic you that you can share with them. It's more of a revelation than the reveal they had hoped for which is disappointingly lacking in dramatic affect.

I first realized I was trans when I was nineteen and a roommate sat me down on our hand-me-down couch with a copy of the book *Body Alchemy* by Loren

Cameron. My roommate had just learned about transgender identity and wanted to speak to me about the possibility that I was transgender. She was the first person I had met when I moved to Georgia over a year earlier and just the kind of witty, gentle soul that was put on this earth to deliver such information. I had known about trans women since I was around seven and heard an NPR report about a woman who sold her rare and seemingly valuable violin to pay for her gender affirmation surgery. I became obsessed with this sort of grand metamorphosis at that moment, but I had never known that trans men existed until our conversation over a decade later. The weight of this discovery was unbearable. The awful part of this information is that it made perfect sense. It was a diagnosis—the dark spot on an MRI that made sense of the years of pain. It was like finding out you were adopted and finally understanding why you look nothing like your parents.

Once you have named the source of your incongruence with this world, you go to bed calling its name. I became the antagonist in my own story. I couldn't trust myself to be alone with my naked flesh. Showers were torturous in their intimacy. Seldom do I find myself aligned with the notion that trans persons are trapped in the wrong body, but, over the next two to three years, I felt suffocated by my very own skin. I would imagine myself tearing off my flesh like a gory Chippendales model and finally feel free and giddy within my grotesque exposure.

Transition is a multistep process. It looks different for each person going through it. It's more of a stir fry than a soufflé, more of a study in humanity than a lesson in the hard sciences. For me, the first part of my transition was emotionally coming to terms with the fact that everything I ever feared abut myself was right, mostly, that I'd never be "normal" and to add insult to injury, the fact that that was evident to everybody around me.

During this time I felt overcome with self-hatred and desperately envious of cisgender men. I wanted a restart button. I wanted to be reborn. Transition begins with rebirth in so many ways. The first question asked to new parents is "girl or boy"? Even as a transgender person with full knowledge of the ramifications and intent behind the inquiry, I have to resist the urge to ask my pregnant friends the very same question. Asking my friends to use male pronouns with me was the first step to me being reborn. This is easier said than done because language is largely impulse and muscle memory. Reflexively they'd use female pronouns for me. For them it was a simple misstep but for me it cut like a knife. It made me feel impossibly misunderstood. I couldn't help but feel like a joke. It felt incredibly personal at the time, but, years later, I'm a bit more empathetic. If I was the only transgender person *I* knew, certainly this was all new to them as well. I didn't even know you could ask to be called by your chosen name/pronoun until I dated another trans man and he told me that you could request that the people in your life change the language they use referentially toward you. He was in college at Oberlin, a magical land of gender expression freedom. I was a lone genderqueer in Athens, Georgia and stood out like a sore thumb. I felt like a court jester fumbling to find my footing in the Wild West.

A year or so into the personal/social side of my transition, I met another transgender man who was in a similar point in his transition. The relief that came with the camaraderie was epic but it was also difficult to see your pain mirrored in front of you. In addition, it was my first encounter with the realization that the trans experience is incredibly singular and each individual has a different relationship to their identity and varying desires for the outcome of their transition. At the time he felt staunchly male and I felt that I was neither male nor female, something yet unidentified by the sciences. I was hesitant to begin medical transition for many reasons, one being the fact that I feared becoming externally male would feel as uncomfortable as wearing this female skin suit—that the trap door wouldn't release. I was also reluctant to begin medical transition because I felt righteous in my struggle. Battling the world had become habit and I couldn't fathom a life were I wasn't swimming up current in the mainstream notions of gender. If I'm going to be totally honest though, I was mostly terrified to talk to medical facilitators. Just the idea of facing their ignorance and transphobia made me dizzy and numb. Lastly, I knew that medical transition would eventually mean that I had to talk to my family about being transgender.

Before I was a man, I became a woman twice by an act of God. My first Bat Mitzvah was scheduled two weeks after Hurricane Andrew. Because there was sewage in the water mains, I bathed in our pool with the majority of our roof shingles before putting on my culottes (the marriage of a skirt and a pair of shorts) and walking the mile with my family to our temple. I had my Bat Mitzvah in the older, smaller temple because a palm tree had shot like a cannon through the exterior walls of the newer synagogue. Our out-of-town relatives couldn't come because the local hotel was destroyed so there was barely a minion there to witness me becoming a woman in the eyes of God. My parents scheduled a repeat performance for the following January. It was important, they implied, that people get to come and watch me bloom. It took me five years after coming out as transgender to medically transition for this very reason. I feared that the people in my small city in Georgia would ogle and stare because this transition would also be public. I wanted to keep it to myself. I had already gone through puberty once and knew it was not a pretty sight.

When kids go through puberty, their hands and feet grow first. They trip over themselves like Great Dane puppies and people notice that they are awkward even when they are not moving. When I was a kid, being a girl was a painfully obvious effort.

I didn't know you could be something other than what you were told. I am, by nature, a people pleaser and a kiss ass, and I wanted more than anything to be good at being one of the girls. But I am also impulsive and my first reflex was always to turn away from girl things. We—my family and I—were all hoping I'd grow out of it.

I've always hated starting my story from the beginning, from when I was a kid, partly because I can't honestly say I always felt like a boy or a man. I think that invalidates me somehow, and when people find out you are transgender, they are always looking for validation. Everybody wants his or her own say. I tell them that we will all end up different people than we thought we'd be when we were little. We all change ourselves in search of comfort and peace.

By Georgia law in 2005, to begin medical transition I would first need to be diagnosed with a Gender Identity Disorder (GID) by a licensed therapist. He asked me to describe my failure to thrive within gendered expectations. He asked me to step clumsily back into the gender boxes of my youth. When I went to the psychiatrist to get the doctor's note that would let me medically transition, as mandated by the state of Georgia, he told me to start from the beginning and I told him lies. He was a complete stranger with all the power and I was a scared twenty five year old dependent on a diagnosis that would deem me ill enough to legally seek self-care. You get used to answering questions in a way where you don't open yourself up to questioning, especially by doctors who hold your fate in their hands.

After my chest surgery, I called myself a monster. I thought of myself as an unlovable freak, and wondered who would ever desire a person like me. The feelings didn't last long though. In retrospect they were more symptoms of loneliness than those of self-reflection. Two weeks later I put on the thinnest T-shirt I had and rode my motorcycle down a highway. The wind whipped against my chest like it was a wall, like I was the poster boy for the anti-aerodynamics movement.

Deciding whether or not or when to medically transition is an extremely personal decision. For me, what finally made me decide to begin hormone replacement therapy was my desire to be seen as a man instead of a boy by the world. Recently I began working on a book called *My Tenth and Final Year as a 14 Year Old Boy*. And I did look fourteen for at least that long. At twenty-five, flight attendants would gently remind me that the exit row was reserved for those over fifteen and strangers at bars would harass me to see my ID. Worse yet, I would find myself being hit on by high school aged girls getting off the school bus that stopped near my house. Hormones would end my Peter Pan existence.

If my life were a movie, I'd skip to the montage now. Through the length of an acoustic medley you'd watch me try and fail over and over again to find a doctor in my small city that would help me with my medical transition. You'd watch me call doctors and be turned down, or visit them and be turned away. Then the music would ramp up and you'd watch me as I drove, fatigued from failure, to a doctor in Atlanta. As the beat and darkness of the song began to crescendo, you'd watch me take my first shot, the needle shaking above my naked thigh, the doctor beside me, his face red and angry, yelling through gritted teeth that if I wanted to be a man I needed to be able to take the first plunge myself. My movie montage would be filled with drama and puns and unsound medical practices.

Puberty isn't graceful, but it's fascinating to endure. Becoming comfortable with your transition is like breaking in a pair of leather boots. When I look back at pictures of myself during both of my pubescent eras, I'm filled with the same sense of embarrassment and dread. Puberty is undeniably awkward. You have to humble yourself to its takeover and maintain confidence that things will eventually settle and you'll be handsome like your dad was at twenty-two.

Testosterone heightened my appetite for everything. After years with little to no sex drive, suddenly the world felt alive with lust. I felt electric and limitless but frustrated at a world that tried to douse my fire with its rules and nuanced gender expectations. Becoming a man doesn't come with instructions and when you leave boyhood behind at twenty-five, you face a steep learning curve.

When I was a boy I got away with certain things, but men face a volatile world. Entering the men's club came with a new set of rules. Once on a date during the early stages of my medical transition, a man outside a bar overstepped his welcome into my girlfriend's personal space and made her feel uncomfortable. I laid my hand on his chest and asked him to please step back. I quickly learned that in a man's world, this movement that I knew only as gentle just a few months ago, was now a gesture of hostility and he became violent in an instant. Other lessons were more subtle but equally affective. I changed the way I walked behind women and confronted misogyny from other men. I swelled with privilege and entitlement and was ashamed by my enjoyment of it. Male privilege is alive and well in this country and it equally disgusted and thrilled me. For as long as I could remember, I had been unwelcomed by the world. I was odd as a girl and awkward and visibly non-categorical from the time I was fourteen until slowly, but also with alarming speed, I was losing the only identity that had felt certain, my identity as an "other" and was becoming the thing my community devalued the most, a middle-class, straight, white man, but the type of person society presented with the most privilege. It was and still is confusing. It remains, for me, the most difficult part of my entire transition process.

During the school year I teach Trans 101 workshops at colleges and universities, so the summers are my time off. After three months without one mention of dysphoria, I can almost forget that I am a transsexual at all and life seems so bitterly easy. It's hard to get used to being trans, but one day it happened to me. I just woke up and forgot. I felt remarkably not special and disturbed by the normality of it all. I taught a workshop last week and found myself stumbling over my words when telling my personal gender story. I have scars on my hands whose origins I can't remember. Certainly it was traumatic when the knife slipped while I was cutting something, but over time the only evidence is a thin white line that crosses knuckle creases. The retelling of my personal gender journey felt contrived because remembering it has become a clumsy process.

Kai Scott

In my twenties, I became increasingly dependent on alcohol as a means of escaping an underlying and inexplicable uneasiness in my daily experience. I had a gnawing sense that there was something seriously amiss, but I could not put my finger on it nor could I piece it together. I tried everything outside of myself to correct what I ultimately discovered lay inside. I worked hard and played hard. Binge drinking on the weekends provided an escape from the crushing pain I felt from dysphoria. I drank to cope and get a break from it all. I was deeply hurt by things I could not explain. Getting together with my then girlfriend, who previously had only been with men, magnified my sense of inadequacy and my gender issues. I doubled my efforts and was determined to work harder and keep a stiff upper lip. Family issues from the past were also welling up inside. I did not know how to handle it all.

At first, drinking was light-hearted fun and a source of great stories to recount later with friends. Then, it became more frequent and there was a greater sense of urgency to get away from past and current troubles. I started to let people down and I became more and more distant. I felt trapped and alone. Booze was an easy fix for the seemingly insurmountable and continuously amassing troubles. I got fixated on other people or circumstances as the root cause of my pain—my relationship, my job, my this and my that. I also turned on myself with a lot of negative speech and self hate. Then, it got dark and my world seemed to cave. I had emotional outbursts about particular situations or deep echoes of the past. I engaged in risky behavior. I started to resort to self harm to channel the hate I felt towards myself and calm my nerves. I drank more and more to cover up the shame and confusion caused by bad drinking episodes. I didn't want to face what was inside—it scared me.

Typically when I started drinking at the beginning of the evening, I could not stop, even if I intended to have just one drink. There seemed to be an insatiable appetite that could not be stilled. I would drag myself through horrible hangovers vowing never to drink again and oddly find myself in the pub the next night or weekend without even a thought to the consequences of the previous drinking episode. How could I have such a mental gap in my memory that should have been strong enough to dissuade me from picking up another drink? And yet I continued unabated, even picking up the pace and frequency.

Then my girlfriend broke up with me after several attempts to discuss the effects my drinking and the associated behavior had on her well being and her concern for me. Many times before I had brushed them off as her being oversensitive or controlling. But that time, in December 2009, she had had enough. That woke me up to the gravity of the whole situation. I could plot the rest of the drinking trajectory to a horrible end. I did not want that. I knew about 12-step programs that help people with addiction, but I did not know what they entailed. I was desperate enough to try something new; anything was better than the state of despair and constant pain I was in.

Despite intense fear and trepidation, I went to the next meeting in Vancouver I could find, on my own. I surrendered at that moment; I knew that this was where I needed to be. I did not want to be lost in my own nightmare anymore. They asked if there were any newcomers, and, with a racing heart, I said the first thing that made any sense in all this confusion: "Hi my name is Ka—and I'm an alcoholic." Instant relief rushed through my body. I could finally let go of controlling and figuring everything out on my own. These people seemed to have a glow in their eyes and they expressed genuine concern and love! It did not seem so daunting or overwhelming. I cried the whole way home with a sense of relief and renewed hope. I began with the steps, got a sponsor, and a home group.

Early sobriety was tough. I still felt a lot of anxiety without my usual coping mechanisms. I was also in an unhealthy relationship dynamic, some of which was a remnant of the chaos created from my drinking days. This posed additional challenges and obstacles to my fledgling sobriety. With a lot of support from others in the program, I began to understand my patterns and develop healthier ways of responding that respected others and myself.

The journey through the program is not something I can easily describe in words, but it has been profound and life changing. This type of work with others, who also suffer from the same disease, is so grounding, soothing, and confirming. It has enriched my life way beyond what I thought was ever possible or what I deserved. Getting sober allowed me a first glance at what was going on for me in terms of my gender. It gave me the courage to look deeply and be unafraid at what I saw. And ultimately it taught me courage to be who I really am inside and share that with the world. In addition to the program, I got professional help and guidance from a psychologist. I had a lot of baggage to unearth and needed to develop specific tools and alternate coping strategies to the harmful ones I learned along the way. I began to study Buddhism, including a regular meditation practice, at the local Shambhala chapter. This trifecta of recovery, counseling, and Buddhism has really worked well to breathe new life into my being.

Without booze in my system, I was able to get clarity and peace of mind. My emotions balanced out. I began to take an interest in taking care of myself, including restarting my favorite athletic endeavor growing up; cross-country running. I also began to understand that I wasn't the root cause of all troubles. I wasn't less than, I was the same or equal to everyone else. I fostered a trust in my own intuition. I started to understand what I was feeling and communicating that to others. I began opening up to people, knowing that I was strong enough to be vulnerable.

Sobriety has also afforded me a calm and steady route through gender transition. If I had continued drinking and tried to transition, I would have a much harder and more treacherous path. It takes a lot of resources and energy to transition, and alcohol sapped the life out of me, leaving me in a stasis that would have led to my demise.

At the end of 2013, I celebrated four years of continuous sobriety with a heart full of gratitude and excitement. I am so glad I took the chance on myself, and my fellow humans to get the help and support I needed to move into a more balanced and fulfilled life. There will still be ups and downs, but now I know I have the tools and wherewithal to rise to any occasion.

## Emmett Lundberg

For as long as I can remember, I've been interested in Buddhism. I was raised Unitarian Universalist, which, as I like to tell people, meant I got to learn about a great number of religions, in addition to having one Sunday devoted to building time machines out of old refrigerator boxes. Isn't that what church should be—learning about the variety of what's out there and letting your heart decide which is right for you. I know that idea goes against a lot of people's beliefs but it just seems right to me. For a short period of time I had a fascination with Judaism, but was promptly told by a conservative classmate at school that I could not be Jewish. She had no problem trying to convince me to come to her Baptist church, but c'mon, I could never be Jewish.

I think I first began to read more intensely about Buddhism when I was in high school. *Going to Pieces Without Falling Apart* is one of my favorite books and had a deep impact on me when my sixteen-year-old self read it. In college, I read more books and was lucky to see the Dalai Lama speak in Central Park in one of my early years in New York City. I don't remember specifics about his talk that day, but I do remember his energy; so vibrant, content, the purest form of "happiness" that I've ever seen. After that, how could I not want to become "enlightened"?

I struggled, though. I felt as if I could not call myself a Buddhist. I wasn't Buddhist "enough," whatever that meant; I had too many emotions, I wasn't in the moment. But still, I read on and even permanently marked by body with a tattoo of a Buddha. Permanent for this life, that is. Even if I felt some pressure to be something more, I still connected quite deeply with this spiritual path.

Prior to transition, I was also incredibly emotionally scattered. I have always been a sensitive soul, which was apparent in my day-to-day life, as I was likely to be brought to tears by many things. My anxieties were so great that I often went to the doctor with any number of vague ailments. For years I struggled with "physical" symptoms without explanation and I was convinced something was seriously wrong with me.

A few years ago, before I really accepted that transition was the right path for me, I had an ongoing series of chest pains. I was convinced that there was something wrong with my heart. To make matters worse, I did not have health insurance at the time and went to a clinic on the lower east side in New York. There's nothing scarier, in my mind, than fearing the worst for your body and simultaneously feeling like a prisoner to the United States' health care system. I had test after test and one showed an irregular heartbeat, which seemed to back up my theory. They said I could have an enlarged heart. Dear god, I was going to die! I was sent for an X-ray of my heart to take a better look and the technician, after doing the X-ray, said, "You've been having chest pain? If it gets worse, make sure you go to the ER." That is not something you tell a hypochondriac. I was terrified for the two days I had to wait for the results. And then I received the standard call: "Everything looks normal." What? How could that possibly be? The doctors must have missed something. There was no way that I had a clean bill of health.

I was left in the same place I had started. With no more information, except for one doctor telling me offhandedly it could be "Anxiety," I had to look into myself. I had to know deeply who I was and what I wanted. I don't think a single trans person can go through this process without taking a serious look at who they are at the core of their being. The act of transitioning is not something you do on a whim. It is not easy and it is not quick. It takes time, it takes energy, and it takes pain. Emotional and physical limits are pushed. And yet, it didn't feel that way for me, from the inside.

Even as I started my transition, I was not in a place that I considered being *aware*. I was obsessed with the changes, constantly looking and waiting for more and not remaining in the moment. I felt as if this was the most important thing in my life. My close relationships began to the feel the tension. I struggled between reveling in the physicality of finally feeling like myself and still leaving enough space in my mind, heart, and soul for those who I cared most about. I told myself that whether it was right or wrong, I was only going to go through this once in my life and I wanted to be in it the way I felt necessary. What they don't tell you about starting your transition at a point in your life when you've already created an entire world around you, is that there will be pressure to maintain your "adult" commitments, while in a lot of ways feeling like a teenager on the inside. It's quite the dichotomy and a difficult thing to experience. Imagine having the wisdom and life experience of an adult person while going through puberty. You're so much more aware of the things you're feeling and in a way understanding, but you also want to give yourself the space to feel these things as a new event. It's a crazy kind of hyper awareness that as a teenager is not there; at least it wasn't for me.

And then you get to a point in your transition. For me, it was as I neared my one-year on hormones mark. Yeah, I thought, it'd be nice to have more facial hair, or have more of the fat on my hips redistribute, but it becomes less urgent. You're being read as male all the time and even though you look ten years younger than you really are, I suppose that's a blessing of being a trans man.

Life seemed to continue on. My head began to clear. I had space for other things again. My writing flourished. I was able to be more aware of those around me and their needs. I was able to see the way my life was heading. Things didn't feel quite as oppressive as before.

After one final panic attack the night after my very first shot of testosterone, and a week or two of initial anxiety filled with the enormity of my decision, my vague physical symptoms seemed to evaporate. I started to feel more comfortable, more confident and more *me*. I started to feel more "right." People in my life began to notice a happiness about me that was not outwardly visible even in my happiest of days before.

Then something really spectacular happened. For me, it felt like a huge wave of connection between everything in my life. I had never felt that intensity and depth before and I could only contribute it to being able to be true to myself. I felt the energy and connection of the universe inside my being. I began meditating more regularly; I consumed books about this universal connection and devoured documentaries. I started to think about how in some indigenous cultures, the transgender people are shamans and it began to make sense. In my mind, there is no greater experience than having lived in the world being perceived first as female and now as male. It's almost as if you have insider information unavailable to most other people. Obviously, I'm biased but I do like that think that we transgender people have a special place in the universe.

I am by no means a flawless human being now: far from it. I still struggle with anxieties. I am a deeply feeling and thinking person, and along with that comes a certain nervousness. But I am aware, I am present and I am working on it.

Things just make sense in a way that they did not prior to my transition. The world around me is "clear," for lack of a better word. I was worried I might "feel" less after being on hormones. Yes, testosterone does make it more difficult at times to verbalize certain emotions for me, but I still feel very deeply and completely. I have not lost that ability by any means; instead it has transformed into something I genuinely connect with and feel to be an integral part of my being. I am able to be sensitive and I am able to be spiritual, and those things fit wholly into my life now.

Alexander Walker

I hit the *send* button on my email. It was done. Two weeks before I was scheduled for my top surgery, I had finally told my family that I was transitioning. It wasn't very much notice for my family. In my email to them, I expressed my concern of losing them in my decision to finally transition.

I'd been contemplating, agonizing, and trying to wrap my mind around this decision for five years. The anxiety of "what ifs" had always gotten the best of me—What if I lost my family? My job? My Friends? My partner? What if I regretted transitioning? A year before I sent that email to my family, my attitude towards transition had changed. I decided that I was not going continue to struggle with the feelings of standing outside myself, seeing someone I didn't recognize, and of constantly grappling with a level of incongruence that tugged at the deepest strings of my being. I was going to take my first step.

Emotionally, the summer of 2011 was one of the best and worst for me. By August 2011, I'd been living as male in society for close to a year, though I had not taken any medical steps to change my body physically. I was scheduled for top surgery, double incision method, on

August 9, a day that would leave me with no regrets. In my twelve years since hitting puberty, I'd spent countless hours finding ways to hide this part of my body.

Back in 2007, I began contemplating what gender really meant and where I fit into it. I never realized that one could feel "female" or "male." As I began to explore this, I felt alone, scared and unsure of what to do. I kept thinking back to that day earlier in the summer when a friend (who now happens to be my wife) asked me out of the blue, "So, what pronouns do you prefer?" At the time, I wasn't even sure what she meant. In the moment, I brushed off her question. Yet I couldn't stop thinking about it. In the fall, I asked her more about why she posed that question to me. Her response was simple; she saw something inside me that seemed to be hiding. It was apparent in the way I interacted; my spirit was different from others. We had countless conversations about what this meant and I remember her describing a good friend from college who had transitioned from female-to-male.

I began searching for answers using the Internet. At that time, in the mid 2000s, I was a part of Livejournal. I identified as a masculine lesbian and was a part of a group where everyone had a similar identity. One day, I saw a post about someone transitioning and mentioning YouTube. I followed a link and was brought to a digital world of streaming videos. I found a video of a young female-to-male, FTM, who had just begun his transition in Florida. I was hooked. I watched his and others' progressions of changing with hormones, names, and, for some, surgery. As I watched these videos, I felt both relieved and terrified at the same time.

My anxiety, which I had struggled with for my entire life, had reached an all-time high and I struggled with the tasks of daily life. Even checking out at a grocery store was nerve wracking. It wasn't the act of seeing people or buying things, it was something else. It was how those who saw and interacted with me would perceive me. The shopping and socializing were particularly challenging. Initially, I was read as a young boy. More often than not, I was greeted with, "Hi son! Did you find everything alright?" These words sent me into a state of panic. It wasn't the language that terrified me; I liked this way of being addressed. My fear stemmed from not imagining how those people would react when they heard my voice or saw my given name on my credit card. Often, the reaction was a long the lines of "I'm sorry, young lady," accompanied by an embarrassed blush. These interactions put me in a near constant state of panic. After several years of living this way, I was at a crossroads. I needed help but was not ready to acknowledge the deepest source of my anxiety.

My first step was to find a way to navigate my anxiety and help me move past the emotional state I'd lived in since the age of sixteen, when I stopped taking anxiety medication. I began working with a therapist. We focused on understanding my childhood, building confidence, and finding a system with which to be successful in college. Week after week, for three years, I attended sessions and dissected my upbringing and the challenges of living with a parent who was unstable and, at times, a threat. I intentionally ignored the questioning of my gender for most of this time. I wasn't ready to explore my own gender, or rather, accept what I had known for a long time.

By the end of 2009, I had worked through much of my non-gender related anxiety and had a stable, productive life and was motivated to further it. While social interactions and shopping were still challenging, I had found a way to push through these moments. In my mind, I knew that eventually I had challenges coming my way, as I completed my education degree and started teaching—a profession where gendered titles were the norm. Nearly every day, a student would ask me, "Are you a boy or a girl?" I learned to take these daily interrogations in stride and respond with, "You can call me Miss," but their questions made me wonder. What made my students question my gender? Was it my clothes? The way I held myself? I struggled in my profession, already feeling like I was paving the way in the Midwest as a masculine dressed, lesbian-identified person, which I did not hide. As uncomfortable as I was in that role, it was better to deal with constant questioning than to think about the idea of transitioning.

The end of 2010 was a turning point. That December, I switched therapists and began actively working on figuring out my gender identity. The first few months were hard. I had a lot of internalized transphobia to overcome. I didn't want to be a stereotypical guy. I had a vision in my head that, if I took hormones, I would become an emotionless bastard. I realize now that this was incredibly naive, but at the time, that's what I saw.

There was only one narrative being told at the time: "born in the wrong body." I struggled in not relating to that personal narrative. Sure, I ran around my back yard without a shirt as a young kid. I was different from my three sisters. I never wore 'girls' clothing. But why didn't I have the language to express these feelings? I needed to feel congruent in some way. With the guidance of my therapist, I began to work through the nitty gritty of it all. I found that I could be myself— the kind, selfless, loving, passionate person I always was, and also be a part of society and feel whole when I looked in the mirror. It took me years to get to this place. During that time, my then fiancée and I moved to a new part of the country and a new city. We started over. There were many reasons for this move—a better economy, more jobs in our fields, and graduate school. It was also a prime opportunity for me to transition.

In the summer of 2011, we packed up our stuff, our dogs, and moved to our new home. I began a new job and living life fully as male. At first, I was fearful of others asking questions, but soon found that with confidence I was just another hardworking employee. I got used to being called Mr. It felt a little strange, but good at the same time. I had always said it didn't matter to me, but in retrospect, hearing "she" felt even more strange.

I learned a lot during that first year of social transition. One thing was that the young kids that I enjoyed teaching struggle with ambiguity. Even though I was presenting as male, my students picked up on certain traits about me that were different from their other male teachers. They did not treat me any differently or respect me less—quite the contrary. They went out of their way to be respectful, particularly when reminded that "everyone is different," but they just weren't quite sure what to make of me.

At the same time, I increasingly liked the way I felt and my anxiety was becoming more absent from my life than it had ever been. I was more content with life than I had ever been.

I lived for that first year without considering medical intervention. The whole idea of changing my body still felt foreign. I spent a lot of time meeting other trans people in the area, talking with them, and learning about their successful medical transitions.

I started to feel the anxiety again and knew that I was reaching a point where I needed to take another step.

I scheduled an appointment with a surgeon. I set a surgery date and knew that once I took that step I would eventually go down the path of hormones, name changes, and possibly other steps. I was ready. Emotionally, I knew what kind of man I wanted to be. I was going to be a collaborative, passionate, caring person who is ever growing and changing.

The morning of my top surgery, my fiancée sat next to me. She looked in my eyes, hopeful that the next two hours would be over quickly. I was nervous because it's still surgery, but excited to finally have a literal weight lifted that had been holding me back since I was eleven. I was wheeled into the OR and two hours later I remember a nurse saying to me "Wake up, do you know where you are?" All I could say was, "Are they gone?" Her response was, "Yes" and I lifted my right hand in a fist and smiled from ear to ear.

Transition wasn't something that was clear-cut

for me. With my upbringing I have very little memory of my childhood. I needed to dig deep, face my demons, and work through my childhood experiences before I could piece through whether this was right for me. My knowledge of transsexual people had been limited to male-to-female prostitutes. My eyes were opened and my soul was set free, but it took time and effort to figure out exactly what kind of person, what kind of human, what kind of man I really was before I could take any steps to transition.

# SECTION III—FAMILY

Blood is thicker than water, but is it thicker than the physical form?

Coming out to your family can be one of the most terrifying experiences of your transition. Even those who *think* their family will be okay with their identity wonder if this could possibly put an end to the pleasant and supportive relationship they have had thus far. But ultimately, the pros outweigh the cons and this is a step that must be taken.

Our contributors have had a range of experiences with their loved ones. Some have found ways to include them as they move forward with their transitions. Others have found struggle along the path to their true selves.

At the end of the day, it's all about including people in your life who give you what you need to be a positive and productive person. They can be family by blood or those brought into your life as chosen family.

Jack Elliott

After my parents divorced, my mother moved us to New Jersey with her soon-to-be husband. We landed in a rental at the top of a circle with thirty-foot pine trees wrapping clear around the small patch of property. My room, one of the three small bedrooms that occupied the second floor was faded and green. The floor was covered with shag carpet that had once stood upright full of life and volume. By the time I moved in, it had been worn and matted to the floor. The fibers no longer stood on their own, and seemed to have given up out of pure exhaustion.

The year was 1982. The ominous sounds of Black Sabbath poured underneath my door from my brother's room like smoke. With covers pulled up to my chin I waited for something to happen like Satan himself to tear me out of my bed with his part-hand part-hoof. Pins and patches lined our jean jackets, and roach clip earrings swung underneath feathered hair. We had settled in on the rougher south side of town but in context rough meant the comfortable white suburban equivalent of metal heads vs. preppies.

Our new family unit was compact, and simple. Trouble would soon find us, and the warning signs began to appear. They were subtle the way a poltergeist knocks something off the counter when you turn around, and you say things like, "Oh that was probably nothing."

The first holiday season with our new unit began in an exhilarating rush to the finish line that would be Christmas with our new extended family. Year One as I like to refer to it. Our house rivaled the Saks Fifth Avenue window display at Christmas. We weren't privy to the information until years later, but my mother and stepfather's courtship was during a period of which some might say in low voices at parties *while they were both still married to other people.* So our Christmas was an overcompensating hyperbolic rush of reds, greens, and silvers coming right at your face.

Our stepfather had three daughters from a previous marriage. They were much older than my brother and me, old enough to have a mother to place blame squarely on our backs for breaking up the marriage. I was indifferent to the idea of having sisters. I didn't like girly things, and didn't understand their language or rituals. And most importantly the balance that had formed in our new unit was now threatened.

So the fighting gloves went on, and in this case also held an elaborate tray of Christmas cookies. The unit had been breached, and alliances had to be formed. It started with having to go to our new aunt's house for her holiday celebration. My brother and I walked in like a chain gang. We were neatly dressed, quiet and polite. The chairs had been prearranged in a circle, a possible interrogation instead of a gathering. I sheepishly held my sequence of numbers under my chin as I faced forward and then to the side for identification. We settled in and I slipped away into my surroundings. Porcelain clowns peeked out from inside curio cabinets with their hands rested under slightly tilted heads. Shelves were filled with a succession of class pictures of each of the five kids. A permanent record of how ugly progressed every year. A single bowl of peanuts made its way through the room with no accompanying beverage. We sat with dry throats as siblings finished each other's sentences, and listened to the cadence of inside jokes that were traded at our expense. There was nothing louder than the sound of being ignored. So the division began, my kids-your kids, my family-your family and so on. The unit started to take a new shape.

Through all of this complicated business that was developing around me I realized something wasn't quite right with me. How I felt inside, was not in fact who I *was.* There was no language to describe those emotions. There was no social context, something I might have heard on TV, or overheard in an adult conversation.

Calling them feelings was too limiting. This was the very essence of what I was in the world. It was my absolute truth. My body didn't match my self. But how was this possible, that I felt like a boy underneath my girl body? It was so earth shattering to me that there was no other option than to just not think about it. Life had other plans, and everything that touched my world was gendered. It was present in every fiber of my life. The clothes I wore, the toys I should play with, the friends I chose, the length of my hair. It manifested itself in the way I was supposed to walk, talk, and how

I was referred to and about. It was everything. And it all felt wrong. I wasn't prepared to conceal a truth of that magnitude. How were the other parts of me supposed to mature properly around this huge disconnect? How was I supposed to drag this fractured self around with me like one would drag an annoying younger sibling?

Meanwhile, that Christmas morning in the rental house we shared a rare but normal family moment of opening up our gifts. Family interaction was being acted out in a slightly exaggerated way. My mother and stepfather told me I had one gift left, and prior ritual had suggested that this would be my "big gift." They had it hidden in the family room so I descended the four small steps to find it staring back at me. It was an abomination. It was a giant ladies ten-speed bike. The horror.

The oxygen began to leave the room first out of my body then quickly out windows and doors. I began jumping up and down faking excitement. It hadn't been premeditated; my false joy, but once I started I couldn't stop. I was using it as a ruse to give me time to formulate my true emotions. Each thought came in between each over exaggerated bounce. All I wanted for Christmas that year was a BMX bike. I would have settled for the one with the pink seat and tires, a sacrifice to the hetero-normative little girl gods. Instead, this giant brown ladies bicycle mocked my secret identity. Each gift for my brother was perfectly matched to his loves and interests. I got a denim skirt. His collection of pins had been carefully picked out to match his favorite bands. I got a Jean Nate' spray and lotion set. His stereo to my Malibu Barbie, and it went on and on. My legs finally tired of jumping so I sat down on the enormous seat and wrapped my hands around the foamy handlebar grips donning the same beige color. Total defeat.

Four years later we moved to the big white house with green shudders. Our 1874 Dutch Colonial home wore its past on its giant white wooden sleeve. They say places have energy, and this place seemed to welcome our non-working family home like the prodigal son. Our life had gotten an upgrade in the form of our six-bedroom right side of town house. My room had red-flocked wallpaper and red carpet even in the closet.

At the age of twelve I was beginning to lose the war against my body. Puberty, that unwelcomed visitor was taking hold. A decision had to be made, and I was forced to make a choice. Hold on to my boy self, keep my hair short, and do my best to honor how I felt inside, or give in to the girl that was winning the battle over my body? I think there could have been a way to have better understood myself if I had felt safe to tell the truth.

Had I been part of a family that welcomed human emotion as a viable form of currency I would have sought refuge. I doubt that any of us would have had the language to speak to what was happening, but there would have been safety for the feelings and love to serve as the foundation. It is not to say that my upbringing was violent, or unsafe in any way. However, this is a cautionary tale as a warning to the dangers of mediocrity. No emotions were actually expressed, or challenged, or held in high regard but there we lived in a beautiful house, there was food on the table, and clothes on our backs. It was all so fine enough that I didn't realize until years later what *hadn't* been there. There was no closeness, safety, and no one really knew or fully trusted anyone. It was like being raised by your co-workers, some of whom had ulterior motives and career ambitions that included manipulating you out of your job. Our office family politics were exhausting. It made me an expert in outsmarting passive aggressive behavior, but really lousy at collecting happy family memories.

I survived high school with moderate success by further developing my skills to hide in plain sight. I excelled socially, so I couldn't jeopardize that persona no matter what the consequence. What would I have done had everyone found out? I learned to use my girl self to navigate the world even though it felt uncomfortable and false. I grew to understand what was expected of me. I couldn't risk the power I had outside the home, because I lacked so little of it with my family.

As my twenties came upon me, I see now how grossly ill prepared I was to be an adult in the practical sense. I had become so practiced in thinking in abstraction that everyday tasks were sometimes difficult. Returning phone calls, paying bills on time, and the life of a functioning adult became overwhelming at times. Everything that I knew and understood was false, it was a made-up fantasy. I protected myself with layers and layers of untruths to create a self that was acceptable for the outside world. Instead of acknowledging the loss and fear I felt, it liquefied into the rest of me, and became unrecognizable. When obligatory phone calls from family came my response was that I was doing fine out of white-hot rage.

My rebellion came in the way of an impenetrable personality instead. It was a sense of bravado based on the theory that if I pretended nothing bothered me then I would not give anyone an obvious excuse to dismiss or abandon me. I believed that my self-reliance protected me from scrutiny and rejection. So I kept myself on an invisible leash. If I were to have been in need of anything including love and understanding it meant that I had failed.

Underneath this façade were feelings of deep loss, frustration and anger surrounding my life. The central point was the question of self that was deeply fractured. The trouble was that these feelings weren't just isolated around my questions of gender. I didn't know how to give or accept unconditional love. There was a pressure to keep everything surface, and manageable. If a truth meandered its way into our home it would have been like a deadly virus. Any form of self-discovery was like a contagion.

As my twenties came to an end, the gnawing of self that was once manageable became overwhelming. I think subconsciously I knew there would have to be an end to this denial. It was more that I just had no idea when it would be. It ended up coming when I was thirty-four. The moment I realized what this was, it came over me like a club to the head. When I came to, I brought a friend of mine up to the roof of her East Village apartment at sunset and I said it out loud for the first time. The need for self-preservation had finally out weighed the feelings of fear and shame. This truth I carried around with me for as long as I can remember was finally born. The words came out of my mouth and gave him life. He existed outside of me for the first time. I stopped for a moment and realized that this was a beginning. I know now that he was responsible for much of the unrest in my life. He was unnamed for so long, but he was there unsettling, poking, and prodding his way through every part of me just looking for a way out.

There was no right way tell my family. So instead I chose to dig a sizable hole in the ground and stick my head in it for months. There was a definite timeline on my denial, as the physical change itself would relieve me of my need to *tell* anyone. I was able to spit out one awkward word after another to my grandmother, and that is how the family started to unravel. We were so loosely woven together it shouldn't have surprised me something like this would be the end of us as a family. In quite unceremonious fashion, it all went down something like this:

I told my grandmother first and swore her to secrecy. After much guilt and confusion she thought my mother ought to know so she went ahead and told her. My mother then told my stepfather, brother and father. They were all mad because I hadn't told them, but no one was convinced that I would go through with it (whatever that meant). There were many angry phone calls back and forth amongst them. I never spoke to my father, stepfather or brother again after that. And that was it.

I managed many years later to reconcile with my mother and we are able to see each other as people and less as a parent child relationship. It makes things cleaner for me to not have to kick all that dirt around on a regular basis.

In dealing with it, I came to find the strangest

realization was the attachment other people felt to who I was. These fundamental things, being a woman, a daughter, a sister, meant having very specific responsibilities to everyone else based on those roles. Having come through the other side of all of it I have earned the courage to see myself as I truly was. It made me realize I wasn't always ready to live up to my part. I have fallen short in every one of those roles more times than I want to count. At times my confusion made me distant, selfish and petty. My anger and confusion was so all consuming it could get the best of me, and cloud the very judgment that I imposed onto others.

There are always new chapters to be written, and I cannot say with certainty I know how this story will end.

Rae Larson

Sometimes when I look back on my life, I can't help but wonder if my family thinks I'm purposefully trying to keep them on their toes. Ever since I was four years old, it's been one thing after another. I can't remember the number of times I've had to come out to the same people. Every time I say to them, "Can we talk?" they immediately roll their eyes and sigh, "What now??" My relationship with my immediate family has always been very... interesting. Or at least it's been very interesting to me.

I knew I was a boy from the moment I understood that society expects there to be two types of people in the world. It took me quite awhile to figure out why my family didn't think I was a boy. I really thought there might be something wrong with them because I knew, more than anything else a toddler can know, that I was in fact a boy. The day I found a side-by-side picture of a bio man and bio woman in a biology book hidden in my parents closet was one of my most depressing days to date. The trauma of reality can do terrible things to the imaginative mind of a child. I went into a deep depression after that day, a depression that a child my age would have no way of articulating. I started asking my parents questions like, "If I had been born a boy, what would you have named me?" One day, my questions lead to my mother telling me a story that sparked hope into my young and incomplete heart. She told me that very late in her pregnancy with me, the doctors told her I was a boy. She told me they had been expecting a boy. My heart, my broken, incomplete heart was grasping for the invisible pieces of itself that were pouring out of the words she spoke to me. In that moment, everything made sense. Even the doctors thought I was a boy! There must have been some sort of accident, but I most definitely was always supposed to be a boy! But reality kept creeping its ugly head in between me and happiness. I saw those pictures in that book my body was missing a part and reality laughed in my face.

Even still, I kept the conversations going with my parents. What kinds of things did they do to prepare for the son they thought they were going to have? Were they sad I wasn't born a boy? I was desperately seeking for a sign that I was not the only one who wanted me to be a boy. Maybe if someone else felt the same way, we could both pray and God would hear us better.

I didn't ever get the vocalized opinion that I wanted from my parents, but my older sister always let me pretend to be whoever I wanted while we played. I was the dad, brother, son, or dog when we played house, and I was always allowed to be Tarzan when we played "Jungle" while climbing trees. She never asked questions or gave me confused looks in response to my requests—she fully accepted me for who I make-believe was and that was validating enough. Or at least it was during playtime. Nighttime, after my parents prayed with me and the lights were turned out, was the worst. I would cry and plead in prayer that God would fix my body while I slept, so I could wake up as a normal boy. Those tear-filled nights went on for years.

The struggles with my parents also continued for years. Every Sunday was the same fight—I was NOT getting into that dress. You would NOT do my hair in that fashion. I am a boy and boys don't wear those things. I will NOT attend Daisies; that Bible study is for girls and I am NOT a girl! Of course, as a child who had been slapped with reality one too many times, I had no way of articulating those things. I just didn't know how.

During the week, I was free to express myself how I wanted. My parents let me pick out my clothes and do my hair, but Sundays were what nightmares were made of. And the Sunday routine—wake up, despair, fight my parents, cry, give in, go to church, feel utter humiliation, wish that I could evaporate into the pew, daydream about being a part of the boys' Sunday School, go home, take off those stupid girl clothes, and bask in the freedom of a T-shirt and shorts—continued until I was about eleven years old. The only reason it stopped at that age was because we started going to a church that was casual dress all the time and I was able to pick out my own clothes.

My parents never pressured me to hang out with girls, so I hardly ever did. I was dressing how I wanted, expressing myself how I wanted, and I was friends with the people I wanted. Though I was allowed to express myself how I chose, my dad would constantly remind me how he preferred me to be. He would forever say things like, "Remember when we used to put pigtails in your hair? Oh, you were so cute! You should do that again." Or, "You should buy more fitted shirts, those look so much better on you." It was hard to hear those things, harder than I realized at the time, but my friends would often validate me by saying things like, "You look like us, you talk like us, you do the things we like to do; I think you're a boy like us!" And this kept me mostly happy—until puberty.

My dad was the one who brought my attention to the changes my body was starting to undergo. I had bought a shirt without trying it on first. After putting it on at home, I wanted to show it off to my family. My dad immediately commented on how it made my breasts look. I heard the slap of reality across my face from his words. How could I have suppressed the reality that was literally staring me in the face every day in front of the mirror? In was in that moment that everything came crashing down again, just like it had in the past. I remember being reduced to tears while I came to terms with that evil and damaging word that had begun haunting my every day life: reality. I was a girl, that's just how it was, and it was about time I lay down my fantasies and start accepting life as it was handed to me.

In middle school, I dove headfirst into this new acceptance of my life. I figured if I submerged myself in the world of "women" then maybe I'd be more apt to fit into a role I was never created for. I started dressing, acting, talking, and looking the part I was expected to play. The compliments and encouraging opinions from both my parents and the girls at school didn't comfort me in the slightest. I liked the positive attention—for the first time in my life, the way I chose to dress was receiving positive feedback—but it wasn't enough. I soon learned that admiration and approval were things earned by manipulation, false pretenses, and people pleasing. During this learning process, I became intensely set on always maintaining my parents' approval.

This was an emotionally draining full-time job for me. I was literally sustaining my life by feeding off of other people's approval because I sure as hell didn't have approval of my own. I hated myself but others loved me and that was what life was about—or so I had been taught. Shortly after mastering the art of people pleasing, I met a girl. A girl who would shake the foundation of every relationship I had established up to that point.

It didn't take long for us to become friends and it didn't take long after that for us to fall in love. I remember being so confused by it all. Love can be very scary but homosexual love in a conservative, Christian home is even scarier still. Around the same time that she and I finally stopped the denial and recognized our feelings for each other, my father had been deployed to Korea for a few months and would not be returning for quite a while. My older sister had moved in with my grandparents, thousands of miles away. It was just my mother, my two younger siblings, and myself living at home.

My mom turned a blind eye to my new relationship for quite a while. I think she knew but she just didn't want to acknowledge it fully. My father found out by reviewing the footage of the security camera he had installed by the front door before he was deployed. He saw me kiss her goodbye and immediately called my mother to inquire. I'm not entirely sure how the conversation went but I believe my mother denied it all. When my father was given a two-week break from his deployment, he drove me down a dark alley, parked the car, locked the doors, turned and faced me and we proceeded to debate my life choices for a solid three hours. This was the first of hundreds of debates he and I would have.

When my older sister came home to visit, at this time she was a sophomore in high school in a tiny town in Wisconsin, she found out I was dating a female. She locked us both in our parent's room, sat me down on their bed, and broke down. With angry tears streaming down her face, she looked me in the eyes and told me how I had broken all her dreams for us. We would never have children at the same time. What would she explain to her children about the women I was living with? Our husbands would never be best friends. I had ruined her dream of her future—how dare I try to make my future happy for myself.

My extended family chose to ignore everything, for the most part. One time, my grandpa got very intoxicated and said some inappropriate things to me and my girlfriend. Another time, my grandma asked how it was possible to not have an incredible dramatic relationship, seeing as though there were two girls in it. Other than that, no one commented or acknowledge anything, one way or another.

On the other hand, if my father and I were left

alone for more than fifteen minutes, we would begin debating my life. Sometimes it was my hair, sometimes it was my clothing, but most of the time it was how I could possibly justify whom I dated, given my Christian beliefs. He was the only one who ever consistently tried to change my mind. My older sister eventually went to college and began looking at life very differently. She started to support my happiness, though it differed from her own version. My mother loved me and never once questioned whom I dated or how I expressed myself. My younger siblings were proud to show off their "token lesbian sister" to all their friends. And this was how life went, for the next seven years.

After donning the label "lesbian," it didn't take long for me to realize how unfitting it felt. Lesbian: A girl who likes girls. It just never seemed right to me. In a group of women, I never felt like I fit in, even if they all identified as lesbians. When I was twenty-one, I figured out why.

When I came to terms with my trans identity, I instantly felt the fire of liberation, fear, happiness, excitement, and even remorse, all burning in my heart at the same time. Immediately after the flames of these feelings sparked, my heart started to sink; what was I going to tell my father? For seven years we had debated the people I fell in love with. How could he possibly accept my transgender status?

I started going to therapy, hoping that my therapist would help me emotionally prepare for the debate war that would surely ensue after disclosing my feelings to my father. A couple of weeks after my very first therapy appointment, my sister graduated from college; the whole family gathered up in a small town in Wisconsin to celebrate. I had worked a twelve-hour overnight shift and then driven eight hours to get to the ceremony in time. When I arrived, I was in desperate need of sleep and even more desperately in need of a shower. The very first thing my father said to me was, "Your hair looks really good." With those five little words, I felt like someone had pressed the reset button and I was starting over fresh. My father had never once complimented me on my appearance since he and my mom had stopped dressing me. I was ecstatic. From getting in the shower to getting dressed, I didn't stop smiling. I put on the outfit I brought that I was most proud of, did my hair up to perfection, smiled at myself in the mirror, and could have easily defeated the entire world in that moment. I walked tall, my smile beamed, and puffed out my chest as I walked down the stairs to meet up with my family to head out for my sister's graduation ceremony. I stood proud in front of my father, waiting to hear his approval. He looked me up and down and said, "I liked your hair better before." Immediately, pain spread everywhere. I almost wished that he had just sucker punched me in the gut because I could recover from that a lot faster.

I spent the rest of the night in a terrible mood, complaining to my siblings, and doubting the true value that my life really had. Most of the next morning went the same way. At one point, my siblings had heard quite enough. They turned to me and said, "Have you even talked to him about your feelings?" This hit me really hard. How could my dad possibly know how those comments, the comments he had been making my whole life, affect me if I've never confronted him? So I decided I would tell him.

I waited until the very last day of the trip. My father and I were waiting for everyone to pack up their things and we were sitting alone together in a dark room. I started out by bringing up past incidences—all the times I felt proud, comfortable, and confident and he would put me down by saying things like, "We used to put you in cute dressed and pigtails. I miss that. You were so cute. Why don't you grow your hair out again?" I told him how devastating those comments were to me. It felt like he was only proud of the person I was when he could dictate who that was. He only loved the idea of me that he created and not the real me—the happy and healthy me. He paused for a moment. Then, he started stammering. Finally, he blurted out, "Well YOU changed your status on Facebook to my 'SON.' And now I'm sitting here worried you *actually think* you're a *boy*!" I started searching my brain for the command of "breathe." I didn't even know what to say. I had only been to therapy once and I was certainly not prepared to come out to him. I clearly remember how the conversation started and ended, but the middle part is such a fuzzy memory. I do know that a lot of very nasty things were said including things like, "You will *never* be a man. You're too emotional. Your brother is a *man*. The way he gets angry, that's what *men* do. You are no man." I remember never saying the word *transgender* during the conversation. But I did discuss the feelings I had as a child and the feelings that continued all the way to present day. There was a lot of yelling on his part and a lot of crying on mine. But the way my dad ended the conversation went something like, "I don't see you as a man. If anything, I see you as a gay man" (which was quite ironic in my opinion and told me a lot about how my dad views gender and sexuality) "but I love you. I'll always love you. No matter what." That was all I needed to pick up the shattered pieces of my heart and put them back together again. This became the very last time my father and I would ever debate my gender or sexuality.

I ended up officially coming out via video to my entire family five months later. My older sister, the same one who previously told me I had ruined her dreams, immediately jumped to my side. She sent a video to the family as well, coming to my defense and telling my family why they needed to support "her brother." It would be over a year before my mom and I would discuss anything in relation to my gender or identity. I think we were both in an emotional place where we just weren't ready for that conversation right away. I think that had a lot to do with our past experiences with emotional topics. My younger sister and brother took a little time to come around. They don't get the pronouns right 100% of the time, only my older sister does, but they try hard. They are so supportive of my happiness and they will always work hard at validating that in all forms. My extended family has mostly chosen to ignore it all. They try with the name sometimes, and other times they don't really. I think a lot of that has to do with their location and the atmosphere surrounding foreign concepts—just ignore them and they'll eventually go away.

As you can probably assume by now, I was most worried about my father's reaction to my official "coming out" message. His reply was started out with, "I may not agree but by the way you've explained yourself, I think I understand. And I can respect your decision to do what makes you happy." He then continued to list some minor concerns but he never once tried to discourage me. Short, simple, and beautiful. It took a few months for questions and dialogue to come about, but with each passing day, my relationship with my father slowly mends and builds stronger.

My family isn't perfect, but I think perfection is overrated. If my family would have been immediately on-board and supportive, I don't think I'd appreciate the relationships we hold now. Everyone involved in my life has consistently grown. Sure, things could have been better growing up, but they most definitely could have been way worse. They could have turned their backs on me. They could have easily given up and most people wouldn't have blamed them. But they never once stopped loving me and they will never stop trying to show that love in a way that makes me feel validated. I think that's what's most important. My family has taught me that unconditional love can come in many different forms. My family loves me unconditionally, but now they are learning to love me in a way that I can fully receive. There are no words to express the gratitude towards the journey they've agreed to accompany me on. If I had to sum up where my relationship with my family stands at present day, I'd do it with this anecdote:

Thanksgiving 2013. It was simply my immediate family and my grandma on my dad's side. I was in the other room but I was listening to the conversations taking place in the kitchen. My mother said, "Oh, I think Rae's going to handle that." My grandma replied, "Where is she?" Without even the slightest hesitation, my father firmly and simply said, "*He.*" My now-flustered Grandma cleared her throat slightly and said, "*He…*"

Leng Montgomery

When I started my transition I knew I was lucky because I was certain that telling my family wouldn't be an issue. Growing up it was mostly just my mum and I. I never knew my father; he died when I was young, so there was never a chance to get to know him, even if I had wanted to.

I didn't miss having a male presence around me because I never had it to start with, but I did sometimes find myself *missing* having a dad like other kids. Although my mum didn't say it, I knew what the truth was—he never wanted to be a father in the first place. Once he found out that she was pregnant, he bailed. And then he died.

She brought me up on her own, had a few partners, but met the most important one when I was twenty-one. They got married and I called him Dad for some time. Even though they are no longer together, he still acts as a father figure, having put me through University and always accepting and supporting who I am.

In September 2009, I was binding properly for the first time. I was in San Francisco at the time and was having a Skype conversation with my mother. I will never forget how she noticed straight away that I was sitting differently and that I looked different. I proudly told her I was wearing a binder. She could see that my chest looked super flat. She asked if this meant she would be calling me by a different name any time soon. I wasn't sure then, but the most heartwarming thing was her response: "If you do, then it's fine. I will address you however you want to be addressed". Knowing she supported me put me at ease. She is a very rare type of parent to have.

We have been mostly estranged from the rest of the family so there was really no one else to come out to. Some of her friends are like extended family, and I told them about my intentions to transition. The response has been mostly positive. A few didn't understand why I was transitioning, but it was never met with hostility, more of a lack of understanding. The more I have medically transitioned (i.e. taking hormones, or having surgery), the more everyone has come on board and been as understanding and respectful as they can be.

For a while, my mum did feel that she had 'lost' a daughter, which I understand is something all parents might feel when their child transitions. But at the same time she never saw me as a feminine being. For her, the joy of having a son now means that she has a child who is happy with himself.

Adolescence wasn't a great time for either of us; I felt suicidal for quite a large chunk of it and was massively depressed. I didn't feel right a lot of the time and spent it feeling like I was in the wrong identity and wrong life. Realizing where some of these feelings were coming from has played a huge part in healing different areas of my life.

Some of my friends are also family in my mind. Once I came out to them, I wasn't sure how it would go over. I was particularly concerned about some of my lesbian friends, who didn't seem to have any male friends. I had no idea how that would go down. In some cases not so well, and even though nothing was directly said like "I can't be your friend because you're trans," the friendship hasn't been the same. Other friendships became a lot closer, and people seemed to love me as Leng without any thought to the fact that I was now male.

I am fortunate to have found love in a group of people known as 'The Community,' where I met Jean, whom I have been with for the last four years. Despite the movements within our relationship, the love we've shared and have for one another has made us permanent fixtures in each others' lives.

Ian Carter

In order to convey the ramifications my suicide attempt at eighteen years old had on the relationship with my family, I feel it's important to go all the way back to the beginning. A lot of background information is needed in order to put my current relationship with my family into perspective.

My immediate family has never been close. This should not be confused with my relationship with my grandparents, however, as they were the glue that kept us together. Sports and education are the two things that our familial bond revolves around. Affection didn't really exist within the confines of my childhood home. Growing up, if we went a full week with only daily spankings and one harsh yelling at, it was considered a fairly good week. This is not to say that my parents beat the shit out of us... not on a regular basis at least. They did have a knack for screaming at us or shoving us against walls during times when love and nurturing might have been a more productive solution.

Along with the expectations within my family, I was simultaneously battling what the church and society had taught me to be the worst flaws a human being could have. I can't be a boy, I thought, so I will be a lesbian, but wait, I can't be a lesbian, so I'll hide inside my own little world where I can be who I am without conflict. I spent the majority of my early life hidden. Hidden in my own world, with my own pain. I kept the constant thought of suicide a secret. It would be of no surprise if upon being asked about my suicidal tendencies before my transition, my family would have answered, "Ian just had a couple bouts of depression. He mostly kept to himself. He's always been very introverted." All of which would be true, however, my bouts of depression lasted for years at a time. I kept quiet so much because the screaming inside my head was enough noise to deal with. My [continued] introversion is a whole separate thing all together it's who I am and how I expend my energy. Even now, my life-long introversion probably gives my family an excuse to look away from the whole truth.

I was only seven when I made my first suicide attempt. My sister and I do not discuss it and the rest of my family isn't really aware of it, unless they read about it on my blog. I wouldn't be surprised if my sister has even forgotten about the event all together. This all happened around the time that she became wrapped up in her own, all-consuming dark shadows, so there was, understandably, no energy left for her to help me. This would be my own battle to fight, alone, for the rest of my life.

I became so used to the feelings of despair that I found comfort and creativity in it. I would spend hours alone in my room, drawing and writing. And I was really good at it! My depression and emotional pain became a part of me; like a limb, or a vital organ. I thrived on being a tortured soul. My family never saw this though. They just thought I happened to be very talented at writing and drawing for my age. They weren't aware of the battle I fought inside myself, and that this was an outlet, the pen and pencils my weapons.

During my mid- to late teens, my depression turned to anxiety, which became debilitating at times, still unbeknownst to my family. I worked very hard at keeping the magnitude of my emotional and mental struggles a secret, which in turn fueled a number of short screenplays that I never showed anyone because of how dark and telling they were. From the ages of fifteen to eighteen I drew a mural on my bedroom wall as a way to cope with life. It helped to alleviate my daily panic attacks. Some of which were so bad that it felt like something else took control of my body and the anger would simply rush out. I would go through my room like a tornado; throwing things, hitting things, crying, and then I would literally black out for minutes at a time. When I would come to, my room was completely torn apart and I had little recollection of what happened minutes before. It was terrifying, but all I could do was clean my room, and make it look like nothing ever happened.

Aside from writing and drawing, being on the high school and US swim team helped me as well. I could take out my anger and frustration on the water as I chopped my hands through its surface. Using my anger and frustration helped me to become one of the top swimmers in my county and my state. Finally, this is when I got my mom's attention—because I was actually good at some sort of sport.

Prior to my decision to transition, junior and senior year of high school were the most pivotal years of my life. Junior year was when I had my first real girlfriend. After her parents found a "love note" I had given her, they were enraged and decided to make my mother aware of my lesbian identity through a mouthful of profane language. Because we were on the swim team together, and because her parents were major financial contributors to my high school, we were monitored very closely. We couldn't be in the locker room alone together, or anywhere for that matter; we couldn't be seen talking to each other, we couldn't sit on the bus together on the way to swim meets; we couldn't do anything without being watched. Luckily, our friends on the swim team did everything they could to help us have moments alone. They would hold parties or events where we could be together without adult supervision. We somehow managed to do this for two years, which included the summer between junior and senior year when we were allowed no contact whatsoever.

That summer was spent mostly in Europe when I tagged along with my mom's German class. After the students returned home, I stayed with my aunt in Austria for a month while my mom traveled to Spain and France. Upon her return, we went on a walk to a nearby café, and that's when my mom told me she was a lesbian. My dad knew already, and they were in the process of getting divorced. As excited as I should have been about this news, I felt angry with her... thinking if she had only come out sooner she could have helped to prevent some of my own struggles. After seeing the abusive, angry and depressed mother I once knew vanish with this revelation, I let my own anger toward her disappear and was grateful for her newfound comfort. Instead of my mom saving me, I saved her and had given her that courage to finally be herself and be happy.

Senior year, my girlfriend and I were reunited and back to hiding the love we shared. Our relationship began to unravel after I endured harassment from the coaches and death threats from her father. On New Year's Eve, I held a party for the swim team at my house since my parents were out of town. There was alcohol and marijuana and all the typical drama that comes along with high school parties. What mattered most was that my girlfriend and I got to be together. I wanted us to survive; I needed us to survive for my own sanity and well being. Unfortunately, the events of the night would lead to our destruction.

We received a phone call at my house that night from a family member of one of my friends on the swim team. Her mother was in the hospital and they were trying to reach her. This particular friend, however, was not at my party that night. A couple of hours later we found out her mother had committed suicide by way of sleeping pills and carbon monoxide. Drunk and disoriented, I completely lost my mind, and I didn't get it back for a very long time. The next morning we came to find out that not only did her mother commit suicide but also the mother of a guy on the swim team had committed suicide. The two were completely unrelated incidents but they both hit me hard, deepening my own depression, and increasing my suicidal ideation. My relationship suffered, leading my girlfriend to stray. I lost fifteen pounds in two weeks. I couldn't keep food down for months. I needed help getting out of the pool after races because I so weak. My panic attacks were becoming even more frequent. I lost my relationship, and I felt like even my allies were turning against me. I decided one night to end it by suffocating myself.

I really wanted it to work. I placed a pillow over my face and pushed down as hard I could to try to finally end the pain. I felt my breath getting slower, as did my heart rate, and I kept trying to push down as hard as I could even though I was getting weaker. I remember praying, telling God I was sorry for what I was doing, but that it needed to be done. Suddenly, I felt as though the pillow was lifting off of my face. The more I tried to push, the more my pillow became lighter against my face, and a warmth shot throughout my body. Call me crazy (it wouldn't be the first time and won't be the last), but I truly believe it was divine intervention. I let go of the pillow, threw it to the floor in frustration, and began to sob as this warmth cocooned over my body and held me through the night.

While I was getting ready for school, I told my mom what I had done. I told her I couldn't take the pain anymore, and I needed help. I don't remember much about her reaction as I was still so numb and detached from reality. I do remember going to school that day and sitting in my first-period Spanish class. A girl that liked to pick on me, as a way of flirting, was going at it, but I wasn't paying attention to her. My mind was stuck on the night before, and my eyes began to fill up with tears. She realized there was something seriously wrong and pulled me out into the hallway before class began. She pulled me in close and wrapped her arms around me as tightly as she could get them, as if she was trying to squeeze the pain from my body. I broke down in tears, screaming and wailing right there, in the hallway, in her arms. The teacher left us alone and didn't ask either of us to come back into the classroom. Fifteen minutes later, a kid came to the class with a note. It was a request from the crisis counselor to see me immediately. My mom, who worked part of the day at my high school, had gone to the counselor that morning and told her what happened. I spent the rest of the day in the office, being monitored.

Soon after, I was referred to a psychiatrist. In therapy I spilled my guts about my past, my battle with my gender, and how I'd concluded that I was a lesbian. They put me on a handful of anti-depressants and anti-anxiety medications trying to find the one that worked for me. They tried Prozac but that gave me rage. I've been on and off of Luvox, Lexapro, Wellbutrin, and more. I was a zombie for a good portion of my late teens and throughout most of my 20s. When I wasn't a zombie, I was depressed as hell, but incredibly creative and productive! Even though I would not have another suicide attempt, the thoughts would stay with me. There were times I would break down and start seeing a therapist on my own and request to be put back on some medications, without my family's knowledge. I had never been one to put my problems on someone else, and I wasn't about to start if I could help it.

My family only saw my success; getting through my first four years of college and graduating with the best GPA I ever had, holding down a full-time job, and paying my rent and my bills on time without ever asking for help like my siblings did. They thought I was just fine. I've always been good at putting on a show. Everyone had their own lives at this point and they were all too engulfed by them to really take notice of anyone else. The individuals in my family are pretty damn selfish. Like I said in the beginning, we have never been a really close family. We never will be.

In my late 20s and early 30s, I survived a divorce, a bankruptcy, and a short bout of homelessness. My family was there for me as much as they could be, but for the most part I got through it all on my own and without asking for much. On top of that, I graduated with my Master's in Psychology and landed a full-time job at a non-profit agency. My life had finally gotten back on track, and I was doing something that not only I was proud of, but that my parents were proud of, too! I should have been feeling like I was on top of the world, but I was actually feeling like I was buried underneath it. The more stable my career life was becoming, the more I began to lose the battle against my gender dysphoria, my depression getting a hold of me again. How was I going to do this? How could I transition while keeping my job and my parents' admiration?

At thirty-two years old I realized I was either going to die at my own hands or choose to finally live the life I had been yearning for since I was four years old. As much as I wanted to make my parents proud and was afraid of disappointing them, I couldn't live a lie anymore either. It was up to them how they chose to look at it, either losing a daughter or gaining a son. Either way, I was going to pursue my own happiness. This was my life to live. No more hiding behind a facade, no more pretending I was fine in order to protect everyone else. This was my time to be happy.

I began to tell my family one by one that I was going to begin transitioning to male as of January 1, 2013. I started with my brother, and then my mother and her wife, then the rest of my family, once I knew the aforementioned were on my side. I reminded them of the battle with depression I had been continually fighting and opened up about my suicide attempts; tried to explain where it had all come from. Their response, "We figured you would make this choice some day. We still love you and are very proud of you." I felt blessed to be in this little dysfunctional family of mine, and their continued love and support this past year has been amazing.

Both of my suicide attempts seem to have been swept under the rug in my family's eyes. Nonetheless, I feel these incidents and my choice to finally open up to my family about who I am and what I've put myself through out of fear of rejection have been the unspoken drive for us to become more understanding and accepting of each other as individuals. The fact remains, however, that we will never be a close family. We will never be the hug and kiss and I love you types. It's not who we are. But through all of our ups and downs as a family, and as individuals, we have come to realize that having each other in our lives in some sort of way is better than not having each other at all. Even if we have a hard time saying it, we love each other and accept each other as we are; with all of our quirks and differences. And for us, that is enough.

# SECTION IV—RELATIONSHIPS

Does love go beyond gender?

We often look to our significant others for more support than we do anyone else. What happens when we ask them to stick around while we take this journey that is by far the most self-preserving decision we could possibly make in our entire lives? And what if the relationships you had prior to transition became a thing of the past? What if your desires changed?

Transition is all about becoming your truest self. In some ways it is a time when you are almost required to be selfish in order to find a life worth living. Good relationships need compromise, so how does that fit into transition?

Our contributors share what it has been like to be on this journey with someone by their side, with fluid sexuality and changing feelings.

Mitch Kellaway

Today, Valentine's Day, I wake up to blood spatter. She'd placed the hand-made card, drizzled with red drops, right where she knew my eyes would see it first when I awoke. I can imagine her smiling to herself as she painted her nails a wine purple, saving the cherry color for the card. Or perhaps it's finger paint, hastily dabbed between helping her students fashion glittery hearts and Be Mines for their classmates.

I flip the card open and wonder if Jessica got it out of sight before the children's questioning eyes fell upon it and they demanded an explanation. Did she tell them how it was a reference to *Dexter*? *It's a TV show*... she'd begun, and hastily backtracked before having to add that it's about a serial killer who kills serial killers.

She and I have been watching that show, bodies tangled in the dark, every night before bed. Always two episodes in a row, though we should only do one—we can't help but stretch the time we have together after she comes home late from the women's shelter, the second job she rushes to after the school day ends. She gets up early each morning, without that extra hour of sleep, to start the whole exhausting, fulfilling routine once again.

7:30am. Three hours before I'd opened my eyes and saw red, she'd kissed me on the forehead as she always does when she leaves for work—I do the same on the rare occasions I have to open the coffee shop at 6:30am—and whispered in my half-awake ear. "I love you. Have a good day, baby." She paused and added, "Happy Valentine's Day," reminding me, priming me for her little surprise—because she probably knew I forgot. Endearingly, not aggravatingly, of course.

I'm home sick today, so I guess I could claim the mental fog hindered my memory. But we both know it would've taken me hours to recollect the date, and we could probably both imagine how I'd do it: sitting in the living room in front of the TV, eyes half on my writing, snot-filled tissues strewn about me and cough medicine sitting in the cabinet overlooked, distracting myself with Facebook even though I know better.

I place the Valentine's card on her pillow so I can see it first thing when I return to the bedroom. With a groan I roll out of bed and shuffle shirtless to the bathroom, noting that my throat is still as sore and sinuses still as clogged as the day before. I mindlessly run a hand over my chest as I stare at my reflection in the mirror; my nipples still lack sensation from my top surgery six months earlier, but I'm pleased by the layer of thick hair that's grown back.

My hand's motion recalls a feeling: I love when Jessica trails her fingers through my chest's dark curls, and even when she decides to tug sharply. She doesn't mean to hurt me, but probably likes it when I yelp suddenly, then growl and wrap her in my arms to keep her from pulling again. I've discovered that it's scientifically impossible to stay mad at her for more than five seconds.

The mirror reflects three-days hair growth on my head, so I decide to shave myself back to baldness for the second time this week. As far as hairstyles go, I prefer a fade, but I'd long ago stopped earning enough money to maintain that at a barbershop. So I'd started buzzing my own head and, after I'd destroyed the first clipper Jessica had given me for Christmas—choking it slowly with tufts of my dense hair—I'd decided to use a razor. This particular instrument was a birthday gift from her mother; these two big-hearted women seem to take a certain joy in my facial hair care. I lather myself up with the shaving cream Jessica gave me this Christmas and begin sliding the cool blade over my scalp.

*What hairstyle are you going to have at our wedding?* My mind moves idly to a conversation we'd had last week as I rhythmically swipe then swirl the razor in a sink full of cloudy water.

*What about a nice fade? It'd be like when we first started dating.* Her suggestion is not really a suggestion—of course I'll get a fade. Not only because it makes me feel crisp and clean, but because I can't help doing what I know makes her happy.

*You'll have to let your hair grow in before August so it'll look right.* Her voice sounded anxious, like I should start growing my hair right now, even though our wedding is still six months off. I reassured her that everything would be perfect, as soon as we finally send out all those invitations.

Three years ago, we'd been walking hand-in-hand

down a quiet street, pondering a hypothetical I'd casually tossed out. *Would you rather get a same-sex marriage or a straight one? Or what about a ceremony with no legal strings attached?* We chatted and lazily circled away and back towards the question. We were still months away from surprising each other with rings, having both secretly planned proposals in the same special spot.

At the time, I wasn't sure my question even had a legal leg to stand on: could a trans person with, say, an "F" on their birth certificate and an "M" on their driver's license choose which one defines their marriage? Nevertheless, with weddings looming so large in cultural conversations about queerness, it seemed pertinent to wonder. In fact, I quite liked the thought that I could make a political statement if I took the road less traveled.

It'd taken Jessica two years to reach this level of intimacy in our relationship, this place where we could talk about "forever"—though I'd seen it coming almost as soon as I'd met her. I'd been immediately drawn to her style, her humor, her cute nose, and by a shared belief that the medical-legal complex should have no part in defining our private identities. We texted daily, enthralled with each other's mundane happenings, as only a new couple can be. As we flirted and traded impassioned speeches against the system, I'd notice how my chest felt calm whenever I was near her. It was mutual; we floated into love. And once we acknowledge this aloud, we made an intentional, verbal agreement to engage in a partnership.

While my gender changes emerged a year later and began weaving amongst the other new beginnings of early adulthood, so did hers; she began vocally, ecstatically embracing her femme-hood. We each cheered the other along, often through buying each other books and reading them aloud together—our bookworm mating ritual. We hummed along steadily towards other milestones. I changed jobs. She graduated from college. I began writing. We picked a grown-up apartment together. We put time into family get-togethers and weekend trips. And all throughout the ensuing disappointments and joys, we touched base about our senses of selfhood and coupledom. We talked and talked.

When she eventually placed a ring on my finger—beating me to the draw as I fingered the engagement ring still hidden in my own pocket—my mind flashed to a memory of us sitting side-by-side in bed, propped up on pillows and quietly reading. I'd looked into her eyes and told her: "I'm ready to be a man." In so many words, I was asking her to change her life with mine, to engage in a lifelong process of emotional and spiritual transformation. And now she was doing the same with a marriage proposal. I accepted, she accepted: we accepted.

I finish shaving my head, gaze a moment longer at my reflection, and let the water drain slowly; by the time I step out of the shower, all that's left is a dull gray film of hair dust and dead skin lining the sink bowl. I wipe it up with toilet paper and flush it down the toilet, then turn the faucet on and off to make sure I haven't clogged it again. This happens periodically and I blame my beard trims, even though it's usually clumps of Jessica's brown, wavy strands that I'll pull out of the drain. Though she's the culprit, I do the deed because soggy hair makes her almost vomit; my college years as a bathroom cleaner, however, have left me desensitized.

The water drains swiftly, so I wrap a towel around my waist and make my way back to the bedroom, stopping in the kitchen for a box of cereal and a glass of ginger ale. The sink's piled with dishes and I can spot signs of Jessica's hurry and fatigue amongst the heap. For the past few days I haven't been waking up to make her breakfast, something I often do to make her morning routine slightly less rushed than usual.

I pause and look up out the window as I usually do when washing dishes—something we've silently agreed upon is "my" chore, much like putting away the laundry is "hers." She's pinned black-and-white pictures of women writers to the venetian blinds, so I often contemplate bell hooks and Margaret Atwood as I scrub pans. I'd arrived home from work one Saturday to see she'd redecorated our apartment, not telling me because she knew I'd say "no," anxious about change as I am. The women in the kitchen window made me feel warm inside, but the rearranged furniture I found jarring—for all of a day, because she's right: a bit of change is necessary, energizing even. Acclimating to it is something I can practice in the safe confines of our home.

I look down into the sink's basin and see several cups with the remnants of breakfast yogurt, mugs with dried coffee dripping over the sides, granola still sprinkled on the counter where a hurried sponge swipe missed it. I see how she's dumped her lunch Tupperware alongside them, too tired to clean it after a ten-hour workday, too full of washing other people's dishes at the shelter, too eager to spend the little time she has before bedtime curled up with me.

I turn on the water for a moment, deciding to wash the dishes and surprise her, but quickly realize I still feel too ill. I inch back towards the bedroom, smile when I see the Valentine, bright with fake blood, sitting on her pillow, and settle in to write this essay about being a transgender man who is loved.

\*\*\*

This essay contains material adapted from "A Day in a Queer Life in the US: A Trans Man on Love and Marriage" by Mitch Kellaway, from *The Huffington Post* (April 18, 2013).

Eli Bradford

I married my partner of eight years in October of 2012.

Kiera and I were both born in the early 1970s and raised on the East Coast. We are three years apart in age, and grew up just 200 miles away from one another in suburban-like neighborhoods. We share many things in common including the fact that we were both declared female at birth (based on our anatomy). The primary difference was that, like most other people, Kiera identified with the gender she was assigned whereas, from the earliest age I can remember, I did not.

A mutual friend introduced us thirty-five years later, and this is when our journey together began. We started out as a same-sex couple because, at the time, that's how I identified. We share a love of music, dancing, and singing along to the Indigo Girls at the top of our lungs (off key!) in the car. We also enjoy taking daytrips up North, which is considered country compared to where we live. The only downside to visiting a Red state, is the lack of diversity. I always fear having to use a bathroom when traveling because it always means some sort of confrontation. And since,

I'm not totally comfortable using the men's facilities yet, I often hear "Excuse me Sir, you're in the women's bathroom." Oy! This may be the only time my breasts come in handy, and the only time I pull my shoulders back to push them out, which usually ends in an apology from an offended woman who is powdering her nose. Needing to use the restroom is the by far the most difficult day-to-day part about presenting as the opposite gender. Why are there not more unisex bathrooms? Seriously, most of us are in there for one reason and one reason only, and are usually in and out as soon as business is taken care of. I'm not sure I will ever understand why it's such a big deal to have secluded male and female bathrooms. So, after being completely pissed off from using the bathroom, Kiera would kindly remind me that I should take the Sir comments as a compliment that I'm actually achieving what I set out to do every day— pass as a male. Yes, it was Kiera's continued love and support that finally allowed me to feel strong and safe enough to show the rest of world the person I was truly was meant to be.

Besides the fact that I was born female, we are really like any other heterosexual couple. We have two kids, two cats, go to work five days a week, and then enjoy family time on the weekends. I'm not entirely sure if nature, nurture, or a combination of the two are at play, but we follow the stereotypical behaviors that are assumed of boys and girls. For instance, like her mother, Kiera loves wearing dresses, getting her nails painted, and even enjoys a little gossip. My characteristics are more like that of my grandfather; I enjoy driving cars a little too fast, using big power tools, and fixing up the yard. I'm typically the one who opens doors, lets her walk ahead of me, carries the heavy stuff, and prefers to pick up the tab. The only time we really bump heads in this arena is when there is a bug in our house. She yells out "Well, you're the boy in this relationship!" So other than bugs, we're both a stereotypical and old fashioned couple.

I assume like most other trans guys, I found my dysphoria to be at its strongest during my menstrual cycles, which happened every single month of my life since I turned thirteen. My breasts were another constant; a curse that was impossible to ignore. There is not a day that goes by that I am not disgusted by the appearance of my own body because of my breasts. I've always complained about my breasts—alone or in the company of others—it was often a topic of conversation because of my constant awareness of them. You could say that I'm the type of person who, when insecure, will call out what it is that I'm insecure about before someone else can do it, whether it be a pimple on my face, a bad haircut, or feeling that my breasts are standing out like a sore thumb making me appear more feminine. What can I say—I'm human as well as a little vain. Still, as much as I hated my breasts, I promised to never modify my body— this is the body that I was born with and I should be okay with what God gave me. So, when Kiera said to me, "I would miss these if you got rid of them" referring to my breasts, I told her not to worry because I was not going to go under the knife to cut healthy tissue from my body just to fulfill my desire to look more male. The part that's interesting is that I truly believed what I had said to her (thank goodness I didn't bet my life on it because...). Fast forward seven plus years—almost a year into our marriage, I told her that I want to have top surgery.

These words were not easy to say, nor were they easy to hear. The situation became very dark. There was anger—a lot of anger, so much so that we both questioned if the marriage would survive. I still remember the pain I felt when I heard her say, "I would have never agreed to marry you had I known this, you're going to *look* deformed, aren't the kids already confused enough about you as it is (because I appear male—clothing & hair)?!" Then there was silence. I was speechless. I was hurt. I didn't understand. I thought, she would be more understanding, and get it—get me. I mean, I was still the same person she fell in love with and I'm certain, that when I alter my body, it will make more sense, not just to me, but to Kiera, the kids, and the rest of the world.

The problem is more complicated than what I've shared thus far. The timing of this conversation could not have been worse. Three months after our wedding in January 2013, Kiera found out that she carries the BRAC1 gene, which means her chances of developing breast and ovarian cancer in her lifetime were extremely high (90-95%). Her need for stability was never greater. We immediately started exploring options and seeing different doctors for their opinions, which ultimately led to surgeons because they all agreed the best way to lower her risk was to remove both of her breasts and ovaries. Kiera was devastated. Moving forward, we explored different surgeons, and decided surgery was the best thing to do to ensure she lived a long healthy life and watch her children grow.

As we met with different surgeons, it occurred to me that this situation was really twisted. Here we were discussing a hysterectomy and a double mastectomy for Kiera because her life depended on it. The doctor reminded her that her periods would stop after the hysterectomy, which actually upset her. How bizarre that having my period stop is something I only dreamed about for myself? How twisted that when we looked at before and after photos of people who needed to have their breasts removed, that this was something I prayed for for myself? Why couldn't I be the one with this gene? Why my wife? It felt like a cruel joke. Awkwardly, I actually believe this is what triggered my desire to explore transitioning.

Months passed by, and my desire to transition increased rapidly. I did everything in my power to push my feelings back inside so that I could focus on Kiera and her worries. Six months later, I had decided to explore the option of top surgery without Kiera's knowledge, not to be deceptive, but in an attempt to be sensitive to her own situation. It didn't take long for her to notice that something was on my mind. I had a decision to make—to lie or to be honest. I didn't know which was worse—so, I chose honesty. Not good. How dare I suggest a desire for top surgery, when she dreaded the fact that she needed to have hers removed? I've asked myself a thousand times—am I being selfish, inconsiderate, an asshole, all the above? "Why now?" she asked me. I still can't answer that, and at times, I still struggle with it. She exclaimed, "Why couldn't you tell me you wanted to change your name (to a male name) or start taking testosterone—why top surgery?" I didn't have an answer for her. It was not my intention for it to happen this way. I wish I had had the courage to do it twenty years ago, but I didn't. Why do I have the strength now? Is it that I'm finally feeling happy, secure, and loved? Or is it that my psychiatrist finally found the right medication to control my panic disorder, anxiety, and depression? Who knows, maybe it's everything— like the perfect storm.

The anger lasted a few months. She was already seeing a therapist and I encouraged her to join a support group for partners of trans-identified people. Eventually, we both found a group, which helped us immensely. I remember the first time I met and hung out with the guys, a waiter was taking our order at a local pub, and one of guys who had collected our order at the table said pointing to me "and he's going to have…"—Wait, what! That was the first time I was ever referred to as a "he"! It was surreal and awesome to be seen and identified (outside my own thoughts) by my peers as a guy. I think the expression on my face was telling because I was asked if that was okay (they knew I was just coming to terms with identifying as transgender). "Of course!" Kiera thankfully, had a positive experience as well. She pretty much came home a cheerleader after the gals' got together. It was even more exciting when everyone got together and brought their children for a group pizza party—it was enlightening to see the kids play with each other like they would with any other, and to see other FTM's being referred to as "dad." It gave me hope that one day, I will be living the dream. I believe finding other couples and families with children like ours made us feel like we were not alone, and that it was okay to be different.

After Kiera found peace with my newly acclaimed identity (and hers!), she confessed that before our first date, she had done a little research on how to interact with someone who identified as transgender. Her intention was to become more aware of gender-neutral language and to also be sensitive in a way that would not make me feel uncomfortable either physically or emotionally. It's interesting to me that someone who had just met me, knew who I was before I did... or maybe more than I was ready to admit to myself. In any case, we're doing much better. Challenges have presented themselves at unexpected times, and we're just trying to take it one day at a time. And although, she really wanted to be a two-mom family, she's beginning to embrace our unique trans-family.

## Jack Elliott

There is no perfect relationship. Thank god. My part as I see it is to show up with everything I've got and spread it out onto the ground to be inventoried. They are numbered, categorized and put on display to put in a larger context like an archeological dig. My ego puts all the pretty shiny pieces together on display because I am proud of them. The others, the chipped, dirt-covered incomplete artifacts lie there as part of what must been unearthed. If I can see the pieces that lack, and really look at them, I'd better be prepared to fix them. And as strong as this lens is for myself, I learned how to be strong enough to look at someone else's lack. I love through the pieces that don't suit me, as I have no right to separate them from the whole of a beautiful person. I know that now, or it just may be because I have never truly loved.

After getting married I felt an overwhelming sense of relief that I don't have to do any more of this work alone. That feeling quickly turned into an ungodly fear of having to do this work in front of someone. Always being able to deliver? Well, that is a different story all together. But is there any beauty in the terrible things? Can there be unwavering optimism even in the midst of unrelenting confusion? I will always believe that some of the bad can be choked into releasing something useful. I do however look in the mirror sometimes and think, who the fuck is this guy; he's got some nerve trying to pull this off. I straighten my collar around a throat that still holds in words. My suit keeps together my form as sometimes I am afraid it will spill out and lose its shape altogether. I still have limited access to parts of me. I only know this because I am called on it by agreeing to share my life with someone I love. Sometimes I'm great at it. I show up in a way that surprises even me. Other times it is like dismantling a car engine, and then trying to put it back together knowing absolutely nothing about cars. I stand over the mess I have made, and sweat through my clothes.

But when the sound of your partner's voice swishes around first in the air, then in your head, and you can no longer remember a time when you didn't hear it is an incredible feeling. I let that voice inside, dusted off a place next to me and gave it a place to sit down. I look across the table sometimes, and my lungs feel the air being rushed out like a balloon that has yet to be tied. I have been present for the moment when I realized how beautifully fucking hard it is to really love someone, and in return be loved. My only purpose in life now is to not run from it.

An open letter to my wife.

Sometimes I feel unlovable, loathsome, ignorant, a beast pretending to be human. My mind races in circles with self-doubt. I work so hard to be everything to you, and at times I am crushed by that weight. I get up though from underneath all of it. I shake off the dusty, torn, and tattered bits. I know you see the real me not just the architecture I have created for the rest of the world. I dare to stand on the shoulders of giants with my words, higher to go and then further to fall. Some types of love open us up and let in things that swirl and rush and soften us when we land. Other types of love stand over us and expect us to be more than we are. We can cower and hide our eyes from its gaze with hands on hips. Or we can reach around the sharp corners of ourselves for a piece that is untouched by the bad things, the soft special thing that no one could get and let it grow into something beautiful. We met somewhere in that part. In that dark place when the need and desire to heal made a little thumping noise that only we could hear. That is where we found each other.

We are just beginning to unravel and uncurl the truths about ourselves. We hold out each grotesque monster for inspection. They drip and slime through our hands as we hold them up for the other to see. But we never wince at all the ugly things. We force them up the narrow staircase into daylight to be exposed. We stare them down until they are no longer scary to either one of us. Our dark makes us feel depth, the wretched hurt makes us love harder, and the things we didn't get created the space for us to live inside each other's heart.

Our love is encapsulating, and it cannot be punctured by the sharp lines of our past.

Alexander Walker

"To love a person is to learn the song that is in their heart and sing it to them when they have forgotten the words."—Unknown

When I met Eleanor seven years ago, the song in my heart was telling a different story from my daily life. Everyone I got close to commented on my eyes; there is depth to them in their many shades of brown. Eleanor and I met while working at a summer camp. I was an assistant director and she was taking a much-needed break after graduating from a Seven Sister's college. We like to say that we met at exactly the right point in our lives, but waited eight months to actually start dating.

My dating history has always been a little left of center. I was always attracted to people and personalities, not necessarily a sex or gender. I say this, but had only dated FAB (Female Assigned at Birth) women who identified as heterosexual. At eighteen, I met a woman who was twenty-three, fresh out of college, and who could see I wasn't your typical young adult; I had more experiences in me. I had just come out of a six-year haze of a spectacular cocktail of anti-anxiety medication. I was emotionally underdeveloped. I had taken myself off the medication a year prior to meeting Sally. She was pivotal in helping me develop my sexual orientation. I discovered that although I wasn't necessarily attracted to a gender or sex, I identified as a heterosexual male. In our relationship, I fell into a male role. At the time, Sally and I didn't have the language for this, but when I came out to her at the beginning of my transition she told me she saw many aspects of the boy in me. Even though our relationship was good, it could not withstand the 1,000—plus mile distance and individual long-term goals; it lasted a year and a half.

After the end of that relationship, I felt even more disconnect with the lesbian community. I was grouped with them, and felt like it should make sense, but something still felt off; I never understood how other butch women were so comfortable with their bodies. I was still years away from realizing that I felt at home with myself as a man in a relationship with a woman. It's hard to express what it really means to be a man in the relationship because I think it's an individual thing. For example, I do a lot of the cooking and cleaning in our home today, which are societal female traits, but being seen and identified in a male way feels like my body finally fits with what my brain felt all along. Having my external male voice match what I've heard in my ear all of my life makes me feel like a twenty-five-year-old weight was lifted. My transition wasn't about changing who I had become personally and emotionally, it was about finally feeling that I could embody myself. With an estrogen-dominant body, I felt as though I was on the outside looking in and waiting for something to change.

I began to live when I met Eleanor. In the present day, 2014, we are married. In the summer of 2007, we became good friends. I was in a tough spot and had just left college to move back to the Midwest to try to figure out what I wanted to do with my life. She had just graduated and was looking for a ticket into her field of choice. We were both emotionally raw and recovering from our own individual trauma. Throughout that summer, I avoided her like the plague, but she excelled at persistence. I don't know why she dealt with me avoiding her, not answering calls, and at times being just rude, but she did. At the end of the summer, as I prepared to figure out my life back in the Midwest, and as she anticipated travel back toward the coast, she gave me a letter. The letter exposed her raw love for me, in which she said, "I know you aren't ready for a relationship right now, but I would be stupid to not tell you that I want to be your friend." Many years later, she told me that as she drove away from camp, she pulled the car over and cried for several minutes, fearful that she would never hear from me again.

About a week later, I arrived at my new 'home' and called her that night. I don't know why I called her, but I did, and it was the best decision I have ever made; we quickly became friends. Eight months later, I flew out to visit her, and the rest was history, well, almost history. The first eighteen months of our romantic lives together were separated by long distance.

In June 2009, she moved to the Midwest to be with me. I was in a much better place emotionally and ready for a relationship. At the same time, I was still struggling with my identity and unsure of my transition path. Over the next two years, I contemplated the idea of transition to the point of oblivion. Through it, Eleanor was my voice of reason, pushing me to talk to other people, and continue to define myself as a human being rather than allowing others determine who I was.

Our relationship is simple, but at the same time complex, as any relationship is. We are a team; supporting each other through triumphs and tribulations. Eleanor listened wholeheartedly as I worked through my internalized man and transphobia. I feared that I would become a different person, that I would lose even more of my sense of self, along with my profession and family. I had a very skewed version of what it actually meant to be a man, not having much male influence as a child. I needed to hit my personal bottom to be ready to take any further steps. During this time, Eleanor began to use male pronouns in our home, even though we were a lesbian couple to everyone else. This was difficult for her to reconcile. She, like me, had always been attracted to the person, not a sex or gender. In the comfort of our home, Eleanor saw me as a quiet, but passionate person who loves to learn, explore, and engage in conversation. What the rest of the world saw was a quiet, ashamed, and anxiety-ridden person who was sweet, but didn't add to the conversation. I knew eventually it would have to change, but I needed more time. We as human beings sometimes get stuck in a rut and need a push to move on. I definitely needed a push.

In December of 2010 I proposed to Eleanor and we decided that we needed to move for the benefit of our careers. I remember so clearly Eleanor saying to me, "I don't care what you do, but I need you to make a decision. I'll be with you either way." I was floored, but it was what I needed. I had been getting closer and closer taking steps to socially and medically transition in my therapy sessions.

I made the decision; I wanted to live. I wanted to be a person. I knew that it would not be easy and I would have to push through my anxiety, but I trusted that I would come out on the other side a happy, healthy, and lively person, and I did.

Eleanor and I have been together for six years and are now married. Our love has only grown stronger with every step, and none of my concerns have come to actualization. I'm the same person I was before, with a little more balance and a lot more confidence. Eleanor was a rock for me. She told me after I had top surgery and was beginning hormones, "You are becoming the person to everyone that I saw in our home for so many years." Would I have gotten to this point without Eleanor? Yes, but I was ready to be committed and move into the next stage of life. My transition is part of my life and it is part of our life; it sits on the back burner and at the forefront all at the same time. We are the experiences that we live. There are good times and bad, positive and negative, but if you dare to sing your song out loud your soul mate will sing it right along with you.

Nathan Ezekiel

Angela and I were waiting for the bus. It was one of a handful of nights we'd had out together over the two and a half years since our youngest child was born.

It had been on the tip of my tongue all evening. Finally, alone at the bus stop, on the cool early spring night, I just blurted it out.

"I want to start binding."

"What?"

"I want to start binding."

Immediately I backpedaled, "I just, I don't know, I think my shirts will look better. It wouldn't be all the time or anything. Not when I'm alone with you."

She knew exactly what I was talking about. A couple months earlier, we both read the book *Nina Here Nor There* by Nick Kreiger, a memoir of the author's early transition, which included a description of binding. We had picked up the book at the suggestion of a friend, and Angela still thought she had just read it because it was an interesting book. When I first picked up the book I had thought the same, but by the time I finished reading, I knew I had seen a reflection of myself in those pages.

Since childhood, I had glimpses that my gender was not what was assumed. Sometimes it was just a brief parting of the clouds, the boyish childhood outfits I loved and wore over and over. At other times I had more clarity. When explaining my family to a new friend, I would say there were three kids in my family— my two sisters and me, but that really, I was more of a brother. As I got older, I emulated my father, taking up jogging so that I could run with him around our neighborhood. In middle school and high school, I was the kid most willing to brave the elements to go on backpacking trips with him in the Colorado mountains. I imagined that by these feats, I had a special relationship with my dad; that I was like him in ways my sisters were not. But I bargained and explained these moments of understanding away. I was a child in the 80s and a teenager in the early 90s, without ready internet access and living in a family culture in which any kind of queerness was unacceptable. It wasn't until adulthood that I fully realized what was possible, and that the uncomfortable truce I had worked out with my body didn't have a prayer of holding.

At age thirty-four, the lifeline I had been clinging to began to dissolve in my hands. I had told myself off and on for years that I couldn't possibly be trans, that it would have been clearer sooner, that I wouldn't have ever had a doubt. I thought that if I was happy with any part of my life (and I was happy with many) I couldn't possibly need to transition. What could possibly be worth such a risk?

The risk felt impossibly high. Angela and I had been together for over ten years, married for over seven. Angela was a lesbian. She had not signed up to have a husband. We had two small children. I was balanced precariously on a knife's edge: certain that if I pushed too far, I would irreparably hurt our children, Angela would leave me, and she would be justified. Yet I felt I had no choice. The gravitational pull towards a body and a life I could truly inhabit seemed inescapable.

That night at the bus stop, Angela met my comment that I wanted to start binding my chest with her typical nonjudgmental curiosity. She seemed like she was turning the idea over in her head, asking questions about how I felt. She then simply said, "Well then, you should get a binder."

In many ways, my understanding that I am male grew out of my relationship with Angela. The feelings that have driven my decisions around transition are deeply personal, but our relationship was where I was first able to access and understand these feelings, and feel safe to let them grow.

Angela is always thinking, naturally drawn to new and interesting things. She is always trying on new ideas and is drawn to the exception to any rule. She has a kind of energy, openness and intellectual flexibility that I have never seen in anyone else, and indeed this is much of what drew me to her when we first met. She is also fiercely driven to improve, always striving for better ways to live, better ways to work, better ways to connect with people she loves. This improvement often takes practical forms and sometimes seems like an endless stream of new systems and structures to organize and improve our lives. I can't always keep up, but I've learned that it's worth it for me to at least try to follow along. Most of the time her new ideas really do make things better.

Starting about two years after our youngest child was born, as part of this ongoing campaign, Angela decided we needed to have more sex. Like many couples, our sex life waned once we became parents, and she pushed to reinvigorate this part of our life together. I somewhat reluctantly agreed to her plan of sex once a week, no excuses.

I was happy to please Angela and have always been extremely attracted to her, but our increasing physical contact highlighted the ways in which my own body was still a mystery. I had never experienced anything else during sex, so I thought nothing of the way I would at first recoil from physical contact. I knew I was supposed to enjoy touch, so I allowed myself to be touched. I tried hard to relax and willed myself not to pull back. And when we were in bed together, after I while, I usually could enjoy myself. But I spent a lot of time wondering what I was missing, feeling like I needed to ask an important question, but I couldn't quite figure out what it was.

It was sometime after this increased physical intimacy that I picked up Nick Kreiger's book. In it, he writes about how his experience of sex changed as he came to understand his gender. Something clicked and I realized I might have found both the question and the answer. With this clue, instead of suppressing the part of me that recoiled from certain kinds of touch, I asked Angela not to touch me in the ways that felt wrong. I found that when I kept my shirt on (and later, my binder), that when I thought of and experienced my body as male, sex wasn't confusing at all.

Even before I had the words to say what I was beginning to understand, before I ever understood how I was feeling in a way I might ever hope to explain, there was a fundamental shift in how Angela and I related, a change in how both of us thought of and interacted with my body, and the change was electric for us both.

I think this experience of sexual understanding and connection gave us both a visceral sense that a powerful change might be in store. I think it also showed both of us that even as we struggled to understand the right path forward, that ultimately what I was coming to understand was very good, not just for me, but also for Angela, and for our relationship.

As I navigated transition, I gradually shifted my appearance. I came out to my parents and siblings, to all of our friends and neighbors, our kids schools and teachers, and to my employer and colleagues. Angela and I had ongoing conversations with our children. I started hormones and, about two years after that first bus stop conversation, I had top surgery. There was no aspect of my life left untouched.

During this time Angela experienced her own transformation. It was clear to both of us early on in my transition that our relationship was strong, and growing stronger, but beyond the identifiable "tasks" of transition, we both had intense work to do to figure out how we would fit into the world, about what was the same and what had changed between us. Angela also bore a heavy burden of support work, both for me and for our kids. This was not an easy time for our family, but it was an exciting time.

I know that not all couples experience transition

in this way, as a positive shift, not just for the trans person, but together as a couple. I've tried to figure out why it worked this way for us, though in reality this is not totally knowable, and certainly depended in part on luck. I also want to be careful not to imply that preserving a pre-existing long-term relationship is somehow a marker of a "successful" transition. Success takes many forms and all people change over time. Some relationships continue and some don't, for all kinds of reasons. In our case, Angela and I both chose to stay with each other, and I'm glad that we can carry on together, closer than we were before, knowing each other more fully. I do think there were some aspects of our relationship and how we each acted and treated each other that helped us make it to where we are now.

I think we benefitted from the decade of solid work we had already done taking care of our relationship, building trust and habits of frank honesty with each other. We learned over those years how to approach challenges as a team. Transition was hard for us, but it was not harder than other things we've gone through together, and both of our lives got better in tangible ways as I became more comfortable in my life. Another part of why transition strengthened us as a couple was Angela's approach to life, her flexibility and curiosity. While she identified as a lesbian prior to my transition, the changes in me and in our relationship prompted her to explore a shift in her own sexuality. She ultimately decided that a bisexual identity better aligns with who she is. She was willing to look at herself with new eyes, just as we were both seeing me with new eyes.

I think it also helped both of us that even as I felt like my life was being turned utterly upside down, I tried hard to remember to leave room for Angela— even if she was telling me something that was hard for her. I saw any hint that she shared with me of how she was really doing, what she was really thinking, as a success. Navigating the social, emotional, legal and medical hurdles of my transition took a lot of energy from our partnership. I was aware that the intensity of my transition experiences could easily push Angela's needs and voice to the side, in effect silencing her even though that would never have been my intent. Even though I didn't always do a perfect job, Angela understood that I really wanted to know what she was thinking and experiencing, and that I appreciated the work she was doing to keep us all afloat while I found my way.

My relationship with Angela was the first place I felt a physical understanding of my body as male. Our everyday interactions were the first place I experienced a social reflection of my gender. Angela was the first person to use my name, the first to use masculine pronouns, laboriously changing back and forth in the time before I was out to the rest of the world. But it wasn't just that she humored me, using the name and words I asked—she truly *saw* me. That reflection back from her, of a self who was male both socially and physically, a reflection I had spent a lifetime craving but not experiencing, drove a deep intimacy, almost as if she was the sole witness present as I was being born.

## Jaguar

If you told me ten years ago that I would be dating men, I would have laughed and called you silly. You see, if there was a gold-star card they handed out to a lesbian who's never had sexual intercourse with a man, during the time she's been a living as a lesbian, I'd be a proud owner. It's actually not that uncommon for lesbians to be having sex with men. I know, that sounds surprising, but I've met a few through the years. I was proud that I was not one of those.

I came out as a lesbian in 1996. It was my junior year of high school. This was a year before Ellen Degeneres came out of the closet from her TV show sitcom *Ellen*. I knew I liked girls since I was a little kid, before being a lesbian was cool and hip. It wasn't just the typical girl-girl crushes, I knew it was something more serious. I would leave flowers and "secret admirer" poems to girls in school. Courting girls was my thing. The girls never knew who it was coming from, I wanted to be able to see the twinkle in their eyes or see them blush while they smelled the flowers. It also made me blush from far away.

In my 20s I only dated women. I've had a few girlfriends throughout the years. My relationships with women each lasted between one and four years. It wasn't a phase. What happened after transition, however, I wasn't prepared for. A year after my first shot of testosterone, something shifted. The attraction I had for women slowly faded away. I started to look at men more and more. It's not like the male attraction began right away; at first, it was mere curiosity of the possible changes that would happen to my body as I morphed from girl-to-boy-to-man. I started to look at men, trying to see the variety of men and where I fit in that spectrum. I also started to look at how men walk, talk and what hand gestures they use. The more I looked at men, the more I realized that I was attracted to them. I had never been sexual with a man. The last time I kissed a boy I was thirteen, and that was on a dare.

The first guy I kissed as an adult was a transguy. I don't quite know how it happened. Perhaps it was the few beers we had consumed. There was a sexual attraction and we became intimate. This was the first time I had ever kissed a guy with facial hair, and it wasn't all that bad. Next thing you know, we were dating. Being with Robert made me realize that I could possibly be a gay man. Looking back I'm sure there were other signs I had either refused to see or didn't quite think would lead to dating men.

When I was a lesbian, I was androgynous. At first glance I look like a boy, but my soft features gave away that I was a girl. Others would classify me as butch because of the clothing I wore and the short buzzed hair I sported. However, that was all exterior. Personality-wise, I was soft, and feminine. I was also attracted to masculine women. Even though the women I dated had long hair or wore dresses, their energy was masculine, and I actually balanced them with my feminine energy. Meeting Robert, I suppose it wasn't that surprising that I was attracted to him. He identified as Butch and masculine, and of course, the masculine part is what I was attracted to.

The real adventure was when I started to take this "gay thing" further and tested the waters. I sought out cis-gay men. How would they accept me as a transman who was pre-top surgery? I came to find out that cis-men validated my maleness more than women. It made me feel good that the men I were involved with only sexually saw me as nothing short of a man. It helped that I was small-chested to begin with, even before top surgery. When I would apologize that I hadn't had top surgery, the men were even quite surprised; they thought I'd already had surgery.

Looking back at my first experience with cisgender men, I understood why it was easy to be with them. With cis-men, even though the sexual experienced involved penis-to-vagina (yes, that's how I refer to my "original plumbing"), the energy exchanged was that of two men having sex. These men never made me feel less of a man, instead they respected me as a man. It was a man-on-man sexual exchange. Unlike the times I did hook up with butch lesbians post transition, who were still treating me as a female and referred to my body parts in female terms. Besides my vagina, I refer to the rest of my private body part in male terms; my cock (clit), my chest (breasts). The cismen I had sexual experiences with did the same, which was very comforting. Being seen and treated as 100% man felt good. It helped me become more comfortable with my body with men because my sexual experiences were positive. I sometimes wonder if I would have enjoyed the same experience had I been female? All I could think about is that, I probably wouldn't, simply because with testosterone, my sex drive is in high gear. Sex is simply that, sex. We fuck. When I was a woman, my sex drive was very low— and sex meant, "making love." I was riddled with too many emotions. With men, I was able to explore not only my sexuality but also myself in entirety. I can comfortably voice what I like and don't like to do in bed. I feel more confident as a sexual being and as a person.

I like to think I'm 98% gay and 2% bisexual. I still look at women, but I'm not sure I would be sexually involved with one now. Who knows, maybe I've not met the right woman who would convince me otherwise. I do know that I am sexually attracted to men, cis or trans, doesn't matter.

When I tell people I'm trans and gay, I get the confused look. Often I get asked why I even transitioned. The thing is if I were still a woman, I would never have had sex with a man. As a female, being physically intimate with a man doesn't feel natural. However, being intimate with women felt natural, when I was a woman. Now as a man, having sex with another man also feels natural. I often joke that no matter which gender I am, I'm simply gay.

# SECTION V—MEDICAL COMMUNITY

What does it mean to teach those who are expected to care for us?

Medical interactions can be confusing and stressful for most people. Because there is a wide range of information available about what happens when trans masculine folks decide to use medical intervention, we asked contributors to focus on how they navigated different healthcare systems.

Within this section, there are two individuals who discuss their experience with socialized medical systems. In these stories, they discuss the decisions of utilizing a system that covers medically necessary procedures, along with the difficulties of wait times and emotional necessity.

Two other individuals discuss navigating the U.S. heath care system. These stories outline the many layers of red tape that have been established, as well as medical professionals who have little to no experience treating transgender/transsexual individuals.

Kai Scott

Three Bridges Community Health Clinic, located in downtown Vancouver, provides trans-specific health care to people seeking assistance with the medical aspects of gender transition and/or confirmation. The clinic has several doctors who have experience with trans and gender-variant patients, including hormone treatment and surgeries. Some of them collaborate with other physicians and surgeons throughout the province and across Canada to advocate for changes to the health care system to better accommodate trans and gender variant needs, including reducing/removing requirements and making more surgical options available.

They are equipped to help trans folks through the paperwork and maze of requirements in the medical processes. They also provide timely updates on changes (often frequent) to health-care standards and availability. They are a critical lifeline to keeping trans people up to speed in an ever-changing environment. For those crippled by dysphoria, it is difficult to navigate and adjust to changing goal posts and there is often a sense of frustration and confusion among trans people with the health system.

My experience to date with the Three Bridges Community Health Clinic has been focused primarily on hormone treatment. My first visit to the clinic was in January 2012. I felt nervous and scared about the unknown, without much clarity about the process or timelines. I wondered if I would be "trans enough" for the doctor but my fears were dispelled during the first visit. My doctor was approachable, informative, and genuinely cared. He understood my sense of urgency mixed with reservations. He had heard my questions and impatience from other trans guys before. He could take it in stride and give me assurances and realistic timelines. He took the time to explain the informed consent model. During our visits in which he conducted "assessments" to inform the next steps in my treatment for gender dysphoria, he listened to my story but did not pry unnecessarily or ask inappropriate questions. His starting point was that my feelings and identity were real and that he wanted to help me identify the treatment I needed to live a happy and fulfilled life. That allowed me to relax and develop a trust with him. I was prepared for an interrogation where I had to prove myself and instead got full support and understanding. What a reprieve on this already tricky gender journey.

Once I got my prescription for testosterone in March 2013, the clinic assisted me with how to do my own injections, including the steps and equipment needed. At first, I felt scared and overwhelmed. They helped me become more and more comfortable and confident. They understood and supported my desire to self-inject given my travel schedule to remote areas, where there is a lack of trans-experienced or positive medical staff.

I did not go through the provincial health care system for top surgery. I opted to go down to Florida to have surgery with an experienced surgeon. I had many reasons for my decision, of which time was the leading one. Once I came to terms with being transgender, the dysphoria related to my chest became shockingly intense. While I took the necessary time to make an informed and grounded decision regarding surgery, I also knew that it would be difficult to maintain the status quo. The two-year wait list for the provincially funded top surgery seemed daunting and scary. I did not think I could make it that long without severe physical pain (from wearing a binder) and/or emotional anguish. I needed to consider my ability to work and be present in my relationships. Fortunately, I had the financial means to cover the cost of my own surgery in Florida. I recognize this as a tremendous privilege. I also understand this to be a controversial matter in Canadian society, where socialized medicine for all is a nationally espoused virtue (distinguishing it from our southern neighbour). I think it is more complicated and nuanced, especially trans-related surgeries. I struggled with this decision for a while, but opted to go forward, knowing that I was removing myself from the queue and freeing a spot for someone to go earlier. I also give where I can to other top-surgery fundraising efforts, knowing that there is no greater gift than freedom.

In the future, I am considering two other surgeries, which the provincial health care system covers, including: Hysterectomy and a metoidioplasty. There are long wait lists (sometimes up to 10 years) and many requirements for these types of surgeries. I have started to discuss these with my doctor. After a year on testosterone (for me in March 2014), I can commence the process of getting on the lower-surgery wait list. Currently, there are no surgeons in British Columbia that conduct these types of surgeries for trans men. As such, the province funds trans men's travel to Montreal. From my discussion with trans men who have undergone these procedures, there are many challenges, especially if complications arise after the surgeries. Many of the doctors in British Columbia are not equipped to deal with them and the men are left in limbo without adequate health care. This scares me a lot and is a real consideration for me in determining my path forward. I know the procedures are continuously evolving so by the time it is my turn on the wait list, perhaps there will be fewer complications.

Mitch Kellaway

My therapist blinks placidly as I sob on his couch. With infuriating poise, he lets his next query land carefully: "Do *you* think there's something wrong with not knowing if you need to be a man, but being sure you need to be a father?" Our back-and-forth on the matter had already led to my current weepy dead end, but this time his curious therapeutic magic does the trick. As if holding up a mirror, he repeats back my concern as a calm-voiced question, and I finally hear in it what I need to.

"No?... No." I respond shakily. "It has to be okay, because I know it's what I need." I feel electrified to release the knot of guilt and confusion I've carried until now. I take a deep, clarifying breath and steady myself. I'm unashamed to cry in front of him, as I've been succumbing to it for the past several weeks. But suddenly I know that this is my last time.

Tears had burst forth unexpectedly the first session—one second the quiet, the next second the storm. That was about four months into our six-month therapy stint, right on time for a clichéd Hollywood "breakthrough" moment. And what a breakthrough it was. Having come to his office to simply obtain medical clearance to begin testosterone therapy, I balked as soon as my goal was in sight: one of my patented self-sabotaging moves. *Can I really handle gender transition?*

I knew then, as I know now, that I'm a man. I've known so ever since I first read the word *transgender*, setting my heartbeat racing as I shuffled through the rest of my high school library shift. A light bulb had clicked on within the dusty gender attic of my head, illuminating the possibility that the sex designated to me at birth didn't need to remain static over a lifetime. Though I didn't despise my body or being a lesbian, I felt an immediate certainty that I would be a *man* someday. It shone like that far-off fairy tale ending I've been reaching for since childhood, filling me with the same satisfied warmth I felt whenever I thought about finding the love of my life or creating my own home.

Why, then, did the same trusty thought I had once turned to for comfort now halt my therapeutic progress in its tracks, sending waves of anxiety screeching through my body? My inexpert diagnosis: adulthood. I'd spent the intervening years in college, then almost failing college, then on an extended sanity-gathering hiatus. For seven years that same dream of manhood had called out to me, but I'd shelved it for when I had more time. But there was never more time, until my need bubbled over, throwing me into an existential crisis and academic nosedive.

When I unceremoniously hit the "real world" of apartment-hopping and bill-payment-postponing, I quickly saw the framework of the "system" that I had long suspected was keeping me from my gender-actualization dreams: it wasn't that I had no time, it was that I didn't have money. Or much goodwill towards men. I'd been theorizing about this ever since I made the joyous discovery that I could obtain a whole degree in studying gender, but there's nothing like the daily grind to put abstract notions into practice.

*Patriarchy*. The unseemly social system that hierarchically places men above women, working hand-in-glove with capitalism, the beastly economic system that hierarchically places the rich above the poor. Oh, how I loathed it all! I saw injustice everywhere I turned, and male bodies doing most of the dirty work, intentionally and unintentionally acting out the roles handed to them. My demanding restaurant job was like an incubator, compressing the worst of it into a cramped, sweaty space.

The weekly onslaught of newly-hired female hosts and male kitchen staff fueled an established undercurrent of sexual harassment that we all, scarily enough, acclimated to quickly. We inherently understood that management wasn't going to intervene without a unified protest, and even then none of us wished to be the reason that a man, should he happen to be an undocumented worker, be deported. So, flying by the prep cooks with trays of steaming food and piles of greasy dishes, I withstood a barrage of comments about my body, unrelenting flirtation despite firm rebuffs, and a cacophony of other men heaping similar attentions on female co-workers. They agreed on how to split us up between them.

When I envisioned my man-self, I was nothing like this. In fact, I held the same sensitive, pensive, feminist core. The deluxe upgrade was that I could externally carry the facial fur, resonant voice, blocky frame, and flat chest I sensed under the surface, needing only a drop of hormonal potion to unfurl. But the cat-call gauntlet I walked daily from kitchen to dining room— an experience which, according to my femme—presenting friends, is amplified exponentially on city streets—gave me serious pause.

If I had lived in a vacuum and been handed a gender-swapping switch, I would have flipped it without a second thought. But these new social interactions, unbuffered by the polite reticence of my upper-middle class hometown or political correctness of my university campus, exposed me to some of the lowest of what people might surmise about me whenever I entered a room, exuding manhood through my beard and baritone. And I wasn't sure I could tolerate the weight of assumptions. I vibrated with uncertainty as I envisioned men considering me their confidant in sexually objectifying women, or a feminine shadow hastily crossing the street as I came up behind her during my nightly home commute.

Besides, I'd worked as a server until I was bone-tired and emotionally raw, and I still couldn't afford health insurance. I was blessed enough to manage therapy out-of-pocket, but my wallet couldn't sustain a full-blown medical transition. The $8,000 price tag on chest reconstruction loomed, getting further and further out of reach as I calculated the cost of the bi-monthly hormone injections, regular check-ups, and periodic blood work I'd need for the years I scrimped and saved.

Desperately, I tried on gendered combinations in

front of my mind's dressing-room mirror. Could I see myself as a butch in a binder? How about hairless, high-voiced, and staunchly reissuing a daily demand for male pronouns? Could I begin testosterone and only partially transition, halting at the highest pinnacle of my voice's cracking, at the downiest dusting of facial hair, foregoing the plunge into vocal depths and daily shaves? I'd seen others pull off these masculinities, and every embodiment in between and beyond, with such panache. But on me, they were that ill-fitting shirt I wanted to make "work," but would never quite satisfy me when I donned it, rendering me self-conscious and restless.

Trying a different tack, I bounced words of my mind's sounding board. "Sir" aged me. "Mr." did the same. "Dude" and "bro" left me as cold as the frat-favorite beers I didn't like to drink. "Man" worked okay, though I already got that casually from other twenty-somethings. "Husband." Getting closer, but it rang awkwardly as I struggled to imagine my queer girlfriend voicing it after a year of us simply being "partners" to each other. "Father." Yes, I could imagine that. In fact, I was delighted to discover a whole related set of fuzzy scenes mentally stored away, only waiting to be sharpened into focus.

*A young body toddling towards me, reaching upwards with open arms and tiny splayed fingers. "Dad!" she exclaims, beaming with the simple joy of seeing the only man who can fit the title. I smile down, scooping her up to hold tightly against my chest. Dad.* Dad.

"I know I have to be a father because I can't imagine it any other way, and I would be incomplete without having children," I continue to my therapist. "But," I hesitate, mental gears working overdrive to find a way—any way!—to avoid the next conclusion I draw.

"Is this just a way for me to make up for not having my own father?" At this point, we could recite his reply in tandem. "Do *you* think it is?"

I don't. Not really. And I kick myself for pushing our session to its clichéd "daddy issues" max. But if I'm going to take the wary leap into new social territory—something never done lightly by this confirmed introvert—I have to consider every angle. I'm gripped by the urge to *know* if transitioning has anything to do with my absent father—and I need the answer *right now* and unequivocally. This, of course, is the cue for our appointment to end. My therapist's reassurance that we'll pick up our conversation in two weeks is anything but comforting.

Sniffling and puffy-eyed, I descend the carpeted staircase into the lobby. A heavy cloud of doubts hang about me l as I absentmindedly emerge onto the sidewalk. *Why is "father" the only thing I know for sure I want to be in life? How can I be so certain when I don't have a clear idea of what it feels like to* be *fathered? Is this something I need to figure out before I start transitioning?*

I search myself for signs of an internal father-shaped hole, and come up empty. Whenever past conversations about paternity had sprung up around me, I had performed this ritualized precaution, just to confirm what I've been since birth: whole. Even I marvel at how little angst I've felt about my lack of a male role model, having been heaped with the requisite social messages about the natural logic of a two-adult, heterosexual household. In fact, I had always found my single mother more than enough, and I believed her earnest claims that a marriage between her and my biological father would have given new meaning to the word "dysfunctional." Before this panic-stricken hour in my therapist's office, I'd even carried a certain pride that of all the insidiously limiting social prescriptions, I had *least* internalized the fiction of one family structure reigning above all others.

Just like that, what I was apprehensively starting to consider the next wall between me and transition falls, a welcome anti-climax. *The only father I will ever know in this lifetime is me.* Within the ten minutes it takes to reach the subway station, I've become buoyant with the thought of the precious blank slate I've been handed. My fatherhood has no predecessor, no flawed archetype to continually refer back with a sighing *"When I have kids, I'll never be like that..."* refrain.

I dig in my pocket for my cell phone and jot off an email to my therapist suggesting we up our visits to every week. It seems to me that all of the processing from here on out can only be a mere formality. So when, over the next two dry-eyed months my medical—clearance letter fails to materialize, I call an end to our therapy sessions. The distant beacon of fatherhood has set my compass firmly due north, and I have no time to squander.

It could induce *deja vu*, this experience of sitting in front of a man who holds the key to unlocking the next door to transition—but it doesn't. This time I'm the opposite of a tearful puddle; I'm a stone monument of determination. I will not leave the office until I get the medical clearance I came for.

Then again, it's easy to be dauntless when the goal is guaranteed. My latest medical home is a large, urban LGBT health center, offering providers who are up to date on the latest standards-of-care. Their approach, following the "best practices" model agreed upon by experts in trans health, places trust in the patient to know the right time to transition.1

The only requirement I face is articulating an understanding of all possible outcomes—something I'm duly prepared for, having spent many an evening poring over other men's transition narratives—and signing an "informed consent" waiver. When I enter the building to meet my new doctor, the fresh breath I take in comes as much from the air-conditioning as it does from releasing the burden of being at my therapist's mercy.

"Hi there, I'm Dr. Miller. I understand you're here to begin testosterone therapy?" My doctor's kind eyes meet mine over a firm handshake. We exchange formalities and within minutes I'm within sight of the goal that had so unnecessarily eluded me for months.

Not wishing to sway my consent process, Dr. Miller keeps his face as blank as my former therapist's and hands me a paper checklist. As I place "X"es next to each box on the form, he politely averts his eyes towards the floor. My heart warms at the attempt to give me privacy, but the small space can hardly afford it. Besides, I don't need any more time to think. The unquantifiable amounts of physical, mental, and spiritual energy I've spent over the past half-year spill out with the ink, sealing my hairy, low-voiced, paternal fate.

So I'm not anticipating, as perhaps he is, that I'll

be blindsided by my first reason to grieve. About halfway down the page, my eyes halt their forward march.

_X_ *I understand that it is not known exactly what the effects of testosterone are on fertility. I have been informed that if I stop testosterone, I may not be able to become pregnant in the future. I have been advised to undergo gamete (egg) banking if this is a concern of mine.*

"Do you have any questions?" he asks after I nonetheless sign off with little fanfare, save the flourish I still excitedly give to writing my newly legalized name. I see no option but to take a chance on my body's ovarian potency: without the prerequisite manhood, I'll never achieve the fatherhood I personally envision.2

"No, I don't." I focus on keeping my voice even.

"Did you read the portion about banking your eggs?" I exhale a deep breath into loaded silence.

"Yes, I did."

I hadn't imagined discussing my distantly-planned pregnancy any time soon, much less right now. I fear that, much like weighing my mixed feelings about my father, considering my potential impending sterility will only stall my momentum. If it won't cause my doctor to withhold transition from me, my own overactive imagination could.

"Well," I begin. His eyebrows rise expectantly. "I just thought guys could give birth if they stopped testosterone." He nods slightly. "At least if they haven't had a hysterectomy."

"That's right," he assents, pausing to let my thoughts flow now that I've broken their dam.

"I've never heard that T makes you sterile. I know men who are pregnant. And I see there's the option of egg banking, but I imagine that's expensive."

We share a joyless chuckle at how preposterous the financial demand is, probably enhanced by our previous phone conversations about just how little money I have to put towards my medical care. I'm not sure why I carefully avoid centering my own desire for pregnancy in our conversation; perhaps I feel that if I don't offer it, it can't truly be taken away from me.

"There just haven't been long-term studies done on the effects of testosterone on trans men's fertility. While it's definitely not guaranteed to render men sterile, I also can't say that it *won't*. Without proof, I'm bound to inform you that it might. If you ever want to try to get pregnant, we'll stop your hormone therapy and get the ball rolling, okay?" "

I nod, heartened but tight-lipped. It seems a cruel twist of fate to possibly lose out on the future joy of carrying a life within me so that I may be at peace with my gender now. I have only a moment to consider retracting my hormonal green light, and I instantly feel the weight of potentially becoming an invisible man once again descend upon me.

My spirit cannot endure the years of misgendering that would inevitably pass before I could even get *close* to being financially and emotionally ready for in vitro fertilization. I simply cannot wait any longer to embody the mannish aura I catch glimpses of when I stare hard into the mirror. It's calling to me, siren-like and visceral. I place a prayerful bet on the numerous success stories I've heard from other men, wagering that my fertility's chances are as good as any other.

"Yes, okay."

"Alright, that's all I need to know!" He claps his hands together, flashing the genuine smile of a doctor who knows he's about to change a patient's life. "I'll go grab the testosterone."

\*\*\*

---

1 The World Professional Association for Transgender Health first established the international Standards of Care (SOC) for providers working with transgender patients in 1979. The

document has evolved ever since to come increasingly in-line with the needs trans patients articulate for themselves. The most recent edition is SOC Version 7, published in 2011. In it, the WPATH updates the pre-transition requirements they had held since the previous edition's publication a decade before. Rather than the formerly required three to six months of talk therapy, the current SOC asserts that as long as a trans patient is determined to be in sound mental health, they should be able to access hormones after being informed of all side effects and signing their consent. Should a mental health concern present itself, the patient should be treated, and once stable should still be allowed informed access to hormone therapy.

Eli Coleman*, et al, "Standards of Care for the Health of Transsexual, Transgender, and Gender-Nonconforming People, Version 7,"* International Journal of Transgenderism 13 *(2011): 181.*

2 It should be noted that all transgender, transsexual, and gender-nonconforming individuals do not need to medically transition (i.e. undergo hormone therapy, chest reconstruction, and/or genital reconstruction) to attain fatherhood. Each individual knows what's right for themselves; it happens that I know my path is to transition hormonally and have my chest reconstructed before I become a father.

\*\*\*

This essay contains material adapted from "Transgender Sterilization: Sweden and Beyond" by Mitch Kellaway, from *The Huffington Post* (July 1, 2013).

Leng Montgomery

As a Londoner, I have access to the National Health Service (NHS), which in some ways has made access to medical assistance and healthcare a less-costly option compared to other places in the world.

I distinctly remember the first time I saw my doctor at the time to talk about transition; I had been putting it off for quite some time as I was keen to start going to the gender clinic and more importantly, unsure that transition was the best option for me. I knew I hated my breasts and that I wanted them gone, but, what I didn't know was that I might have more than one reason to do so; I found a lump. When I saw the doctor, I knew I wanted to be honest about everything. I told him I had two problems: The first was very male, and the second was female. I felt at ease being straightforward with him. He checked the lump in my breast and referred me to a breast-cancer clinic for more testing. As for my transition, he told me to make a new appointment in two weeks' time. He'd never cared for a patient that was transitioning and wanted to read up on the ways in which he could best support me. I definitely wasn't expecting that. I saw him two weeks later, after being cleared from the breast cancer clinic and we discussed what my next steps would be.

First, he had to diagnose me with 'Gender Identity Disorder' and that had to go on all my records. I wasn't thrilled about the idea of having this permanently attached to my medical history; to his credit, neither was he, but it was standard procedure. I was referred to a community psychiatrist who asked me about my mental health and gender issues. We discussed what I wanted, which was to go to the Caring Cross Gender clinic. She wrote a letter stating that I had GID, which was added to my doctor's referral and sent to the clinic. They told me the next available appointment was ten months away. I was heartbroken. The waiting time on the NHS list is extremely long, and in that time I was able to change my name legally via deed poll, save up some money for various transition-related costs, and see a private gender doctor, who started me on hormones and wrote a letter so I could change my passport.

By the time I entered the gender clinic I was well into my medical and social transition. At that point I wanted their assistance to assess me for top surgery. I had an initial appointment and a consultation four months later. After that I returned to my primary doctor at the clinic who discussed surgical options with me.

Before my surgery application could be submitted to the Primary Care Trust (PCT) who authorize funding for surgeries—not just trans procedures, but for other elective surgeries, I had to deal with a complication that arose. One morning I was trying to get my testosterone—the pharmacy didn't have it, even though I had a repeat prescription, and they insisted the doctor's office hadn't sent it. The doctor's receptionist blamed the pharmacy, and in the end the receptionist asked if I could come in. When I got there and went to sign in electronically, my age and gender wouldn't come up in the system. I gave them my NHS number and the receptionist literally <u>gasped</u> at what she saw on the screen. She told me that the Health Trust had given me a name that was different from Mr. Leng Montgomery. In fact, it was a name that didn't even exist.

'Miss Leng Leng' appeared on all of my medical records. Not only was it the wrong name but it was the wrong gender too. What a fiasco! My Doctor was very sympathetic. I brought in my documents—passport and name-change certificate—to show them, and they sent it through the system. But, "Miss Leng Leng" was stuck there and remained to taunt me for five more months.

My application for funding couldn't be done. Major budget cuts happened within the NHS, from the government, and my first application was rejected. Because top surgery is considered to be a core procedure available to trans patients my doctor appealed the decision, but depending on where you live, it becomes a postcode lottery.

PCT doesn't want to spend money if they don't have to, and in my case they claimed to need evidence in support of the fact that I needed this, additionally saying that they don't cover gynaecomastia, which is something I couldn't biologically have. My respective doctors sent them letters of appeal and clarification. They had been given all the correct information the first time but they either went silent or rejected my application.

They decided they wouldn't fund my surgery because the surgeon I chose had left the NHS but still charged the same rate as NHS surgeons. It would be at the discretion of the PCT whether or not to grant the funding to have surgery with him. The PCT had authorized funding to him on several occasions prior to this but mine was the exception. I was denied! This battle went on for almost a year, until a miracle happened.

I had been keeping an online blog about my battle with the NHS and a complete stranger contacted me via Twitter, offering to pay the full cost of my surgery. I thought someone was winding me up. Who gives a complete stranger the equivalent of $10,000, just like that? We exchanged a few emails, they wired me the money and within two months I was in Brighton with the surgeon of my choice.

On that day, I felt I was born again. It was partially because it involved being in a hospital, and also because all my movement post surgery was so delicate that it was like being a newborn baby. Never in my life have I felt that vulnerable, and yet, at the same time unbelievably powerful. I was a year and a half on hormones by then, and was seeing myself changing before my eyes.

My follow up appointments with the gender clinic have been very positive. They have worked in partnership with my doctors to make sure they are managing my hormones well, and so far it's been great.

This year (September 2014) I will be discharged from the gender clinic and will not require any further assistance from them. This is a huge milestone. I turned 30, hit five years in my transition and feel like I am finally living as me.

Dylan Farnsworth

As is true with every profession, a variety of different kinds of people choose to work in healthcare. I have been fortunate in that the majority of my experiences have been as positive as they could have been, though that has certainly not been a universal experience.

In 2007, while I was living in Washington state, I found myself in need of a letter from a therapist stating that I was of sound mind to make the decision to have top surgery. At the outset, I thought that this was ridiculous since people have surgery all the time without ever seeking permission from a therapist. I realize why the requirement exists in concept, but to me it was just one more roadblock I had to overcome in order to get where I needed to go. I looked up psychologists in the area and began making phone calls and leaving messages. Out of more than a dozen messages only one therapist called me back. Perhaps the words *transgender* and *surgery* scared the others away. Throughout my psychological evaluation I felt very much like a bug beneath a microscope. At the end I was writing out a check to pay for the uncomfortable experience and apologized for taking so long, to which she replied that I shouldn't apologize so much, that it was a feminine trait. I honestly think that she was trying to be helpful but to me it came off as sad that she had such a warped sense of gender roles.

Armed with my letter I proceeded to San Francisco, California, to have my top surgery with Dr. B. Accompanied by my best friend Sally I felt unstoppable. At last I was going to make a change. Never again would I have to put on a binder over sunburn. No longer would I have to avoid going swimming, one of my favorite hobbies. The pain of that recovery was dwarfed by the pure and overwhelming sense of peace and calm that overcame me. It would be three months before I took my shirt off in public, and the stares at my obvious new scars were deflected by the newfound pride I had in my body. It was during this time that I first began to feel a new self-esteem begin to grow within me.

One of the most dreaded appointments for me a trans man must endure is the check-up with OBGYN doctors. Many trans men avoid taking care of this part of their body, but it is still important. After moving to Monterey, California I made an OBGYN appointment with a new doctor's office. When I arrived, I walked up to the receptionist's desk and said that I had an appointment to see the doctor. She looked at me incredulously and said, "No, you don't." I had communicated to the doctor and nurse about my unique situation when I made the appointment, but they had apparently not mentioned this to their reception staff. "Yes, I do." I told her, not wanting to explain myself in full hearing of every person in the small waiting area. The receptionist smirked and remarked that she thought I was in the wrong place. "Trust me," I said, handing her my ID card, "I have an appointment. Look it up or go ask the doctor." Smugness quickly turned to consternation as she typed my name into the computer. She shook her head and handed me some paperwork to begin filling out. I walked to an open seat with as much dignity as I could, all too aware that there were more than a few sets of subtly curious eyes on me. As for the receptionist, she wasted no time in going to tell the rest of the staff about the anomaly that had walked in the door. This experience was far different from the times I had to see my OBGYN in Washington. That office was polite, respectful, and even changed my gender in their records before I was legally male. I think that the solution to avoiding situations such as the one I had is to educate medical professionals about transgender issues. Not just about the unique medical needs of the trans community, but also about how to train their staff to be respectful and professional. I harbor no bad feelings toward that receptionist I only wish that I'd had the confidence and self-assurance then that I possess now, so that I could have educated her.

With my move to California I had to find a new doctor to prescribe my testosterone. There were no doctors on the peninsula who specialized in transgender care so I decided to pick the most friendly-seeming doctor that I could find. At this time the Defense of Marriage Act was alive and well and I did not use my military insurance for this doctor. I paid for my prescriptions out of pocket. I still remember her surprise during our first appointment when I told her about my situation and what I was seeking. She had seen a transgender woman once a few years prior, but that was the extent of her experience with trans healthcare. Fortunately I had chosen well, and she was all too happy to help. Willingness and experience, however, are very different things. It wasn't a big deal when I was doing testosterone injections, as she could simply copy the prescriptions that I'd previously received. Things got more complicated when I told her that I wanted to switch to a topical testosterone cream. I knew from my research that she had experience with hormone replacement therapy for women undergoing menopause, and hoped this would translate in some way. She said that she often prescribed creams for her female patients, even low dose testosterone creams, but had never prescribed anything with such a high dose. I think that beyond her determination to do her duty as a physician she was genuinely curious and fascinated by this challenge. She collaborated with a local compounding pharmacy and they gave it a try. I switched to the cream and we tested my testosterone levels every few months and adjusted the dose accordingly. Eventually we got it dialed in to what seemed like an appropriate level. It certainly would have been easier if there had been a local doctor who had experience in this area, but there was something exhilarating about figuring it out on our own. Much of my transition has followed this theme; there is something to be said for forging your own path.

After a year or two in Monterey I was ready for the next step in my transition: a hysterectomy/oophorectomy. Time was running out because I was months away from losing my private insurance, and with it I would lose any hope of not having to pay for this surgery out of pocket. I knew that I needed a letter from a therapist and a physician in order to have this surgery, so I wasted no time. I scoured the Internet for a therapist within an hour's drive, who had experience with transgender patients. As luck would have it, I was just under an hour from Santa Cruz, where there was more than one qualified therapist. I looked at their websites and picked one who I thought seemed the most compatible with my personality, and made my first appointment. I had assumed that this would be a multi-stage process, requiring a few visits for him to get to know me enough to ensure that I was capable of making this decision on my own. I had grown accustomed to the gatekeeper mentality of many healthcare professionals. I was pleasantly surprised when, after an hour of discussion, there was no hesitation in his willingness to write my letter for me. He even recommended a local doctor who I could see for the other requirements for surgery. We got along so well that I continued seeing him for the remainder of my years in California.

During those years I had to endure a lengthy litigation process due to a car accident I was involved in. The defendant's insurance company was unwilling to reimburse me for even those medical expenses I'd had to date, not to mention the future projected costs due to a permanent neck injury that I sustained. After a great deal of legal back and forth we decided to go to trial. Being deposed by their lawyer was an experience that I will never forget. I won't get into the details, but she had no qualms about prying into the most sensitive parts of my life and exposing everything that she could dig out of my past in order to embarrass me and/or make me look bad. Think about an antagonist combing through your medical files and confronting you on things from your past that you've tried desperately to forget; I felt deeply violated. They are not bound by the rules of admissibility during a deposition the same way that they are during the actual trial, so it was all fair game. Afterwards I asked my lawyer if the trial was going to be like that. He told me the things that he would have disallowed due to relevance, but made sure I understood that they would make absolutely certain the jury knew about my transition in an attempt to discredit me. The only defense against this, he said, would be to be proactive and attempt to preempt their attacks on my character as a transgender person. Following this deposition I had to be examined by their physician in order to ascertain the extent of my permanent injuries. Perhaps my negative experience with this doctor was not abnormal considering the circumstances, he is after all employed by insurance companies seeking to discredit victims of accidents. But he treated me with scorn and my medical complaints with unveiled derision.

This litigation went on for a total of four years. In the end it was my chiropractor who did some research and sent my x-rays off to a diagnostic company that ended up finding the evidence that eventually forced the insurance company to take me seriously and settle. He was a constant advocate during that process, always seeking to look after my whole person, not just my spine, and I will forever be grateful for the friendship he offered me. As you can imagine this litigation experience was extremely stressful for my wife and I, and the anxiety issues that had long since disappeared with the start of my transition came back with a fury. It was during this time more than any other that I was grateful for having found a therapist who was not only experienced with transgender issues but compatible with my personality. Therapists are not one-size-fits-all, and throughout my life I had seen several who did not work for me at all. This therapist, however, was a perfect mix of equality and expertise. He respected my experiences and spoke to me as an equal, and over the years I began to think of him less like a therapist and more like an older brother who had wisdom to share with me. I don't know how I would have handled the awful experiences of that long litigation had it not been for the support and compassion that she offered me.

The doctor that my therapist recommended was Dr. H at the Santa Cruz Planned Parenthood. This recommendation proved to be some of the best advice I've ever received. For the first time in my life, I felt that I was sitting down with a doctor who was more knowledgeable about transgender health. I was relieved and felt that I was getting the care I needed by qualified medical professionals. Somehow I knew that from that moment on she would have my back, and be an advocate for me if I ever needed one. She wrote my letter for surgery and recommended a surgeon that she knew, since a transgender specialist was not needed for a hysterectomy. I met with the surgeon and she was more than happy to accommodate me, and her staff was very friendly. She said that she could perform the surgery in one of two locations: a Catholic hospital or a Woman's Surgery Center. Needless to say these were not the best choices I could have asked for. Nonetheless it was not a difficult decision to make; my break with religion ensured that. So I became, to the knowledge of the receptionist at the surgery center, the first male patient to be admitted to their facility. All in all I can say that I was treated with dignity and respect. The only surprise was when, on the day after surgery, one of my wife's relatives walked in the door to my room. Unbeknownst to us she was a nurse and worked there. It was a moment of pure incredulity; what are the odds?? Our first reaction was panic, since Kathryn's family had no idea that I was transgender at this time. They spoke, though, and she was completely supportive and reassured us that none would find out about this from her. Once that stress was averted my recovery went wonderfully.

A year later, in 2012, I was planning to have my metoidioplasty performed by Dr. Miroslav Djordjevic in Belgrade, Serbia. Some people choose to go overseas for surgery because it's cheaper, but I chose him because of his results and the testimonials of his previous patients. Since I needed more letters and some pre-op tests done I went to Dr. H and told her about my upcoming surgery. She was genuinely excited for me and made certain that everything on that to-do list was completed, and that everything was sent to Dr. Miro as soon as possible. I was struck by how simple it all was; I didn't have to educate and explain, and more importantly I didn't have to convince anyone that this was important and medically necessary. I had confidence in my doctor that she knew how to help me and had my best interests at heart, an experience that I was still getting used to. I felt cared for, and that was so very nice. That place was an incredible oasis of understanding and compassionate care. I have since seen this doctor present at Seattle's Gender Odyssey, and watched with gratitude as she advocated for patient's right to have a greater say in their own care.

My mother was understandably nervous about me traveling to Serbia for a major surgery. She was reassured that Kathryn would be by my side caring for me, but I don't think her anxiety dwindled until she got the "Dylan's just fine" text. There are some things about Belgrade that had the feel of what one might imagine the old Soviet Union was like, but the medical care that I received there was certainly not one of them. My wife and I were picked up from the airport by one of the doctors on Dr. Miro's team. She took us to the police station to be registered and then took us grocery shopping before showing us our apartment. She was sure to let us know that the apartment was just downstairs from her parents' residence, and that we should not hesitate to let them know if we needed anything. My mother should have been more concerned with my medical experiences in the United States; I was in very good hands here. We were provided with Serbian cell phones to use during our stay, with all of the personal phone numbers of all of the doctors programmed into them. They had also set us up with a taxi driver who we called George. He knew where the hospital and apartment were, was familiar with the situation, and spoke enough English to amuse us during our trips. We would not be taken advantage of due to not knowing where we were going or how to speak the language. It seemed Dr. Miro had thought of everything. The doctors came to me at the apartment for follow-up appointments, and even stopped by to bring Kathryn some medicine when she got sick. I was astounded by their attentiveness.

My single complaint about the medical care that I received in Serbia was that Kathryn was not allowed to stay the night with me after surgery. I understand their reasoning that patients need their rest, but it should be allowed if requested. I didn't sleep at all the night after surgery. The nurse would come in and check on me every hour or so and admonish that I should be sleeping, and I would shrug and say I couldn't. I was restless and extremely uncomfortable. Not just the normal "I just had major surgery" discomfort, but mentally very uncomfortable. The next day Kathryn stayed with me as long as she was allowed to, then left. Once again, I spent a sleepless night. I was able to doze a little bit in the late morning, but only briefly. It wasn't until that day that we realized that I was experiencing withdrawal from one of my medications. The doctors gave the okay for me to begin taking it again and at last I was able to sleep comfortably. The entire process would have been so much easier on me had Kathryn been allowed to stay with me. The rest of my recovery was exciting and uneventful. I felt whole and complete for the first time in my life. It wasn't just my body that was healing, but there was something deep within me that was healing as well.

Overall I would say that my experiences with the medical community have been better than most, but there is certainly room for improvement. There are those within the transgender community who are actively striving to educate healthcare professionals about the unique issues that we face, and I am grateful for the work that they do. I think that it is important to demand respect from our caregivers, and to speak up when that respect is not given. We must self-advocate and be educators in our own small communities, and the aggregate of our efforts can make meaningful change in the world.

# SECTION VI—TRANSITIONING ON THE JOB

Can our livelihood remain intact while transitioning on the job?

Writers, educators, office workers, activists, and service workers; trans people are all of these and more.

Sharing their experiences of working while living life in different states of being "out" can be challenging. How do you find a balance? Many contributors feared discrimination, misunderstanding, and unequal treatment in jobs due to their gender identity.

While many have found acceptance, there have been challenges for all to varying degrees. By sharing these stories, contributors hope that as future employers you may consider your professional practices, identify diversity, and understand the vulnerability of this process, while remaining professional.

Mitch Kellaway

"...Many transgender men have been conditioned to deny our deepest needs."
—Shannon Minter, *Hung Jury*

As I reach the door of my undergrad program director's office, my autopilot butterflies begin to subside. This new feeling overtakes me: a *lack* of feeling, actually. A mental fog has been lowering all semester; I can't seem to care, and I can't quite determine if it's self preservation or self sabotage. It's recently culminated in a slew of missed classes and ignored homework.

Over the previous month, I'd felt such trepidation approaching my final papers that I simply hadn't done them. A familiar dread had crept in, suddenly no longer reserved for socializing. It had latched onto writing: the one task I threw myself at with the gusto of all irrationally passionate hobbyists.

I've been perseverating on flashing thoughts, certain that last week I'd finally passed the point of no return in Masculinities—my favorite class, no less!— likely prompting this call down to the department. Though I know it's not an official reality until the director tells me I've failed, my guilty conscience is already living hours ahead.

I knock quietly, calm as the earth-toned walls surrounding me. I'm told to enter by Dr. Hoven' bright voice. Closing the door behind me, my eyes dart to the woman standing beside her desk: the assistant director. *Maybe this is about more than one missed class.* The women's faces are blank masks as Dr. Hoven motions me to sit opposite her in the room's second chair.

Pleasantries exchanged, she cuts to the point. "We think you're an incredibly adept student." The women share a look and nod—they're tag-teaming a prepared monologue. "You're more than capable of completing a thesis next year…" the assistant director continues. I feel my throat forming a lump. Even though I'm not sure being a high-performing student matters to me anymore, it hurts to hear it taken away— to know I did it to myself and not understand why. And to realize abruptly, in the presence of scholars I respect, that I don't know who I am without our shared identity. "But we're not sure, given your class work this semester, that you can keep up with the deadlines." I nod silently.

After a pause, words tumble out of my mouth before I can finish thinking them.

"Well, I was considering taking a leave of absence."

It's the first time I've said them aloud despite how often I'd pondered them over the last couple months.

In response, they both nod heartrendingly. It must be a relief to hear me make the first right decision in a semester riddled with poor ones.

"That could do you good. A lot of students choose that path. We'll support you whatever you decide."

They smile warmly; I can sense how much they care. Still, my heart sinks with the feeling that I'm letting us all down.

My mind, newly given to carrying on without the rest of me, floats above the scene, watching dispassionately. I go through the motions of thanking them, depart, and over the next few weeks I file paperwork confirming my indefinite leave.

For me, as I suspect it is for many other trans folks, "transitioning on the job" meant "transitioning *between* jobs." I was perhaps exceptionally lucky, however, in that I didn't *have* to change employers when I started medically transitioning. This wasn't only because my town had recently passed a gender identity non-discrimination ordinance. My co-workers and bosses were actually fully on board with my shifting gender, and I had the all-too-rare liberty of choosing to switch occupations when I desired something new.

Biding my time until I felt I'd figured myself and my goals out, I stumbled into food service at age twenty-four, a newly official college absentee. I didn't have any experience or a friend to vouch for me; I simply walked into the address listed on a help-wanted ad and was lucky enough to receive an on-the-spot interview. I was hired immediately and started answering phones the next day.

For almost a year afterwards I dispatched delivery orders in the less-than-ideal nexus point between the kitchen, dish room, and service station. My role was a mix of wrapping greasy bags of ribs, straining to hear customers over the restaurant's din, and staying out of the way as servers, dishwashers, and food runners flew by. Adept at staying focused in chaos, I was soon promoted to supervising the take-out station; when the restaurant needed a new floor manager, I was promoted again and trained in everything from bussing to hosting to serving. That's when I realized something management had, in retrospect, probably banked on my not knowing: our servers and bartenders were making double to triple my starting hourly wage. So when the stress of floor managing outweighed the benefits, I took the out that most of my peers had: I asked to be switched to the floor.

As a server, I excelled. It's a role I had never imagined myself taking on or enjoying so thoroughly—not because it was grueling and filthy...*that* I could handle. But I'd doubted my ability to endure so much face-to-face small talk. I was still an agonizing year away from realizing my anxiety was a self-destructive pattern that could actually be broken.

Fortunately for me, it turned out that there was something very asocial about interacting with customers, a couple hours into the shift, they were a faceless sweet tea-guzzling mass and I was on cruise control. I also found welcome relief in having a mind-boggling amount of coworkers—a number fluctuating between seventy and eighty at any given moment. Out of necessity we broke into cliques and I settled comfortably into developing intense friendships with only a handful.

At pique efficiency, I could work seven days a week. And I did. It wasn't exactly the same as being my former college-student self, but it was akin. The feeling of productivity, and the accompanying sensations of stability and safety, were something I had never before put words to needing; having gone straight from home to college, I'd simply had them until they were gone.

Finding myself without university-provided meals, housing, or health insurance, I experienced a previously unknown urgency: *It's up to me alone to survive this.* There was a tangible connection between my labor—how many hours I put in and doubles I pulled, how sore my muscles and how stained my T-shirts, how fatigued and sweat-soaked I was as I crawled into bed each evening—and my ability to keep clothed, housed, and fed. It was a *realness* that I needed to go through, and that connected me to my working-class parents before me.

I embraced the change wholeheartedly and wound up spending the majority of my waking hours at work, as it came to sustain my spirit with a sense of purpose and belonging. Knowing that I hadn't lost my ability to be productive was profoundly healing.

Then again, it would be disingenuous to say I merely got by; at a certain point I became quite prosperous. After a half-year of serving, I was earning more money that I'd ever had and this, along with the stability of my apartment, job, and loving partner, unexpectedly set the stage for my gender transition. Though I hadn't opted for the restaurant's health insurance—at 15% of my income, it felt too steep—I realized one day that I could comfortably afford $100 therapy sessions out-of-pocket.

I walked towards my first appointment still short-sightedly believing I was seeking therapy to address my depression. Nonetheless, I had purposefully opted for the closest therapist who specialized in gender. By the end of our first meeting, I knew I was really there to pursue the transition I'd always imagined myself undertaking (even buried under heaps of schoolwork as it once was). It appeared, as must happen, that the future had finally caught up with me.

The following morning I decided upon a first and middle name and, with little fanfare, bundled up to catch the train downtown. Walking in the crisp winter air towards probate court, I stopped for a coffee since I'd heard the long lines there could be grueling.

"What can I get you, sir?" the man behind the counter had asked as I entered.

I read the subtext gratefully: *The Universe Supports Your Gender Transition.*

"Have a good day, sir!" he called as I emerged onto the sidewalk.

In minutes, I'd ascended several flights of stairs, handed over my birth certificate, and taken my place at the end of a long line of folks mostly there, it appeared, for divorce certificates.

Though I initially feared the worst, especially after having heard stories of men being required to publish their new names in local newspapers before being granted a legal change, no one batted an eye. For my official "reason" I simply listed "personal preference" and, after forking over $185, I was told to expect the court-approved legal documentation to arrive in five weeks.

A little over an hour after I walked inside, I exited the courthouse feeling like a changed person. And although I knew the wait would be interminable, I was giddy with the feeling that I'd finally *done it*. I'd started a ball rolling I had been contemplating for years, and it was only a matter of time until I'd be fully presenting outwardly who I was internally.

I knew work would probably be less awkward if I waited a couple months to announce my transition—better yet, why not the six-months-to-a-year it'd take for me to start exhibiting testosterone's effects? But as I breezed through Meat-N-Three's back door the following afternoon, I was taken by the urge to march straight down to my assistant manager's office.

"I legally changed my name yesterday. It's Mitchell now," I announced before the conversation could turn to anything else.

"Really? Wow. What do you want me to call you?" Lisa sounded genuinely pleased.

"Mitch is good. I'll give you a copy of my legal name change paperwork when I receive it, so you can switch my name on my paychecks. Can you ask Sammy to change it in the computer?" I answered.

*If I act like this kind of thing happens everyday, perhaps she will too*, I thought to myself.

"Sure," she responded.

I left to walk upstairs, confident that every other manager would know the news within an hour. Right on cue, after the forty-five minutes I spent prepping the dining room for our dinner rush, my head manager trundled up the stairs and called out my name—"Mitch!"—a little too cheerfully.

I trotted over as if this were any other instance he'd barked my name and I'd stood at attention awaiting orders. Looking uncharacteristically lost, he lowered his voice.

"I'm not sure what to call you," he admitted, his tone vaguely embarrassed.

"Just Mitch," I replied, offering no elaboration.

"Mitch," he said slowly, as if feeling for something. "Alright, then!"

This was a man who never made a move without calculating its losses and gains; though I'll never fully know his inner machinations, it was clear he'd made a decision to simply go with the flow. This turned out to be emblematic of nearly all of my coworkers' reactions.

I chalk such institutional nonchalance up to being in the middle of a liberal city and working in a fast-paced job where smoothly adapting to minute-by-minute changes is the pinnacle of expertise. The career servers and bartenders—"lifers," we twenty-somethings called them—were especially adept at taking my gender change in stride, with a grin and pat on the back or a quip about my downgrade to using the restaurant's dingy men's bathrooms. Months later, following the city's new nondiscrimination ordinance, they marked all single-stall bathrooms gender neutral.

Shortly after I began my social transition at Meat-N-Three, and right before they changed those daunting bathroom signs, I realized the work environment was too toxic for reasons, happily enough, complete unrelated to my gender expression. I started dreaming of renewing my deep enjoyment of labor in an environment free of suspicion and resentment. Across the street was a cafe known locally for hiring queer folks, and I'd also spotted a couple men among them I pegged as trans. Aware, too, of the owners' reputations as fair and thoughtful managers, I finally let myself apply. Their hiring manager, Cliff, recognized me immediately as a large-latte regular—I'm sure she also remembered the day, not too long before, that I'd excitedly asked her to change the name on my order to "Mitch"—and put in a word. Within a week I was hired at their other location a twenty-minute walk down the road.

Haven Cafe was an abandoned bank playfully repurposed by my new employers, two environmentally minded women with a gift for bringing independent coffee shops to life. Keeping its frame, they'd torn down the insides; today, the space invites droves of customers who often remark upon a unique structure that incorporates the bullet-proof teller window and vault of its former, less welcoming incarnation.

When I first stepped into Haven Cafe as an employee, I was experiencing a luminal reality some trans friends and I refer to as the "Gray Space." It was that finite, though indefinite, amount of time after starting T in which the mental and emotional actualization of my true gender had not yet been matched physically, and was therefore not reflected back socially without me making my maleness explicit.

On my first day as a barista, I hadn't yet stopped carrying the safety-blanket of my name-change document around to prove myself. My new state ID, freshly marked with an "M," only arrived the day after I filled out my new-hire paperwork. I wavered each morning between the men's or women's restroom, usually opting for the latter and kicking myself afterwards. I seemed to have a knack for using it when a female coworker happened to be in the only other stall. I was surrounded by coworkers I knew to be queer—and trans-friendly or even queer themselves. But somehow my response—and this is still, to me, one of the greatest mysteries of my early transition days—was to silently hope that they would intuit from my male-sounding name that I needed their gender affirmation, rather than ask that they use male pronouns upfront, despite being 100% sure they would have all responded supportively. Yet I'd been able to ask seventy-plus Meat-N-Three'ers and open myself to their predictably scattered responses only months earlier. In other words, it was harder for me to ask for what I needed at Haven knowing I'd receive it than to ask at Meat-N-Three and receive the kind of lukewarm or bemused response I'd come to expect as a trans person vocalizing my trans-ness.

This was a difficulty, compounded personally by my anxiety, which I've heard from many trans men. In part I attribute it to being socialized into a gender where I valued other people's comfort over my own. It's part personality too, no doubt; I know more than one pal who would ascribe my non-action to my being a quintessential shelled-in, other-nurturing Cancer moonchild. I also suspect it's part internalized transphobia: fear of speaking my gender transgression publicly, unable to foresee what others would then take and do with that. *Who else will they tell? Who's listening? Will they hurt me? Will they reject me?* I felt such fears even in what was arguably the safest work situation I could have hoped for, in one of the trans-friendliest towns in the state—possibly within the whole world.

Within a couple of months, though, my voice dropped precipitously and I sprouted a dark goatee almost overnight. I began being read as male by strangers as quickly as one could hope for with testosterone therapy, essentially eliminating the conundrum—one I know many of my brethren experience for longer—almost as quickly as it arose. I barely slowed down as I passed through the Gray Space.

Still, I was left asking myself why I hadn't been able to discuss my transition with my Haven coworkers. I've come to some understanding now, through much reflection. I believe already knowing my gender would become awkward and fumbled at Meat-N-Three helped me charge forward with announcing my transition there. I was mentally prepared to have fun correcting the dozens who had never met a trans person before; I felt the power of creating gender confusion, even while I still felt inklings of shame for not speaking up more for myself.

At Haven, however, I was among my own queer and gender nonconforming people, where errors would have cut deep, and I just could not make myself that vulnerable, open myself to such gender intimacy. It's still a moment, like so many come-and-gone on this transition journey, that I muse about with wonder at how it's helped me understand myself more fully. And then I practice grace by forgiving that young man for not allowing himself the space and the joy of sharing his transition with those who would have cheered for him.

---

References: Cotton, Trystan. T. (2012). *The Hung Jury: Testimonials of Genital Surgery by Transsexual Men.* California: Transgress Press.

Alexander Walker

Freshly out of college, and just embarking on my teaching career, I stood terrified in front of thirty-seven first graders, wondering how I could possibly transition in this environment.

Shortly after beginning my first job, I realized that being called 'Miss' all day would wear me down quickly. I had never met or heard of anyone successfully transitioning on the job as a teacher. In my research, I found nothing but stories of teachers being fired and treated inhumanely for changing genders. My anxiety went through the roof! All I had ever wanted was to be a teacher. I felt like I had no one to turn to and could only hope that someone would give me a chance.

The first year of teaching is challenging for many reasons. First, you're entering a new field; young, fresh, and learning your way (although teachers are never done learning and certainly are always trying to figure out a new way to teach things). I was constantly being asked, "Are you a girl or a boy?" This question baffled me. I felt like these young people were staring into me and saying with no harmful intentions, something isn't matching up. My walk home through the city streets intensified my daily life. I felt like I was lying every time I answered that question with, "I'm miss" I lacked confidence and needed a way out. After two years of struggling, my then fiancée and I decided it was time to move.

We moved to a brand new city and this created an opportunity for me. My fiancée began her Master's degree and taught full time while I started at a tiny, new independent school. When I interviewed for the job I was presenting as female. Since then, I had begun my social transition and wasn't about to go back. I sat down with my supervisor and explained that I was going through a gender transition and I would like to be addressed using male pronouns. She listened and understood, saying we needed to talk with the principle, but she didn't think it would be an issue. The principle, my supervisor, and I made a plan to email all of the other teachers. We agreed that this information was not necessary for parents, students, and others who weren't around when I interviewed. I appreciated their desire to work on my terms, but knew that moments of awkwardness were unavoidable. I felt completely respected by my colleagues who, for the most part, took the information and kept it to themselves.

Throughout the school year, I helped the administration develop and implement a series of workshops to educate faculty about what the umbrella term *transgender* meant. The teachers really appreciated this as it isn't the kind of thing that's talked about in professional settings. I felt it was important for my colleagues to know that not everyone connects with the body they were born into. More importantly though, I feel that children should learn about the range of diversity in the world, that includes transgender as well as cisgender.

As a teacher in this position, I struggled with how much I really wanted to be 'out' at work. This was especially true when I had not yet started my medical transition. I am currently in a new job that I came to after just before starting hormones and having surgery, physically changing in front of my colleagues to whom I was introduced as male. When I began the job, some of my colleagues questioned my age and identity. Never directly to me, but with my administrators. They wanted to be respectful (or that was what I was told). I had several meetings and wondered, "Do I need to come out? Does this distract from my work?" Weighing these questions I had an open conversation with my administration. We decided that no one needed to know about my past. Their curiosity and wanting to be respectful would slow down with time. And it did. I have changed visibly in front of my colleagues, students, and parents. The first year of medical intervention was drastic for me. My voice dropped dramatically, creating awkwardness when I tried to speak loudly. More than once I had a random SQUEAK come out. I learned to control my voice and be mindful of my volume. Students sometimes made observations from the first year to my second. Some would say, "You look different; not in a bad way, just different." These observations are interesting, but even without intervention the students didn't question me before hormone therapy.

I have a small group of colleagues who are good

friends outside of work that I have let in to this part of my life. This helps me to have an outlet if needed at work. These individuals have embraced this information as information not shared and understand that I have unique challenges, but don't expect to be treated any differently. For me it is important to have privacy with everyone I choose. It is my decision to disclose my past. I'm not ashamed and will not deny my past, but instead choose carefully how and with whom I share it. I have 'grown' into myself. I have more confidence and don't really think about who I am anymore. I am there and doing my job.

I am lucky to have had a positive experience in my workplace. I approached coming out in an open and honest way, and was firm about negotiating my own terms. This is <u>my</u> life and <u>my</u> career. When I look back now, it was important to be clear about what I wanted, set boundaries, and have a few people close to me in that setting to discuss anything that might arise. As I walk down the hallways now, I am myself. My colleagues, the students and administration respect me. I am me.

Rae Larson

Growing up, nothing remained constant except two things; my gender confusion and the overwhelming need to obtain my father's approval. Everything else was constantly evolving and changing around me. I grew up in a military home. My father was in the Air Force. When I was in middle school and high school, I began to brainstorm what my dreams for college and a career might look like. My dad was constantly telling me to join the military—they would provide me with school money and a stable lifestyle. It was the logical option. But as a teenager, I was the furthest thing from logical. Against my father's wishes, I ended up graduating high school a year early and attending film school. This, however, lasted a grand total of two weeks.

Upon returning home from my two weeks away, I began attending a local community college, racking up more and more debt. My dad continued to breathe down my neck about finances, my dead-end job, and other questionable life choices like my sexuality and gender expression. I tried so hard to ignore his constant lectures. I made every attempt to suppress my need to win over my father's approval, but there was nothing in my life that seemed to make him happy. On top of that, I was completely unhappy. So, on a random day in October, I decided I was going to join the military.

At the time, "Don't Ask, Don't Tell" was not repealed and I was not looking forward to being closeted, but I saw no other option. On January 5, 2010, I was introduced to my drill sergeant's spit and the bed I would sleep in for the next sixty days at Basic Training in Lackland Air Force Base, Texas. In a short eight and a half-week span, I was completely transformed from an individual with aspirations and dreams into a military machine. I woke up "Air Force," lived "Air Force," and went to sleep "Air Force." It had completely consumed every inch of my being. At one point, I had even decided it made sense for homosexuals to have to serve in secret. I took on the Air Force as my opinion, emotion, expression, and lifestyle. That's what the military wants from you. When you go, they force you to leave yourself at the gates. It worked on me, at least at first.

I remember when I had my military life plans and goals all laid out in front of me. I knew what I had to do in order to make my promotions on time, excel in my work, and embody the values of my military. I was ready to dedicate a minimum of twenty years to "my country." I was actively forfeiting my values and feeling good about it. I was dead set on giving all my time and energy to the military.

Then, shortly before "Don't Ask, Don't Tell" was repealed, things at work started going south. While I was following all the rules and busting my ass to show how dedicated I was, leadership was still trying to find faults in me. It took multiple incidents for me to start realizing that the military wasn't as perfect as it all seemed in my head.

After the repeal, I heard a lot of opinions among my military brethren. Nasty, awful opinions. There were no attempts to censor the harsh, homophobic comments by any rank, branch, generation, and background. People were throwing out harsh and bitter opinions as if they didn't care who heard. At this point, not only was my hard work being ignored, but apparently, some of my peers would have rather had me thrown out than be allowed to breathe the same air as them. The imperfections of my military life immediately started steamrolling out of the shadows.

After "Don't Ask, Don't Tell" was appealed, it was nice to be able to talk freely about my life without the worry of being punished. I never realized how much fear I harbored until after I was finally allowed to discuss the types of people I dated. About four months after "Don't Ask, Don't Tell" was repealed, I came to terms with my trans identity. When people learn new things about themselves, it's really easy to start seeing the ripple effect it will have on the rest of their lives. I started worrying about my friends, family, daily interactions, but also about the security of my job.

The military views transgender individuals as being mentally unstable and "unfit for duty." Transgender people are not allowed to join the military (unless they hide their identity very well and have not undergone any medical transition) and they can be discharged under any category (medical, less than honorable, dishonorable, etc.) that leadership deems appropriate.

It was really rough, spending so much time in an extremely gendered environment. Everyone is expected to use "sir" and "ma'am" while also keeping the two distinctly disconnected from each other. For example, men will typically be expected to have certain responsibilities at work, while women have different responsibilities. It's just the way the military runs. I started having traumatic panic attacks at work and feeling stressed out all the time. My biological sex was constantly being shoved in my face, which wreaked turmoil on my emotion so early in my gender discovery process. At that point, I turned to the only place I knew: the base's mental health office.

I walked in nervous and terrified. The therapists at military health offices are required to tell the patient's leadership if there are any signs of complications that would make a patient unfit for duty. Technically, my story could fall under that category. I sat down with a nurse before I talked to a therapist. She "analyzed" the emotional struggles I was having so she could pair me with the right therapist. At first, I was hesitant and vague. Then, out of nowhere, my worries, fears, and stresses just poured out of me. I spilled my guts out to her. When I finally stopped, she said, "You know, you aren't the first person to come in here feeling this way. We definitely have someone here who can work with you." I immediately felt safe and hopeful. I truly believed I had made the right choice in coming to that clinic.

They brought me to another room and I sat with the licensed therapist. She asked me why I was there and I immediately began spilling my heart out to her as well. When I had said everything there was to say, she looked at me for a really long time. The creases in her forehead told me she was struggling to think of what to say. She took a deep breath, looked deep into my eyes and said, "How long have you liked women?" I immediately regretted my choice of coming to the clinic. I said, "I'm sorry?" She paused again and then said, "Sometimes it can be difficult for women who like women." I just nodded my head in agreement until my time was up and then never went back.

It was clear to me that I wouldn't find any help or support on base, so I started looking into other options. The military controlled everything. My health insurance was through them so I couldn't use it without them knowing what it was for. I decided my only option was to pay completely out of pocket.

I started going to an off-base therapist and general practitioner to receive adequate support. It was very expensive and time consuming. All the while, I couldn't help but resent my employer more and more. I needed them. I needed the support and guidance of the job that had become my life and I had no one there to turn to. I had given the Air Force my commitment and my dedication. I had sacrificed so much—my real dreams, my personal life, and much more. All of that and in return, those I worked for basically told me, "Sorry your life is so difficult but we don't really care."

The two years I continued to serve in the military after acknowledging my gender identity were the most difficult years of my life thus far. Not only did I have to fend for myself while coming out, social and medically transitioning, and learning to navigate brand-new environments but I was also still forced to live my life and work in a gender that never felt right. I was trapped in the closet without the possibility of liberation from the contract. An employer I had given up so much for was ostracizing me and there was no option in the matter.

When I started hormones and things began to change, I got a lot of questions. Thanks to HIPPA, there was only so much I *had* to provide. I had some very close calls with the one year I spent on hormones in the military. I know quite a few people who have been discharged from the military for being transgender. I like to think I was more fortunate, but when I really think about it, was I? Was I really fortunate to be spending so much time under emotional turmoil, forced to submit and subject myself to unnecessary emotional bondage? I left the military after my four-year contract was up, under my own terms, and honorably but the painful memories will linger forever. I hope and pray that one day I'll watch the military make a statement that transgender individuals can serve openly. But for now, there is nothing there for transgender people. There is no support system, nowhere to turn, and no escape from the mistreatment. The oppression is real and the idea of the military being there for all of its employees is false.

Emmett Lundberg

I have been a freelancer for the seven and a half years since I graduated from college. This kind of work offers its own struggles, but it has a number of perks. While I don't have the traditional "safety" of a steady nine-to-five job (I say safety loosely because I feel like that is not necessarily true for anyone given the economic state of our country), I am able to be much more in control of my time. I decide what jobs I will take and what time I will take off to work on projects that are emotionally fulfilling.

First and foremost, I am a writer. Communicating via the written word is what I excel at. But I live in New York and I've still got hefty bills to pay, so my day job is that of a production assistant for the Film & Television industry. I am lucky. I have been lucky to be able to sustain myself with work in my field, even if it is not necessarily what I ultimately want to be doing. I found great people to work alongside and have been with them for several years now.

Before I delve completely into what my transition experience has been like at work, I want to talk about something I have not yet reconciled with emotionally. As I said, I have been very lucky with the work that I have had. Part of that work means that my name is credited for almost every movie I've worked on. You know when you're in the theatre and the credits roll at the end of the movie? If you stay and watch them, that's where my name would be. So my old name, my birth name, is out there in the film world, many times over, for eternity. Well, for physical and digital eternity, I suppose. It is not something I feel disturbed by but there is a part of me that wishes it could be changed. I have the power to change all the important documents in my life, my social security, my driver's license, passport, even birth certificate, but I cannot change the credits of all those movies. Not only is it about changing the name in the credits for some personal comfort but how do I explain my work history to potential new employers without outing myself in every situation? Now that I've written this out, I see that this one piece is just as integral a part of my transition experience at work as everything else.

When I decided to start hormones, I was working on a short-lived TV show. When I made the appointment for my first shot, it wasn't clear whether we would be working on a half season or a full season, depending on studio approval, so there was a discrepancy of three months. I wanted to start hormones desperately but was also worried about transitioning in the middle of a job. A luxury of my work life is being able to have months off in between jobs and for the beginning of my physical transition, this felt comforting. I jokingly wonder if my wish to not transition on the job was what caused the show to be canceled after airing only two episodes. I can't possibly have that kind of power. Or can I? I was only two weeks on T when we were out the door and I had a substantial four months off before I would have to go on to my next job, which would be the first one presenting full time as male.

I told the co-workers I was closest to individually before I started any medical transition. Everyone was supportive and even worked to use only a shortened version of my birth name since I was not completely out yet. I did not feel that this changed how they felt about me as a person or a fellow co-worker. I am thankful for that.

Since I freelance, I do not have the protection of a central human resources department for something like this. Coming out was and continues to be on me. That has been both freeing and frustrating. There are definitely times that I wish I were able to have one coming out at work and be done with it, but it's not that simple. Let's just say that every job has 200 people. While these people are not always the same, crews tend to stick together and you can end up working with people you've worked with years before.

The trickiness of my situation became quite apparent in the first job I took after starting my transition, about four months after I started hormones. Initially, I was quite pleased that I was read as male, despite the short time I had been on testosterone. There were a handful of people that I had worked with prior to transition on that job. Those in my department already knew about my transition and were on board. There was a woman in a different department whom I knew from a previous job, and with whom I was going to be working closely. I had emailed her about my transition many months before, not knowing we would be working together in the near future. Before I was on the job, she seemed to be all good with it. When I started working with her, it was another story.

Since I was still early in my physical transition, I was not as confident as I am now and I struggled more when people misgendered me. The first week was rough. There were countless name and pronoun slip-ups. I wasn't sure I would be able to continue with the job, which put me in a very difficult place. I needed the work since it had been several months since my previous job. Emotionally, I felt as if I was going to war every day. I was constantly on edge, readying myself for a female pronoun directed at me or a slip in my name, which both seemed to happen often that week. It was draining and my inability to focus on the job was hurting my productivity. While all the people I had just met had no issues, when this woman would err in front of them, I felt it diminished me and my identity. When my frustration was at its worst, I corrected her heatedly in front of our colleagues. I had to stand up for myself. I was the only one who was going to.

After that week, I emailed her personally, letting her know how hard her inability to use the correct language had been for me. I told her that if there was anything I could do to help her make the switch, to please let me know. She responded diplomatically and appropriately and we worked to move forward. She became fine with my new name after another couple weeks; it was just the pronouns that continued to be an issue. She explained to me that it was harder for her when talking to people we both knew previously. I tried to understand while still being firm in what I needed to feel emotionally safe. I am thankful that for the most part her pronoun slips in front of the people I had just met did not seem to have an effect.

Additionally, there was a guy coming onto the job at a later point that I had worked with a little over a year prior. I knew he was starting so I emailed him directly to fill him in on my transition. I have found this strategy to be helpful. If I know I will be working on a job with someone whom I have not seen since transitioning, I reach out to them and explain what has gone on. Therefore, I'm kind of in this continual coming out process, which makes it difficult for me to move forward at times. I often wonder if I might one day feel the urge to change career paths so as to start all over.

On the other hand, I do not feel as if I have faced any sort of discrimination in the work environment because of my trans identity. My field is not a conservative one and while it does tend to be one which sometimes feeds on gossip, I say, go ahead, tell so and so I'm on my way to manhood! It's one less person I have to personally come out to.

I have had two other short jobs after that one and on both of them I was able to be stealth, which was a completely new experience for me. The first was a commercial, which even though it is in the same realm as the film and TV world, for the most part, the crews are totally separate. I heard about the job on a list serve and was hired based solely on my resume—something that felt great. It was my body of previous work that spoke for who I was as a production assistant and that was it. I was brought on the second and last day of shooting and was there mostly to help move furniture and other items. It was a physical job and now, being read fully as male, I felt a new pressure to be able to lift and carry certain things. I don't think I am a weak person physically, and never have been, so it was strange to now feel this expectation. I know I was only putting it on myself and yet it was still there. I had to act in a certain way to make sure they did not misgender me. Even though a stranger or a new acquaintance has not misgendered me in well over eight months, I still fear it. Though I know it seems ridiculous, I'm afraid they will look into my eyes and see something, something "female."

The other job I had since medically transitioning was also quite physical. It was a lot of packing and moving small items and boxes at a prop house that was moving to a bigger warehouse space. While I still felt some of that pressure to be able to show a certain amount of muscle, it was less so on this job. Instead, I had another experience that was a new one to me in my transition. Most of the other people they had hired to help out with the move were female identified and while it was easy to get along with them, I caught myself a few times before sharing something that I felt would have either confused them or gave them some inside information into my gender identity. There was a specific interaction where an older French woman asked about the origin of my name. "What does it mean?" She asked. Not wanting to out myself in that moment, I gave some answer about my parents being Swedish. I had chosen a name that had the same meaning as my birth name, "Universal," because that was one of the reasons my parents gave it to me. This must have made sense to her because she replied, "Yes! You look like a Viking!" Okay, thank you?

I do not think there will be a time when I am ever completely stealth, but upon first meeting people, I am not one to spill my whole life story, transition or otherwise, so it's nice to know I have some flexibility there. I will continue to judge each situation as it is presented and work my way forward from there.

## Jack Elliott

I was raised with the notion that work was what one must *do* but a very separate thing from dreams or goals. This was my family's middle-class ethos built from fear and a long history of underachievement. It seemed safe and typical. I found safety in knowing I would be in the crowd held shoulder to shoulder with limited movement. There was no direct line that could be drawn toward success from any particular set of actions of my own doing. Achieving something great seemed the work of divine intervention or some such other. It appeared to me that adulthood was just a mere set of circumstances that one was dealt. There used to be this chest at school and during recess everyone would pick an item like a stethoscope for a nurse, or a hat for a fire fighter. I thought that was how life worked, you pick your prop from a few pre-chosen items, and you went about your business.

### 1991

I had my first real job as a legal secretary for a law firm when I was nineteen. I took a semester off, and I told myself with staunch conviction that I would go back to school at night. I convinced my not-yet-adult brain that this was only temporary. I swayed back and forth on the train with the adults in a sea of beige coats and commuting sneakers. I ordered the biggest coffee with two sugars I could hold with my one free hand, and hung on for dear life with the other.

I took to the rituals rather quickly, and in one year's time I was barely recognizable as the child I still was. There was something soothing about the routine of it, and being able to hide in plain sight. I soon made the decision that I would go to law school. I didn't really want to be a lawyer, but it sounded so far off in the distance and far fetched that it made the present safe and doable. Everything seemed palatable, just as long as I was *going* to law school some day. The first step towards a pattern was forming, and I wasn't even aware. The act of coming up with a plan meant I never really had to go through with any of it. It was used to ward off any truth seekers.

The halls of my life were lined in taupe with speckled gray carpet of an office building. Giant conference room tables showed me a reflection of this new person. I weaved in and out of cubicles in an inexpensive pantsuit, making small talk with ease. I was learning how to use my words. Office politics much like high school came easy to me. I obediently lunched with new friends in the break room as days crashed into months and met each other in the middle.

The future has a clever way of showing up eventually. If you make a plan she will come to collect, and you'd better be prepared to deliver or run. I ran. It was an unidentified and unrelenting feeling that something was wrong and it felt as uncomfortable as it did familiar. The pangs began like the beginning of an arthritic knee, but soon became louder and all consuming. A succession of jobs followed, and as it seemed nothing I did was on purpose. All was not completely lost, I developed a quit wit and a wild sense of resourcefulness. But I just kept tripping backwards into the next phase. The restlessness would always come back. My future just kept coming to collect, and I wasn't ready to pay.

## 2006

New England, an Ivy League campus, and the smell of old library. I tucked myself into the literary criticism section deep in the balcony. I read, I wrote, and I hid somewhat defiantly. I listened to my music so loud through my earphones some Waspy kid actually threw a pencil at me so I'd turn it down. I was in my thirties, and my in-between gendered self made me not only androgynous, but somehow ageless amidst the undergrads. After making the decision to transition I knew an exit from New York City was best. I couldn't reconcile myself with the thought of changing in such tiny increments. The first year was peppered with cockeyed looks from everyone. I needed to put some distance between me, and who I was to become. I didn't yet know who that would be, and so the chance to hold it in secrecy made sense at the time. Being in a relationship with someone getting a Master's degree, and the need to get out of New York led me north.

As much as I would have taken to a life of leisure I ran out of money. Six months into my transition I had to get a job as my disappearing female self. I wasn't strong enough to tell anyone I was transitioning so I used my old resume, and my old body to get work. It felt like the prostitution of my soul.

I began to uncover some aspects of my personality I had never put into context before. Even though I wasn't supposed to be in my female body, I knew how to operate it. I understood the social cues, and had been trained over a lifetime of what was expected of me. I was now slowly handing away piece by piece the armor I had built for survival. In its place was this androgynous person unaware of how to move or act. I hadn't planned on ever being my old self again, and this felt like an exercise in cruelty. I was forced to deal with the fact that poor planning, and some ill-timed decisions led me here with very little support financially or otherwise. The vulnerability and exposure I felt was unparalleled to me at that point in my life. I had no anchor to tie it down and make sense of it.

I had always been affable at work, likeable, and easy to get along with. Now I felt as if I was wearing an ill-fitting suit. I was quiet, unsure of myself, and barely spoke to anyone. On my very first day at an Ivy League school I had my own office, and a quiet little breakdown. I was told that in order to get an outside line I had to dial nine. My hands were shaking so badly I dialed 911 by mistake. I was forced to explain to the emergency operator that I was not being held against my will, I was not under any kind of duress but in fact was just very, very nervous on my first day of work. Disaster.

I twisted and turned in my chair trying to get

comfortable. I hated sitting down because my body seemed to be taking on an entirely new shape. I was now thick and square. I was equally uncomfortable standing because I had no idea how to hold my angular body. My short hair now swept its way around my head in a pattern I did not understand. I remember staring into the mirror in the ladies room to see if I could wish a full-grown beard to appear during my break and put end to all of it. I planned to have the job just long enough to pay off some bills before anyone would realize my secret. The pulleys and levers of my body creaked up and down like a machine and I had lost the manual. I was convinced everyone could smell this lie on me like a foul odor. Inside my mind two genders were fighting for the same space.

Every day one of the male employees would come into the room and say, "Hey, ladies," in a sing-songy voice. He just hovered there waiting for my response. My rage towards him was entirely misdirected, but I had no other viable outlet. He sang at me, and I loathed him.

At the end of work each day I would shed my pseudo-feminine clothes and try to resume my other life. I wondered what would happen if I would have just told the truth? Would I have been strong enough to be *seen* through the transition? I wish I'd had a support system to help me not see this as a shameful secret.

As it turned out I wasn't strong enough to see it through. I left New England broken, and headed safely back into the arms of New York and the friends I had learned to call home. I soon began the search for a new job. First came the wardrobe. My body now ten months on hormones was still a strange and gangly creature to me. I poured it into a suit and hoped people would just look past my man-child awkwardness. Shirts looked strange buttoned around my neck. My shoulders were slight, and didn't quite live up to their role inside the jacket. I worked tirelessly to synchronize my thoughts with my movements and hoped everything lined up properly. I prayed for normal eye contact during interviews, which didn't happen often. But I kept going back. I pushed through the sideways glances until I had the strength to stare in return.

I watched as my neck and my shoulders began to fill out my jacket. As the years went on, I focused on what it was I was good at, and I got better. My body and my mind were finally running parallel. The relationship I had with my old self began to fall away.

Eli Bradford

I have been working at the same company for seven years. I spend my workdays in a corporate environment where I feared I wouldn't be accepted because of my dyke-like appearance. I have super short hair, I don't wear make-up (unless original flavored Chapstick, that I keep in my back pocket along with my wallet, falls into that category), and I tend to wear oversized boy clothes to conceal my feminine curves whenever possible. My intention when I was hired was not to pull a bait and switch on my colleagues, but the more I come to think of it, I may be guilty of just that.

In the fall of 2006, I was desperate for a job and health insurance. An opportunity in a fancy office became available, but I wasn't sure I wanted to work in that kind of an environment. Wants aside, I knew it would be foolish not to try. My mother and my friends, mostly lesbians, told me that if I wanted to get the job, I needed to look "professional." They told me to suck it up and dress for success. Eventually, they convinced me to wear a "women's" power suit, no matter how awkward it felt. Well, it wasn't my idea of dressing for success, but according to today's societal standards, it was the way to make a best impression. Therefore, I conformed.

I would have much preferred wearing a man's suit and tie, but that's not the way things work in this day and age. So, I broke down and pretended to be somebody that I wasn't in an attempt to get hired. It was an ideal look for any woman in corporate America. But I've never fit into a female category. Although I've always interviewed well, my confidence was compromised this time because I was physically and emotionally uncomfortable being dressed up in a fitted women's outfit. Despite this, I was offered the job and accepted it.

I knew that starting in this company meant I needed to go shopping for women's business clothing. And as hard as it was to spend money that I didn't have on clothing that I didn't want to wear, it was imperative that I do it…or so I thought. I managed to dress the part for several months. Had fridays not been a dedicated "jeans day," I may have broken down sooner. I essentially didn't leave my desk Monday through Thursday unless absolutely necessary. Wearing jeans opened up a world of loose collared shirts, undershirts, and tight fitting sports bras, which allowed me to cover up my body, and my breasts. Fridays were different; no longer dressed in what felt like a costume, I was free to be myself the last day of every week.

I eventually ventured out of our little department to the other side of the building, and discovered others like myself but who were dressed in masculine attire. Were they tomboys, lesbians, trans-guys? I wasn't sure, but I was very excited to know that if others were dressing that way, then I could get away with wearing men's business clothes as well. The next day, I tried it out. It didn't take long before my manager commented, "Why don't you wear a pretty blouse to work?"

Damn, what a nerve!

I snapped back, "Why don't YOU wear a blouse?!"

I regretted my comments pretty quickly, not because I got into trouble, but because I knew that my manager, long past retirement age, was very old fashioned. Thankfully, he was hard of hearing too. I may have lucked out there—I would have been really bummed out if I got fired for my impulsive comment. Regardless of his opinion, I continued to dress the way I wanted. It felt really nice to just be myself.

Last spring, all employees were required to attend a sexual harassment and discrimination orientation. This is when I learned Gender Identity had been added to the list of people protected under Massachusetts' law. I couldn't take my eyes of the PowerPoint slideshow projected on the overhead, not sure if my eyes were playing tricks on me. I kept re-reading it over and over again. Wow, I thought to myself. If people who don't identify with the gender they were assigned at birth are protected under law, then my job should be secure if I decided to transition. For the first time, I felt I didn't need to hide anymore. Being transgender was okay, and it was becoming more accepted not only in society, but within the workforce as well.

It took me a couple of months to make a realistic

plan (i.e., name change, hormones, surgery, etc.) and find the strength to share this information about myself to my employer. I first told my manager because she is like family to me. I asked her if we could talk, and we sat down in the main kitchen. I spoke candidly, and she listened. Her response was: if transitioning will make you happy, then I am happy for you. I went to human resources next, wanting confirmation that if I transitioned on the job, my job would be secure. Their response "of course." The owner of the company offered his support as well as the general counsel and said the company was behind me 100%. They've known me as a loyal, dedicated, and respected employee for years, and that's whom I'll stay even after transitioning.

I will always be me, just a more comfortable, confident version of me in my own skin. I understand it's not every day someone tells you that they are going to switch genders. So, I tip my hat to my company and colleagues for handling the situation with such grace.

Gabriel Pelz

Transitioning on the job has been, and continues to be, one of the most challenging aspects of my transition. I work as a cook at a restaurant. With the responsibilities I have as a single parent, it takes courage every day to stand up with pride and absorb the negative, discriminatory comments some of my co-workers continue to make.

I've been working at this restaurant for seven years. They claim to be a "Christian Establishment," but are far from that. The two owners are sisters and work beside us every day. They are polar opposites in demeanor. Judy is very down to earth and I knew her prior to my employment at the restaurant; Tina is holier-than-thou and judges everyone. Since it's a small company, there is no HR to go to if you have a complaint. After making the decision to begin medical transition and informing my family, work was the next place I needed to come out. I couldn't risk losing my job because of my responsibilities.

I decided to talk with Judy first, hoping that she would be understanding and keep the information to herself for a while. Judy didn't understand at all, but by the end of the conversation she assured me that there would be no judgment. I asked her not to tell my other boss because I was worried about her reaction. I walked away feeling okay about the situation. I knew I still had a job and someone who would be aware of why some changes were happening. After that I felt comfortable coming out to a few co-workers. Things were going okay, but I could still sense that something changed as I did.

One day while I was cooking I heard Tina walk in the kitchen and say loudly, "I don't care what she changes her name to, I will never call her by it." I knew they were talking about me, but I just kept my mouth shut.

Bashing the LGBTQ community among others was a common practice at the restaurant. Pushing my head down and getting my work done was all I could do. I felt betrayed, Judy, or one of my other co-workers, must have told Tina about my transition. I legally changed my name in November of 2013, but at work, my paycheck is the only thing that has been changed. I walk in the door and am greeted daily by a mix of my old name as well as Gabe.

Over time, things have gotten worse. The comments have become more blatant. We often discuss our goals and dream jobs. I shared that my mother always wanted to work on a cruise ship. Tina came up really close to me and said, "If my daughter told me she wanted to be a boy I would run as far away as I could, too." I felt so hurt and upset. Later that day Judy walked out to my car with me, so I told her what happened. She said, "Tina has a point, and you have a daughter to think about." She continued on to say that I'm making a hard life harder for both my daughter and myself. I wish I had some protection to defend myself, but I'm stuck being at the whim of these two sisters.

The final straw came when I received a phone call at work. The boss' niece answered and she yelled my birth name through the kitchen in order to get me to pick up. "Who did they ask for?" I asked. "Gabe, but I told them, 'No you can talk to [birth name] though.'" I was furious when I hung up the phone. I asked her not to do that anymore. After I walked away she told her friends how it makes her so mad when people call me Gabe, and she used God to justify why it makes her mad. That was it—I couldn't take it any longer. After three years of medically transitioning, and more than a year after legally changing my name, I finally made up my mind that I needed to have a frank conversation with my bosses about being called by MY name at work. There have been others at work that went by nicknames. Why couldn't I be called my legal name? Judy and Tina explained to me that they simply didn't want to make others feel uncomfortable. They have and continue to do everything in their power to deny me being who I am, including "correcting" my friends when they call me Gabe.

I was so fed up that I finally sought help from the Transgender Law Center (TLC). Within a week I was contacted by one of their employees and I let them know how I was being treated at work. Since I live in Georgia, I figured I had no rights, but that wasn't true at all. They emailed me a lot of helpful information to give to my bosses. After talking to TLC I decided not to proceed with anything legal, because my mother worked for the same restaurant, and I couldn't risk both of us losing our jobs. I thought maybe I would try to talk to the sisters first. I returned to work armed with information and ready to demand respect. I told my colleagues to call me Gabe. Most of them were very respectful, but some were scared of the owners.

A new job is a must for me. They will never come around or accept me for the person that I am. All they feel is that I have sinned and they do not see how happy I am with everything but my job. It has been hard holding in how I feel, but I have to because my daughter Rye comes first.

Ian Carter

Growing up in my family, education and career were extremely important. Success was measured by your ability to become something great. This often meant, "become something that gives you bragging rights," not necessarily something where you make an actual real-world difference. T would be good, too, as long as you could brag about it. No pressure, right?

The whole "transitioning" thing was unattainable in my mind as a young adult just out of college. At that time, I settled for a butch lesbian identity, which was challenging enough in the work place. Interview performance anxiety aside, my appearance was not up to society's standards of what a female *should* look like. It turned employers off; I could sense it during the interviews. My mom, a butch lesbian herself, even encouraged me to grow my hair out and dress more like a woman. She would say, "I'm just trying to make things easier for you." That was definitely NOT going to happen. I have a horrible taste in my mouth just typing those words out. As a butch I faced a lot of difficulties getting new jobs. I didn't even want to apply for the jobs I truly desired because I was so afraid of rejection. After being let go from a job on my career path because I "didn't fit in with the others" due to my appearance and "lesbian lifestyle," I expected nothing less from any other employer. I finally settled on retail jobs where my appearance didn't seem to play a part.

The retail world was very accepting of me as a lesbian. I owned that role, they seemed to respect it, and I became pretty comfortable working in that realm. For the moment it was safe, though I knew I would eventually need to move on to something "bigger and better" to appease my parents, which made the thought of actually transitioning seem impossible. I was expected to succeed and to become something great.

In my mind, transitioning to male would be a hindrance to advancing my career, so, on the side, unbeknownst to anyone; I spent hours at night writing full screenplays (compared to the shorter screenplays I wrote as a teenager). I fantasized about being the next big thing, making millions of dollars by directing and acting in these roles that truly represented who I was. Eventually, even that dream faded away into the dark abyss of unrealized potential. There I was, once again, settling for a life that made me miserable with not even a dream to turn to. On the outside at least, people accepted the facade. I did my best to "be okay" with this choice, but again, I knew it wouldn't last forever.

I always had a strong interest in psychology, particularly because I battled my own mental health issues and it felt fitting to pursue this path. Going into it, I thought maybe I could save somebody from him or herself; somebody who was in so much pain they wanted to end it. Maybe I could be someone's guiding light out of the darkness. What I didn't know was that that person would be me.

In 2007 I enrolled in a Masters in Psychology program at Chapman University. I spent the next four years of my postgraduate program being the token LGBTQ person in my classes; standing up for "my" community, giving us a voice in the mental health field, and educating others about sexuality and gender. By taking the time to research and learn different terms and concepts around sexuality and gender, I was not only educating them, but I was educating myself. I think if I took anything from those four years, it was learning who I was, and realizing I wasn't alone. I still wasn't ready to make any decisions about transitioning, but I was beginning to accept that maybe I would survive if I ever did decide to go through with it.

After four years, I completed my postgraduate courses, finished my practicum at a partial hospitalization program, passed my oral exam (which I failed the first time due to that damn performance anxiety of mine!), and passed the written exam. FINALLY! I graduated with my Masters in Psychology with an emphasis in Marriage and Family Therapy. I registered with the Board of Behavioral Sciences in order to receive my registered intern number and began looking for jobs. Within three months I was hired as a Personal Services Coordinator (a fancy term for "case manager") at one of the Wellness Centers for the non-profit agency at which I am still working.

After a couple of months with the agency and positive feedback aimed at me, I learned that my boss was retiring. Co-workers encouraged me to apply for her position, although I felt nowhere near ready for that sort responsibility. I was still new at this job and considered "green" in this field! Because of the continued external pressure, I went for it. I applied for the position. Soon after receiving my application, one of the directors of the agency questioned my motivation for applying, as I had just graduated and was not even licensed yet. In reality they had already found someone they wanted to hire for the position, but he said he would be willing to interview me anyway, if I really wanted it. Completely embarrassed about the whole ordeal, I withdrew my application. I'm glad I did; the woman they hired as my new boss would turn out to be my saving grace and the motivation I needed to move forward with my transition despite the fears I had of losing my job and "ruining my life."

The moment I saw my new boss walk through the door, I knew she had been put in my life for a reason. We developed a close relationship through our supervision meetings and our time working together. I would find myself confiding in her about my depression and gender dysphoria. She made me feel safe and comfortable enough to continue to come to her. There wasn't a single act that convinced me to move forward; it was just her being there and accepting me for who I was that made me feel like transitioning could be a reality.

After seven months at one of the agency's Wellness Centers, I was offered a job at the main office as a case manager for a homeless outreach program. Aware of my own experience with homelessness, they thought I would be a perfect fit. I remained in contact with the boss I had at the Wellness Center throughout the next ten months, and I continued to confide in her about my battle with my gender dysphoria. She supported me and made me feel loved and accepted as a transgender person. Unfortunately, she was fighting her own personal battles and decided to move back to Minnesota to find refuge with her family. The one person who I really felt knew me and accepted me was now gone. It was in November of 2012 that I found myself once again in a deep depression; drinking more than a bottle of wine alone each night. As the days and nights passed and the wine bottles stacked up, I realized that continuing down this path would be very difficult to return from, if ever, and I needed to make a decision. My life depended on it.

I started planning how to make this transition feasible. First, I decided I would tell people that I was going to start seeing a therapist to talk about the possibility of transitioning to male. Then, I began planning who I was going to tell first and when I was going to tell them. If anyone asked why, I figured that was easy enough; I would just tell them the damn truth. Encouraged by the fuzzy feelings of wine and Indian food, the first people I decided to tell were my then roommate and her boyfriend. They both work at the same non-profit agency as I do, just in a different program, so I had planned that they would be the first to know. I felt close to them, and figured I could get a feel for how other people at the agency might respond based on their reactions. Thankfully, it went over very well. Then, I told my close friends Beth and Dan over

Thanksgiving. Beth and I became close friends during postgraduate school. I was pretty sure they would be accepting, especially Beth since she knew how much I spoke on sexuality and gender in our classes and I figured she wouldn't be all that surprised by my confession. Plus, I felt if I lost my job over this process, I knew they would be there to help me get through it. They're like family and I knew I could count on them.

Excellent. I now had people who knew about me "possibly" transitioning and were accepting and supportive. What next? It was time to make this transition happen. I confided in the human resources woman at work, and sure enough, she supported me 100%, offering to help in anyway she could to create a safe environment for me. I told my clinical supervisor, as well as my direct supervisor who were also both supportive and proud of my decision. Finally, I met with the Directors of the entire agency and told them what I had planned for the New Year, as well as what they could expect to happen with me (i.e. HRT, emotional, mental, and physical changes, etc.). With everyone's support, we started planning how I was going to tell my clients, and they asked if there was anything they could do to make the transition less frightening for me in the workplace. I was completely blessed and amazed by the support I received.

I asked that they not start calling me by my chosen male name until I came out to the rest of my co-workers and clients, and to let me come out to my clients on my own terms and at my own pace; they agreed. I also felt it was important to make everyone aware that I would still be using the women's restroom at this point because I felt more comfortable with it. Something about accidentally seeing my male co-workers' and/or clients' penises or making them uncomfortable in any sort of way frightened me! The directors offered to make the multiple stall restrooms unisex, but I declined because I felt it was too much change and possible awkwardness for people to handle over one person transitioning. I told them I would figure that part out as the transition went on. It's been a year now, though, and I still haven't figured that restroom part out.

Honestly, during this first year of work and transition, each day just seems like any other; except everyone calls me Ian instead of Kirsten now. My clients have a difficult time remembering to use the right pronouns. Sometimes I correct them, other times I don't. My co-workers usually get the pronouns right, but if they don't, they correct themselves almost immediately. I still use the women's restroom, but now I get the, "Why are you still coming in HERE?" along with a laugh. The idea of making the other guys uncomfortable with me being in the men's restroom makes me uncomfortable. Plus, there are male clients at that office that don't know I'm transitioning because they're not *my* clients, and I don't feel comfortable telling them my business. The women (mostly co-workers) I give my reasoning to seem to understand. However, now I'm seeing that I might actually be making the women uncomfortable by being in their restroom, which is an interesting twist for me as I used to be one of them. So, yes, I'm still working on that one. I also feel that having breasts is a huge mental block for me when it comes to using the men's restroom at work. Whether they can see them or not, I know they're there, and it just makes me feel completely out of sorts when I go into the men's restroom. One human act that should be so simple, going to the restroom, has become my biggest challenge in the workplace. I believe strongly, however, that once my surgeries are complete, I will feel confident enough to go into the men's restroom at work without difficulties. Patience, my dear co-workers, patience! Patience and understanding that choosing a restroom is not nearly as simple for me as it seems it should be.

I've been blessed to have an employer that prides itself on the diversity of its employees. In fact, a person who was hired a few months ago has been watching me as I work through my transition and has decided to begin transitioning as well. She confided in me that she is genderqueer (does not identify as either female or male but prefers female pronouns) and said she almost got top surgery at one point but didn't have the guts to follow through with it, losing thousands of dollars in the process. She said it was when she started watching me go through my process that she began to consider it again. I'm happy that she can go through this process in this work environment. They've been more than supportive and accommodating around my doctor appointments and the occasional need for a mental health day, as I am sure they will be with her, too.

Even though I had to endure years of severe depression, suicidal ideation, and extreme fear around making the decision to be who I was born to be, looking back on it, I see that everything fell into place when, where, and exactly how it was meant to. I wouldn't change any of it. Everything in my past has led me up to this moment. And up to this moment, I've been lucky enough to have the opportunity to transition to male while working in a career field in which I can use my experiences to make a difference in someone's life. Through this process transitioning in the mental health field, I've come to learn to not be proud of what I do or earn for a living, but to be proud of my ability to overcome the darkest hours in my life and turn them into a beacon of light for someone else who is suffering. My job now is only the beginning, a bright one at that. One day I plan to have my own practice working with LGBTQ people so that maybe I can help each client I see from becoming a statistic, just like my old boss helped me. Life can and does get better; everyone should have a chance to experience that.

# EPILOGUE

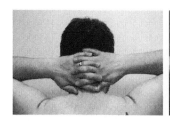

We all want to live happily. We all want the freedom to be ourselves and to be loved for it. I don't think living as a transgender man is really all that different from our cisgender brothers and sisters, or our transgender sisters for that matter. Our path may be one that is fraught with intense physical transformation, but the deepest desires of our soul are still as human as anyone else's. We want to be your teachers, your doctors, your artists, your fathers, your brothers, your sons, your lovers, and your friends. We want to exist in a world where we are included and appreciated as unique yet similar human beings. If anything is apparent from the essays you've just read, it's that we feel as deeply as anyone else; in some cases, even more so. It takes an incredible amount of strength and vulnerability to accept one's own transgender status and even more to move forward with positive changes.

Just as there are all different kinds of cisgender human beings, there is a vast array of transgender individuals. Some of us knew from a young age that we didn't quite fit into the mold that we were given, and some of us came to realize this later on in life. There is not one single narrative that is all encompassing of our stories. It was the aim of this collection to cover as much of these diverse stories as we possibly could, while still showing the common threads that bond us as a group.

Our hope is that this anthology has served as a window into the hearts and souls of this group of transgender men, and that perhaps it has provided some insight into our lives.

# CONTRIBUTOR BIOS

## NATHAN EZEKIEL

Nathan Ezekiel lives in Cambridge, Massachusetts. He has been married for ten years, and is a parent to two school-age children. In addition to parenthood, Nathan is a research neuroscientist. Nathan's writing appeared in the collection *Manning Up: Transexual Men on Finding Brotherhood, Family & Themselves* published by Transgress Press. Since 2008, Nathan, and his wife Angela, have been blogging about queer families, non-biological parenthood, donor conception and parenting through transition on *First Time, Second Time* (http://firsttimesecondtime.com).

## MITCH KELLAWAY

Mitch Kellaway is a Boston-based queer, transgender writer, journalist, and editor for Transgress Press. His work has appeared in Original Plumbing, Lambda Literary, Review, Cliterature, Zeteo, and is upcoming in Jonathan: A Journal of Gay Fiction, RECOGNIZE: The Voices of Bisexual Men and Best Sex Writing 2015. He currently writes for Advocate.com and is the co-editor of *Manning Up: Transsexual Men on Finding Brotherhood, Family, & Themselves* (Transgress, 2014).

## LENG MONTGOMERY

Leng Montgomery is an Ambassador for LGBT charity Diversity Role Models, and speaks regularly in Schools and to wider media outlets about better ways to tackle and combat Transphobia and Homophobia in younger people in the UK. He also speaks to media professionals about better practice in terms of how Trans people are represented in the media.

Aside this he has a background in social media, is a passionate blogger, loves to cook and travel whenever he gets a chance. Being Trans is one element of his life but living life, not fearing change and loving himself and others is the key focus of how he likes to operate. The freedom that comes with transition inspired him to want to connect with others and be visible.

## IAN CARTER

Ian Carter resides in Oakland, California where he also works as a Marriage and Family Therapist for a non-profit agency that is geared toward helping homeless individuals with mental illness. In his free time, Ian enjoys spending time with his dog, camping with close friends, and working out at the gym.

## RAE LARSON

Rae Larson is a twenty-three year old from St. Louis, Missouri and identifies as transgender, pansexual man. He's a four-year US Air Force veteran with a Bachelor's in Psychology. He loves his kids (two cats and a dog), music, coffee, and TV shows more than most things in life.

## CLAIRENCE JAGUAR

Clairence Jaguar is from Los Angeles, CA. He enjoys theatre, libraries, and art museums. He is very grateful to be part of this book compilation.

## WILL M. KRISANDA

Will M. Krisanda is a freelance writer and actor living in Northeastern Pennsylvania. He enjoys writing about his family, what he's learned as a trans man living in a small town and his pets Lincoln and Levi. His favorite authors include Willa Cather and David Sedaris.

## ELI BRADFORD

Eli Bradford lives in a suburb just outside of Boston, Massachusetts with his wife and two small children. Aside from being a family guy, he is a graduate from Northeastern University who majored in Sociology, and is currently working full time a in a corporate office. He has recently embraced the idea of facing his fears and is finally becoming the person he has always wanted to be.

## JACK ELLIOTT

Jack Elliott was raised between New Jersey and Michigan. For the past fifteen years he has worked in printing as a Production Manager, and now consults small businesses in process and operations. Jack believes Transitioning has provided both a physical and mental landscape in which to explore what it is to be above all else, human. He lives in Brooklyn with his wife, and lots of animals.

## HARVEY KATZ

Harvey Katz is also known by his performance persona the Athens Boys Choir. He is a Transgender Jew from Miami who came into manhood in the Deep South. Since 2003 he has been touring the country using his writing as a platform for expression, advocacy, and entertainment.

## GABRIEL PELZ

Gabriel Pelz is a thirty-one year old transman living in small town Douglas, Georgia; with his biological daughter now age eight who was five when he began testosterone. He works full-time as a food preparer in a family owned, second generation resturant. He loves to cook with his daughter when we're not out exploring new places and activities. He was also a model for The 2014 Trans Calendar Project.

## KAI EMERY SCOTT

Kai is a Canadian-American trans man, who was born in Seattle, Washington, grew up in Europe, and currently resides in Vancouver, BC. He is a social scientist working on issues pertaining to the human environment related to proposed resource developments across Canada. He also volunteers as part of the local queer community working towards greater inclusion and visibility of transgender people. In his free time, he is an avid runner competing in half and full marathons.

## DYLAN FARNSWORTH

Dylan is a biologist who calls the Pacific Northwest his home. He enjoys studying wildlife, conservation ecology, and evolutionary biology. He loves camping and hiking with his wife and son in the wilderness, climbing trees, swimming and rafting in mountain rivers, and exploring places where animals outnumber people.

# ACKNOWLEDGEMENTS

This anthology was driven with the help of our contributors. Your willingness to share some of the deepest parts of the human experience is invaluable. Without you, this book would have not been possible. Thank you!

We'd also like to extend our thanks to Don Weise of Magnus Books; Sheyam Ghieth for editing; Yana Davis for photos; Tom Stevens for legal review; and Nick Krieger for his foreword.

Alexander would like to acknowledge Kate for her support in this project. Your encouragement helped to put this idea in action. To my co-editor, Emmett Lundberg, thank you for your insight and collaboration. Thank you Dad, Grandma, Xanthia, and my other siblings for believing in me always. To the educators who have been in my life, Nell, Marie, and Frank, and many more, thank you for your continued support. Thank you to everyone in the diverse transgender/transsexual community; continue to be the most authentic version of you.

Emmett would like to thank Alex, this book would be nothing without your brilliant germ of an idea. To my parents, I am forever grateful for the continuing love and support you have given me. I wouldn't be anywhere without you. To Sheyam, all of my creative endeavors have found their legs with your help; this is just one of many.

# ABOUT THE EDITORS

**Alexander Walker** is a special education teacher, writer, and community activist. He holds a B.S. in Elementary Education and an M.Ed. in Special Education. Additionally, Alex serves as a commissioner on the Massachusetts Commission on LGBTQ Youth working to develop recommend-dations for safe and inclusive schools, community organizations, and legislation for LGBTQ youth. You can read more of his writing about creating inclusive schools for LGBTQIA youth at www. evolvinggender.com. He lives in Boston with his wife and dogs.

**Emmett Jack Lundberg** is an award-winning writer and filmmaker. He graduated from NYU with a BFA in Film Production and is the creator of the original series *BROTHERS* (www. brothersseries.com), one of *Indiewire's 10 Best Indie TV Series of 2014*. He spends most of his time in New York, but remains a Wisconsinite at heart. Please visit his website for more info: www.emmettjack.com.

*Alexander Walker & Emmett J. P. Lundberg*

# If You Liked This, Please Look For These Other Titles From Riverdale Avenue Books

## *Read My Lips: Sexual Subversion and the End of Gender*
By Riki Wilchins
http://riverdaleavebooks.com/books/38/read-my-lips-sexual-subversion-and-the-end-of-gender

## *Two Spirits, One Heart: A Mother, Her Transgendered Son, and Their Journey To Love and Acceptance*
By Marsha Aizumi, Aiden Takeo Aizumi
http://riverdaleavebooks.com/books/3083/two-spirits-one-heart-a-mother-her-transgender-son-and-their-journey-to-love-and-acceptance

## *Growing Up Golem: How I Survived my Mother, Brooklyn, and some Really Bad Dates*
By Donna Minkowitz
http://riverdaleavebooks.com/books/3085/growing-up-golem-how-i-survived-my-mother-brooklyn-and-some-really-bad-dates

## *Transition to Murder*
By Renee James
http://riverdaleavebooks.com/books/4109/transition-to-murder